Island Fantasia

The Matsu archipelago between China and Taiwan, for long an isolated outpost off southeast China, was suddenly transformed into a military frontline in 1949 by the Cold War and the Communist–Nationalist conflict. The army occupied the islands, commencing more than 40 long years of military rule. With the lifting of martial law in 1992, the people were confronted with the question of how to move forward. This in-depth ethnography and social history of the islands focuses on how individual citizens redefined themselves and reimagined their society. Drawing on long-term fieldwork, Wei-Ping Lin shows how islanders used both traditional and new media to cope with the conflicts and trauma of harsh military rule. She discusses the formation of new social imaginaries through the appearance of 'imagining subjects', interrogating their subjectification processes and varied uses of mediating technologies as they seek to answer existential questions.

WEI-PING LIN is Professor of Anthropology at National Taiwan University. She has previously held affiliations at the Harvard-Yenching Institute and the Fairbank Center for Chinese Studies at Harvard University. She is the author of *Materializing Magic Power: Chinese Popular Religion in Villages and Cities* (2015, Harvard University Asia Center) which won the Academia Sinica Scholarly Monograph Award in the Humanities and Social Sciences. She edited *Mediating Religion: Music, Image, Object, and New Media* (2018, National Taiwan University Press).

T0382260

Taiwan Studies Series

劍橋台灣研究叢書

Located in the heart of Asia, Taiwan has always been a critical node for a variety of historical forces and a treasury of humanities and social sciences research. Its economic development during the 1970s and 1980s was described as a "miracle" by the World Bank, and it quickly became a focus of research in the academic world.

However, the important transitions that Taiwan has subsequently undergone have not received sufficient scholarly attention. The establishment of this *Taiwan Studies Series* by Cambridge University Press aims to fill this gap by providing quality publications based on solid research and academic insights that can also make significant contributions to the literature in both the humanities and social sciences.

The series presents a nuanced and close-to-the-ground analysis of Taiwan, a critical node in US-China-Japan competition in the Asia-Pacific region. It studies the island's social complexities and transitions from the geopolitical perspective while also focusing closely on the lives and cultural vibrancy of its people. It is both timely and refreshing.

It will feature books authored by established and mid-career scholars from many disciplinary orientations including economics, law, history, political science, organization studies, public administration and management, sociology and anthropology, among many others.

Island Fantasia

Imagining Subjects on the Military Frontline between China and Taiwan

Wei-Ping Lin

National Taiwan University

CAMBRIDGE
UNIVERSITY PRESS

CAMBRIDGE
UNIVERSITY PRESS

University Printing House, Cambridge CB2 8BS, United Kingdom

One Liberty Plaza, 20th Floor, New York, NY 10006, USA

477 Williamstown Road, Port Melbourne, VIC 3207, Australia

314–321, 3rd Floor, Plot 3, Splendor Forum, Jasola District Centre, New Delhi – 110025, India

103 Penang Road, #05–06/07, Visioncrest Commercial, Singapore 238467

Cambridge University Press is part of the University of Cambridge.

It furthers the University's mission by disseminating knowledge in the pursuit of education, learning, and research at the highest international levels of excellence.

www.cambridge.org
Information on this title: www.cambridge.org/9781316519370
DOI: 10.1017/9781009023481

© Wei-Ping Lin 2021

First published 2021

A catalogue record for this publication is available from the British Library.

Library of Congress Cataloging-in-Publication Data
Names: Lin, Wei-Ping, author.
Title: Island fantasia : imagining subjects on the military frontline between China and Taiwan / Wei-Ping Lin, National Taiwan University.
Other titles: Imagining subjects on the military frontline between China and Taiwan
Description: Cambridge, United Kingdom ; New York, NY : Cambridge University Press, 2021. | Series: Taiwan studies | Includes bibliographical references and index.
Identifiers: LCCN 2021025024 (print) | LCCN 2021025025 (ebook) | ISBN 9781316519370 (hardback) | ISBN 9781009010405 (paperback) | ISBN 9781009023481 (epub)
Subjects: LCSH: Lienchiang County (Taiwan)–History. | Lienchiang County (Taiwan)–Social life and customs. | Lienchiang County (Taiwan)–History, Military. | Taiwan–History, Military–1945- | BISAC: HISTORY / Asia / General | HISTORY / Asia / General
Classification: LCC DS799.8 .L56 2021 (print) | LCC DS799.8 (ebook) | DDC 951.249–dc23
LC record available at https://lccn.loc.gov/2021025024
LC ebook record available at https://lccn.loc.gov/2021025025

ISBN 978-1-316-51937-0 Hardback
ISBN 978-1-009-01040-5 Paperback

For Pinaki

Contents

Figures, Maps, and Tables

Figures

Maps

Tables

Acknowledgements

I first visited Matsu for a conference in 2006. At that time, the islanders were contemplating the varied possibilities for their future, as direct "links" between China and Taiwan would soon be established after years of military confrontation. During that first visit, the islanders' close-yet-distant feeling for the ocean deeply intrigued me. Since then, and over many years of traveling back and forth between Taiwan and Matsu, I have relied on the help and friendship of many Matsu people. To protect the privacy of my informants, I have used pseudonyms for many in this book, but my gratitude to them for talking to and for teaching me goes beyond anything words can express. Not only have I learned to be patient (while waiting interminably for frequently canceled flights to Matsu), I have also improved at playing "bandit mahjong" (though I will probably never come close to matching their speed). Most importantly, I have always marveled at and aspired to match their imaginative powers. My warmest thanks go to my foster mother, whom I call "*laoma*," and to her family for housing, feeding, and standing by me: their love, knowledge, and support has been an emotional anchor during my time spent on these islands.

The fieldwork for this book was funded for several years by the Ministry of Technology, Taiwan, and by National Taiwan University. The Harvard-Yenching Institute and the Chiang Ching-kuo Foundation (CCKF) kindly sponsored the publication of this book, and I completed the manuscript during my time as a visiting scholar at the Harvard-Yenching Institute. Cambridge, MA, provided a stimulating environment in which to think and write, and I would like to express gratitude to all my Harvard-Yenching colleagues, in particular to Li Ruohong, who shared her thoughts with me during my stay.

Michael Szonyi, Li Ren-Yuan, and Lo Shih-Chieh came to visit and travel around the Matsu islands with me. I benefited tremendously from this trip. My thanks especially to Michael for his work on Jinmen, which piqued my interest in doing ethnography in Matsu, as well as for the questions he posed during the trip, which pushed me to think more broadly about the history of the islands.

Earlier versions of some of the book chapters were given at talks, workshops, and panels at Harvard University, Boston University, the University of Michigan at Ann Arbor, Brown University, Xiamen University, Academia Sinica, National Taiwan University, National Chengchi University, and at the annual meetings of the Association for Asian Studies (AAS). Some chapters were subsequently published as journal papers, and are adapted therefrom: Chapter 5 (W. Lin 2016, reprinted by permission of the Department of Anthropology, National Taiwan University); Chapter 8 (W. Lin 2013, 2017, reprinted by permission of Taishe Press and Taylor & Francis Group); and Chapter 9 (W. Lin 2009, 2014, reprinted by permission of The Department of Anthropology, National Taiwan University and Cambridge University Press). I would like to thank Elizabeth Perry, Erik Mueggler, James Robson, Rebecca Nedostup, Cheng Weining, Huang Hou-Ming, and Huang Xiangchun for their invitations, and to them and the meeting participants for helpful comments.

Many people have inspired me over the years, in particular Liu Yuan-Ju and Lee Feng-Mao. Robert Graham and the Chatterjee family were always eager sounding boards for my stories and ideas about Matsu. D. J. Hatfield and Huang Ying-Kuei read several chapters in the early stages and made many helpful suggestions. I am most especially grateful to Robert Weller who invited me to numerous workshops and read the whole manuscript in its final stages. His thoughts and comments have been invaluable. I also wish to express my deep appreciation for Cheng I-Yih's support, in countless ways, during the long process of fieldwork and writing. I am very grateful to her for sharing her wisdom with me.

Many people have helped this book to take shape. My students from Matsu, Wang Chun-Hui and Tsao Yi-Hsun, worked with me and introduced me to their families. I had fruitful discussions with Zhang Guangdong, and I benefited from comments by Shen Yang, Yu Junfeng, En-Ya Tsai, Ning Ge, Peng Handan, Gui Qi, and Hung-Shiuan Yu, who generously contributed their ideas in my class. Peng Jiahong helped to draw maps and figures. Tang Yi-Jie helped with the romanization of the Fuzhou dialect. Eleanor Goodman and Geoffrey Voorhies improved the English of the book. Moreover, I would like to express my special gratitude to the team from Cambridge University Press: to Catherine Smith and Angela Roberts for help with editing, and to Joe Ng for shepherding this book through publication.

My mother and brother have always cared profoundly for my well-being; it is in the minor details of life that they show their love and support. And finally, my greatest thanks to Pinaki; this book would be impossible without his company and his encouragement.

Note on Transcription

The Chinese characters in this book, unless specifically marked, are in Mandarin. Romanization is done according to the Hanyu Pinyin system. The dialect spoken in the Matsu Islands is the Fuzhou dialect, which I have romanized according to the system explained below, but without any indication of tones; this is given only when there is no equivalent Mandarin translation, and is marked by an F.

The phonetic transcription used in this book, based on the International Phonetic Alphabet (IPA) with minor adjustments, is consistent with *Matsu fuzhou hua pinyin fang'an* (the phonetic alphabet program of the Fuzhou dialect in Matsu); see the website of *Matsu mindong (fuzhou) hua richang shenghuo changyong cihui* (Common vocabulary of everyday life in the Mindong (Fuzhou) dialect in Matsu).[1]

The consonant symbols are shown in the table below.

Place Manner		Bilabial	Alveolar	Postal-veolar	Velar	Glottal
Plosive	Unaspirated Voiceless	p	t		k	h (coda)
	Aspirated Voiceless	ph	th		kh	
Nasal		m	n		ng	
Fricative		(β)	s	(ʒ)		h (initial)
Affricates	Unaspirated Voiceless		ts			
	Aspirated Voiceless		tsh			
Lateral			l			

[1] www.study.matsu.edu.tw/1000/images/paper.html

The vowel symbols are shown in the table below.

	Front		Central	Back
	Unrounded	Rounded		
Close	i	y		u
Mid	e	oe		o
Open			a	

Below is a brief explanation.

1. The consonants *b* and *j*, which are respectively equivalent to /β/ and /ʒ/ in IPA, are produced only when "initial assimilation" occurs. Initial assimilation in the Fuzhou dialect is a process in which the initial of a syllable in a polysyllabic word changes under the influence of the coda or the final sound of the preceding syllable. This phenomenon appears only in syllables after the first one.[2]
2. *h* is a glottal fricative when used to indicate an initial and a glottal stop when used to indicate a coda.
3. *y* is a close front rounded vowel.
4. *oe* is a mid-front rounded vowel, equivalent to /ø/ in IPA.
5. This book uses the symbols as shown in the tables above without any indication of tones.

[2] In a word with two or more syllables, the initial of each syllable other than the first one can change based on the features of the preceding sound, i.e. the final phoneme of the preceding syllable. In Chinese, every syllable is composed of an initial and a coda, and the initial is also the beginning consonant. In the Fuzhou dialect, if a word is composed of more than two syllables, then the initial of each syllable other than the first one may change based on the preceding sound.

Abbreviations

BBS	bulletin board system
CCA	Council for Cultural Affairs
CCP	Chinese Communist Party
KMT	Kuomintang, Nationalist Party
PLA	People's Liberation Army
PRC	People's Republic of China
ROC	Republic of China, Taiwan
WZA	Warzone Administration
WZAC	Warzone Administration Committee

Introduction: Imagining Subject

Situated precariously between Taiwan and China, the Matsu archipelago is even more diminutive than the Trobriand Islands. From the islands, which belong to Taiwan, one can see cargo vessels sailing along the Chinese coastline during the day and watch the city lights glimmering across the water after dark—China is but a stone's throw away. In fact, to go from Beigan, one of the northern islands, to the mainland city of Huangqi, takes only half an hour by ferry, while a trip to Taiwan involves traversing the tempestuous "dark trench" (*hei shuigou*) of the Taiwan Strait. Taking nine hours over rough seas, the journey can sometimes seem longer than flying across the Pacific to American shores.

At first glance, one's eyes are immediately drawn to the stone houses that dot the islands' mountainous landscape. Unlike the residential courtyards found in southern Fujian province, most of these homes are stand-alone two-story structures, tucked attractively into the folds of the mountains. Their unique name, *huang ngiang nah* (F. foreign shelters), points to the fact that they display some Western architectural elements (Fig. 0.1). It is said that they were designed both as a response to and an improvement on the Western architecture built in China after the signing of the 1842 Treaty of Nanking and the opening up of the Fuzhou harbors (Zheng 2003). Walking through the villages, one occasionally still comes across slogans attached to the exterior walls—"Take back the mainland" (*guangfu dalu*); "Eliminate the traitors Zhu De and Mao Zedong" (*xiaomie zhu mao hanjian*); and "Cooperation between soldiers and civilians" (*junmin yijia*)—a reminder of the archipelago's history as a military frontline. After refurbishment done as part of village preservation projects,

Fig. 0.1 Strolling along the alleyways of Matsu

many of these stone dwellings have been turned into lodgings for visitors. These former "foreign shelters" have taken up fashionable European-sounding names such as "Mediterranean Villa," "Santorini Inn," or "Aegean Sea of Love Bed & Breakfast." Walking in the circuitous alleyways is like entering the galleries of history.

Towering above the simple stone houses on the peak of a southern island stands a finely wrought, recently finished giant statue of the Goddess Mazu. Since the islands are named after her, in recent years many places have developed according to the catchphrase "Goddess Mazu in Matsu." This enormous image was built in imitation of the Mazu statue on Meizhou Island, China. Now, she not only looks out over the vast ocean, summoning the fishermen home, but the angle of the statue has been carefully adjusted so that the Goddess faces her birthplace in China: Meizhou Island in Putian. The direction of her gaze reveals the ardent hope and imagination entertained by Matsu residents today of reconnecting with Taiwan and China.

Imagination, Media, and Contemporary Society

Social imaginary is the way in which the members of a community imagine their existence. It forms the common understanding of how to carry out the collective practices that constitute social life (Taylor 2004: 23–4). In contemporary times, imagination has taken on increasing significance. Whether in anthropology or in cultural studies, imaginary has tended to take on weight comparable to culture, belief, or meaning (Strauss 2006: 322), if not replace them. Why is this the case?

It is undeniable that the flourishing of modern media technologies has created new possibilities for imagination to develop. But the uncertainty that people confront in the contemporary world also impels various kinds of imagination to appear, as is seen widely in many fields.[1] Arjun Appadurai (1996) in the early 1990s initiated a series of papers exploring the importance of modern imagination. He posits that the world we inhabit today is characterized by a new role in social life for imagination, which is a constitutive feature of modern subjectivity (31). Since the 1980s, the rising popularity of electronic media, as well as mass migration, has loosened the intimate bonds between people and territories in traditional society: the world has undergone a process of de-territorialization and re-territorialization (49; see also Gupta and Ferguson 1997: 50). In other words, electronic media marks the coming of a new era: it intervenes in public life and reshapes society by virtue of its wide reach and speed of transmission. So, indeed, does mass migration. Although mobility has always existed in history, when modern migration was accompanied by the rapid flows of mass-mediated messages, images, and sensations, cultural reproduction could not continue as before. Imagination has thus acquired a new power in contemporary society (53).

Appadurai, however, does not deny the importance of imagination in traditional societies; rather, he discusses how mass media brought about new kinds of imagination and results: imagination has become a part of everyday life, a way for individuals to negotiate with the wider, globalized world, and to constitute modern self and subjectivity (3). By juxtaposing previous works with contemporary global transformations, Appadurai contributed important insights to many later studies. Below, I scrutinize the important issues relating to imagination in the literature both before and after him, since the varied workings of imagination in society is one of the central concerns of this book.

Humans are born with an innate ability to imagine, but in reality only some imaginations are able to develop from one or more individuals into the collective and become shared social imaginaries, that is, common images or representations held by most people that influence society significantly. The role of the mediating mechanism in this process is pivotal. Benedict Anderson (1991[1983]), for instance, in his seminal book *Imagined Community,* depicts how print-capitalism brought about a fundamental transformation in how people "think" the world (22). Taking novels and newspapers as examples, he explicates how these media create homogeneous, empty time and comparable social space (24). These temporal and spatial constructions generate a commonality among people and lay the basis for nationalism.

The significance of collective imagining in the formation of modern Europe is explored more systematically by Charles Taylor (2004). He argues that revolutionary social imaginaries usually come from elites' or prophets' original theories of moral order, which over the long march of history gradually infiltrate into ordinary people's minds. In Europe, it was through three kinds of social forms—market economy, public sphere, and self-governed people—that social imaginary was finally transfigured. It is worth noting that Taylor greatly expands the discussion of social imaginary from print media to broader social institutions. But his analysis, as Crapanzano (2004: 7) suggests, does not delve into "how this infiltration works, nor does he discuss the potential contradictions, tensions, and disjunctions in it." It is not surprising that subsequent research focused on "the technologies of imagination" (Sneath, Holbraad, and Pedersen 2006: 11), that is, the concrete processes by which imaginative effects are engendered. In ensuing works, the function of medium has also received more attention. Belting (2011[2001]: 20) calls it "an act of animation," triggering the transference of the individual imagination into a collective perception, as an appropriate medium can open the door to knowledge, enabling the personal mental image to be apprehended and become the collective "picture" in the public space (15). Meyer (2015) develops this idea in her study of Ghana, discussing how movies function as a "synchronizing actor" to transform individual imaginations into a shared collective imaginary.

In the contemporary era, however, we increasingly engage with, and live in, multiple imagined worlds. Unconstrained by territorial bounds, our connections with others are far more complex and fragmentary than before. Many new elements, such as ethnicity, media, technology, finance, and ideology, have arisen to generate larger imaginaries, or "scapes," as Appadurai (1996: 33) termed them. These scapes are usually unfixed, irregular, and able to contest with each other or even subvert the official regulations. To sum up, the imagined worlds in contemporary time are spaces of contestation in continual flux (4); their relations can no longer be explicated in terms of the traditional political economy or the central/peripheral dichotomy. How should we understand the emergence and interplay of these different imaginaries?

The Invisible Subject

Although many of the aforementioned scholars have raised important points about social imaginary, most of their works are premised on the collective or social without delving into individual imaginations (Crapazano 2004: 1; Rapport 2015: 8; Robbins 2010: 306), or more precisely, the imagining subjects. What their works crucially miss is the active agent who initiates the imaginings. I consider that the imagining subject has been rendered invisible largely for two distinct reasons.

First is a tendency among scholars to adopt a top-down perspective. Anderson, for example, explores the formation of an imagined community in terms of print capitalism, yet his work rarely treats the imagining subject and the process of imagination (Axel 2003: 121). Similarly, Appadurai's research emphasizes how people in the present age can use electronic media to achieve previously unimagined imaginaries. But he mainly focuses on the influence of media and technology without considering the individual imagination. This is shown in how he distinguishes two forms of imagination (1996: 7): fantasy, which is private, personal, and often emancipatory; and collective imagination, which is the force behind the formation of neighborhoods, societies, and nation-states, and which could become the fuel for social action. It is clear that he places greater importance on the latter. Although Taylor touches upon individuals—particularly elites—and how their thinking spreads to the larger community via economics, politics, and the public sphere, he rarely explicates how exactly they communicate with each other, and the process by which ideas are negotiated and reconciled.

The second reason that the imagining subject is invisible is probably historical, and specific to the society under study. In a given society or historical era, there may be a larger institution existing that prevents us from readily seeing the individual imagination. The Matsu archipelago, the fieldsite of this book, is a case in point of how imagination can be obscured for various distinct reasons. Until the eighteenth century, the Matsu Islands were considered by the central Chinese government as a "forbidden outpost," to which officials could exile people at will. The inhabitants consisted of a largely transient population who survived by fishing. Social relations on the islands were based on kinship and ties to their original hometowns in the coastal regions of southeast China (see Chapter 1). Relying on the mainland to fulfill many of their basic needs, the residents' lives were only partially conducted on the islands. Some particularly daring individuals rose to become feared pirates who dominated the sea, but their reigns mostly proved to be short-lived. During the early period, life on the islands was transitory and intermittent. Given the extremely limited data, it is all the more difficult for us to know how individuals' imaginations developed during that time.

The conflict between the Communist Party and the Nationalist Party in China, as well as the US–Soviet Cold War, drastically changed the fate of Matsu. Overnight, Matsu was sealed off from Taiwan and China and turned into a frontline in Taiwan's defensive strategy against China. The archipelago was ruled by the army for more than forty years (1949–92). In order to transform the barren fishing islands into a solid base for the army, the military government during this period carried out large-scale modernization projects, including improving infrastructure, building schools, and even implementing a guaranteed admission program to send Matsu students to Taiwan for advanced education. All of this brought about tremendous changes in the previously desolate islands. However, the dark side of this seemingly bright picture is that local fishermen were greatly restricted in their access to the water and their movements at sea. The fishing economy—the lifeblood of the islands—gradually waned. More than two-thirds of the inhabitants left the islands in the 1970s for jobs in Taiwan. Although some commerce based on army supplies did emerge, and the government also offered some jobs, most of these vocations were at the bottom rungs of the military-ruled society; that the government exerted strict control on the bodies and thoughts of locals goes without saying.

In the face of military rule, the individual imagination was largely concealed and expressed privately. For example, Matsu fishermen knew of places on the sea which were beyond military detection, and where they could snatch brief moments of enjoyment outside state control to meet with fishermen friends from China, but those interludes were mostly secret (see Chapter 3). The islanders also elaborated their gambling habits into a kind of imaginative practice in which they could mock, evade, or even contend with the state; but their gambling had to be clandestinely conducted in out-of-the-way places, such as the dark corners of offices, storehouses, tunnels, or even graveyards, as Chapter 4 will show.

Undoubtedly, the pervasive suppression encouraged many Matsu people, especially the early wave of youngsters who were sent to Taiwan to study and who absorbed ideas of liberty there, to rise up in tandem with the Taiwan democratic movement and take to the streets to demand freedom. After two major demonstrations and peaceful sit-ins to protest the military rule, marital law was lifted in 1992, and Matsu finally won its freedom. Subsequent improvements in aviation and naval transport brought Matsu people in touch with the wider world, and the islands were no longer isolated. The advent of internet technologies offered more possibilities for imagination to develop. When the new social media spread to the whole archipelago in the form of a popular website, *Matsu Online*, which was set up in 2001, the residents were afforded greater freedom to express their opinions, connect with each other in the virtual world, and enthusiastically engage in public issues. The individual imagination has gained a larger space to express itself and explore in the online world.

Subjectification and the Ethical Imagination

It is important to take a closer look at the question of how long-oppressed and confined individuals could become imagining subjects. How does their subjectivity take shape, and what is the process of their subjectification? Many anthropological studies of subjectivity have looked at these issues; I benefit particularly from the works of Henrietta Moore (1994, 2007, 2011) who notes that subjectivity and subjectification have not been defined in a rigorous way in anthropology. Subjectivity in general denotes "inner states or perceptions that engage with affect, cognition, morality and agency" (Biehl et al. 2007: 1; Ortner 2005: 31; see also Holland and Leander 2004: 127; Luhrmann 2006: 345). Of these, agency—that is, how people act in the world—is underscored by most of the scholars.

Among these broad definitions, Moore (2011: 72) identifies two perspectives. The first one is cultural, proposed by Ortner (2005) who reinterprets Geertz and highlights the aspects of how "the cultural and social formations shape, organize, and provoke ... modes of affect and thought" (2005: 31). This standpoint is clearly based on culturally constituted feelings, desires and intentions (34). The second perspective is experiential, postulated by Kleinman and Fitz-Henry (2007). They discuss the variability, heterogeneity, and contingency of subjectivities taking shape in the realm of experiences that are usually intersubjective, involving practices, negotiations, and contestations when interacting with others. Experience for them is thus the medium within which collective and subjective processes fuse and condition each other. Although they do not deny that subjectivity is also constrained by culture, symbols, and meanings as Ortner posits, they argue that experience can reconfigure and repattern cultural contents (53).

Moore, however, indicates that experience in this approach is formulated in a rather loose way: what it entails is not really explored. Intersubjectivity and the process of subjectification are also undertheorized. Above all, these discussions are limited to the frame of subjects, without exploring "the specific grounds for transformations in subjectivities and in the forms and mechanism of subjection" (73). The factors which affect on individuals are usually generalized as "exterior" elements: "interior" self and "exterior" influences are separated. Even when they interact, the consequence is usually termed as "hybridity" of modernization or globalization.

Moore suggests that this interior/exterior dichotomy has to be transcended to reach an understanding of how the process of subjectification, or becoming a subject, evolves. In her earlier works (1994: 55; 2007: 17), she differentiated self and subject, showing that the self is constituted by multiple subject positions. Her later work (2011) develops how various kinds of mediums, or "the forms of the possible" (18) in her own words, can reshape self. She takes new media as an example to show how it can magnify "interior" meanings and feelings, supplementing and extending individual sensations and emotions (Moore 2011: 116), and engendering new agency and social connections. This is the process of subjectification which not only creates new subjects, but also reconstitutes self–other relations. She thus advocates that we should break the interior/exterior division and see new media technologies as second nature to humans, with which individuals are able to create new worlds and become "relational" subjects (78). For her, modern computer-mediated technologies are only one of the possible mediums. People also deploy objects (Latour 1993, 2005) and art forms (Gell 1998) to create new social ties and cultural contents. As she writes:

> Humans use objects and technologies to extend our reach across space and time, to create new forms of self, of social relations and social ontologies. ... New technologies enhance our capacities for virtuality and for making social relations. They not only make new ways of seeing possible, but they are productive of new relays of affect and intensity which in turn produces new cultural forms and cultural capacities. (Moore 2011: 127)

This way of discussing self is undoubtedly much indebted to Foucault's concept of "the ethical subject" (1985; 1998), which concerns the mode of subjectification, technologies of the self, and the mode of being that the subject aspires to achieve. However, she proceeds to elaborate it into the idea of "the ethical imagination" (Moore 2011: 15–21; Long and Moore 2013) in which she delves further into self–other relations, in particular, the forms and means through which individuals imagine relationships to themselves and to others, and the unconscious affects, emotions, and fantasies which are thereby generated. This analytical framework is helpful in investigating the emergence of imagining subjects after the demilitarization of Matsu, the major concern of this book. Going further, I will discuss how their rich imaginations, as developed through different media technologies, enhance our understanding of *the formation of the social imaginary*. The online creation of wartime memory, discussed in Chapter 6, provides a vital clue to this process.

From Deserted Islands to an Enchanted Place

The weblog series *The Wartime Childhood of Leimengdi* appeared on *Matsu Online*, a popular website reporting on Matsu. It began in 2005 and was published over the course of three years. The posts were copiously illustrated by Chen Tianshun, a Taiwan-based emigrant from Matsu, and the text was written by his Taiwanese wife, Xia Shuhua. Their collaborative project was widely read and much beloved during its serialization; when later published in book form, residents voted to designate it a "Book of Matsu." The series records the childhood memories of Chen Tianshun, who grew up in Matsu during military rule. The rich culture and ecology of the islands marked him profoundly, but the trauma of military rule also left permanent psychological scars. Owing to the decline of the fishing economy, his entire family left the islands when he was fifteen. He attended a vocational school of art and design in Taiwan and worked there as an illustrator. He and his family lived a relatively secluded life in Taipei, and for nearly three decades he never set foot on Matsu. He hardly spoke about his childhood even to his wife, and his past was seemingly a painful secret that he tried to forget or hide.

Only when *Matsu Online* appeared as a forum for him to unburden himself by exercising his talent, was he moved to draw upon his deeply buried memories. Throughout the process, he was buoyed by his wife's engaging writing and an outpouring of emotional support from netizens. The co-active structure of internet technology (Web 2.0) quickly engendered intersubjective communication and mutual empathy between him and a growing group of netizens (Dijck 2007; Cappelletto 2005a, 2005b). A shared image of wartime Matsu emerged, and it consoled his displaced heart. By the relay of feelings and affects stimulated by drawing for the public on the internet, the interstices of the inner and the outer, the individual and the social were crossed out. Chen was finally able to surmount the sufferings of his childhood and reposition himself between Matsu and Taiwan. He was invited back to Matsu, where he gave talks and taught drawing to school children. After setting foot once again on Matsu, he was even stirred to fight for the ethical value of the unmourned and unremembered dead who had lost their lives because of military rule. One could say that the creation of the weblog series was Chen Tianshun's process of subjectification: his values, morals, and emotions were reconstituted, and he discovered new momentum to move forward.

This process of subjectification is not unique to Chen Tianshun but can also be seen in the middle-aged generation of Matsu residents, in particular those who went to work in Taiwan or were sent there to study by the guaranteed admission program during the military rule, and subsequently returned home to work. The challenges that Matsu faced after the ending of military rule were considerable. When Matsu suddenly stopped being a frontline in 1992, uncertainty plagued the islands. After more than forty years of military rule, Matsu's economy had already shifted from fishing to a system centered around providing goods and services for the army. As tensions between the two sides of the Taiwan Strait diminished, the number of garrisons stationed on the islands greatly decreased. With military demand sharply down and with the economy dwindling year after year, prospects for Matsu looked bleak. Although its designation as a waypoint between China and Taiwan in 2001 temporarily alleviated anxiety, Matsu was even more marginalized after direct transportation links were established in 2008, bypassing the islands. What could Matsu do to avoid returning to its state a century ago as a group of desolate, isolated islands? A disturbed and restless atmosphere was growing.

At that point, a series of plans for the development of the islands—or put more accurately, different imaginaries to reposition Matsu vis-à-vis China and Taiwan, Asia, or even the world—were proposed to explore possibilities for the future of Matsu. The driving force behind the scenes was the "imagining subjects," namely, the persons who had been sent to Taiwan to study by the guaranteed admission program and who came back to work.

They had grown up in Matsu and experienced the hardships and traumas of military rule. After studying and working in Taiwan, they realigned their warzone experiences with their newly acquired knowledge and proposed a profusion of new blueprints for the islands.

I emphasize that these persons were not just "*thinking subjects* engaged in dialogue with a variety of broader intellectual debates and projects" (Miyazaki 2013: 6, italic original), but *imagining subjects* imbued with strong feelings and attachments to their hometown and the desire to find a way out for their suffering land. Their repositioning of Matsu took on particular significance for those who had lived through the wartime period: as a frontline of hostilities, Matsu was seen as "the Fortress of the Taiwan Strait" (*taihai baolei*) and a "springboard for anticommunism" (*fangong tiaoban*), its value defined solely by its military strategic importance. The process of repositioning and reimagining Matsu after the lifting of martial law became a method for a long-oppressed populace to rediscover itself, and to find a new identity and a way of existing meaningfully in the world. In other words, the pursuit of these new imaginaries is thus not only motivated by politico-economic factors; more correctly, it is a series of *self-explorations*, the process of *subjectification*: the people who were traumatized by the army reconstitute themselves by reconstructing the place in which they live. With this in mind, we can understand why the islanders, in particular the middle-aged generation, during this moment were all engaged in a continuous creation of new imaginaries for Matsu.

Imagining Subject Unveiled

This book brings imagining subjects to the fore and examines the transformation of individual imaginations into social imaginaries from three perspectives.

Imagining Subjects as Individuals or Cohorts

First, the imagining subjects can be individuals. Every person has the capacity to imagine, to develop and refine imaginations over time into one's own values and beliefs. Personal ability and life experience are thus important for my analysis of the formation of individual imagination. As those with unique historical experiences often become "key social actors"

(Boyer and Lomnitz 2005: 113) in moments of rapid change, their struggles, affects, and the new imaginaries they devised are discussed in detail in this book.

Importantly, the imagining subject can also be a social cohort. Having gone through similar life experiences, people of the same generation, gender, or social category are more likely to form common imaginaries. As mentioned above, the middle-aged generation that went to Taiwan to receive advanced education or to work was inspired by the new thoughts and trends they encountered there. When the military government retreated from Matsu, they took official positions in the local government, gaining a chance to develop their individual thoughts into social imaginaries. However, that is not to suggest that they could dominate or unilaterally determine the formation of social imaginary. Rather, I wish to highlight how this generation has been constantly challenged by, and has had to negotiate with, those who have very different historical experiences and social lives, and therefore, social imaginaries. This includes the older generation of fishermen who struggled for their livelihoods on the sea, and the young post-martial-law members of society who grew up after military rule and have no experience of living in wartime. From this perspective, this book differs from previous studies in being concerned with different imagining subjects; their varied senses of self, belonging, and imaginations of the future; and the processes by which they negotiate with each other.

Apart from these generational gaps, differences in gender are also important. The traditional fishing economy of Matsu favored men over women, whose lives were centered on their families and who had little opportunity for higher education. It was not easy for them, nor was it even their major concern to come up with sweeping images of the islands' future. However, their struggle between the competing pull of family and career can be seen as a prism that reflects the challenges that contemporary Matsu society confronts today.

Subjectification through New Technologies of Imagination

Second, this book discusses how imagining subjects deploy different kinds of mediating mechanisms to infiltrate their imaginations into the society. Drawing on Moore (2011), I analyze how people use mediating technologies to enhance and magnify their individual imaginations, expanding social relations and creating new cultural identifications. I define mediating technologies broadly, including general media as well as all kinds of materials, events, and practices (Mazzarella 2004), which engage not only thought and reflection but also affect and fantasy. In the twenty-first century, these technologies recompose religious symbols, practices, and modes of belonging in terms of economic, performative, or scientific forces, and radically extend these traditional elements for a new era (Stolow 2005: 123).

From Chapter 5 to 10, I discuss how imagining subjects have employed different as well as new technologies to create, negotiate, and win support for different imaginaries: some used the internet to assert their freedom of expression when the islands were just emerging from military control; some introduced new cultural projects, attempting to remake Matsu as an "Eastern Fujian Culture Village" (*Mindong wenhua cun*). Some adopted and revised traditional Taiwanese-style pilgrimages and material practices to expand the cultural and social space of Matsu and connect it with Taiwan and China, joining the "Cross-Strait Economic Zone" (*Haixi jingji qu*). Others invited an American casino capitalist to bring the gaming industry to Matsu, hoping to transform the islands into an "Asian Mediterranean" (*Yazhou dizhonghai*).

Many of these projects did not achieve their goals. However, more important than their success or failure, these plans should be considered as both self-realizations of the imagining subjects and persistent collective efforts to "remain in presence—that is, to exist" (Latour 1993: 129). The islanders, in Latour's words, "do not land on an essence, but on a process, on a movement, a passage"; they attempt to reckon with their state of indeterminacy—a precarious existence without the promise of stability as described by Tsing (2015: 20).

Social Imaginaries as Reconfigurations of the Politico-Economy

Finally, this book posits that all imaginative practices have to contend with the realities of global power dispositions. Now that Matsu is no longer a frontline, its residents have been consecutively designing novel ways forward for the islands. We might say that imagination was given an unprecedented chance to develop during this time of drastic change: from the community project to build an "Eastern Fujian Culture Village," to the idea of using pilgrimages to join China's "Cross-Strait Economic Zone," to bringing in gaming to create an "Asian Mediterranean." All these were technologies of "social envisioning" (Peter 1997: 97) for the people who were facing an uncertain future, allowing them to seek out new potentialities by relocating Matsu between the two sides of the Taiwan Strait as well as in the world.

It is undeniable that there are layered grids of politico-economic power relations behind these imaginary creations of place identity (Gupta and Ferguson 1997). In the case of Matsu, it is the political wrestling between the two sides of the Strait and also the expansion of capitalist forces in China and its zoning strategies (Ong 2006: 104–5) which have continually pushed the new envisionings of the de-militarized islands. Many previous studies have already made the connection between capitalism and imagination, and have generally considered the former to give rise to the latter (Anderson 1991[1983]; Harvey 1990).[2] For contemporary anthropologists, cultural imaginations are not just reflections or consequences of capitalism or neoliberalism, but people's imaginary reconfigurations of economic and social conditions (Kapferer, Eriksen, and Telle 2009). These imaginations contain people's experience and criticism of capitalism, as well as their aspirations for the future (Comaroff and Comaroff 1999, 2000, 2002; Weiss 2009).[3]

In Matsu, each time a new imaginary was introduced, the relations between the islands and the wider world were rescaled (Hatfield 2019: 268; Tsing 2005: 58). These imaginings were the means by which the local aspiring subjects resituated their home amid a new hierarchy of political and economic power distributions, as well as responding to a particular historical moment. These responses, moreover, were not just imitations of the way that Matsu subjects envisaged the world, but rather *imaginative reconfigurations* of their place within the new regional and global order. These imaginaries both mediated between people and their local society, and also acted as intermediaries between their lived place and world at large.

In-betweenness, Hope, and the Future

Still, we must press further and ask: are these imaginaries actually capable of producing the outcomes that aspiring subjects hope for? The answer is: not always. In Matsu, the formation of community through temple building is a success. In other cases, the results are equivocal. For example, the "Eastern Fujian Culture Village" project did manage to restore some scenic sites of the village, but because it failed to attract widespread participation from the population, interest gradually faded. The use of pilgrimages and other religious material practices to connect Matsu with Taiwan and China also proved not fully workable after a few attempts because of the rapidly changing politico-economic dynamics and infrastructure developments in China. The proposal to create an "Asian Mediterranean" by bringing the gaming industry to Matsu did not receive much support from the central governments on either side of the Strait, and it remains unresolved today.

The significance of imagination, however, resides not in its immediate or achievable effects, but in its capacity to create open-ended ways of "knowing in being" (Ingold 2013: 747). Imagination is characterized by anachronistic and magical qualities (Belting 2011[2001]: 36) that are related to the real but distinct from it. The appearance of a particular type of imaginary is usually a response to a historical era, so it can be merely a temporary answer that fades over time. But it can also incite more possibilities for the future. Different from culture (Rollason 2014:11) or symbol (Castoriadis 1987: 127), imagination is less circumscribed by the established representation, and more flexible in its form and content. Compared to other similar concepts, such as hope (Miyazaki 2004; Miyazaki and Swedberg 2015) or aspiration (Appadurai 2004), imagination is less repetitive and more free. An imagining activity thus brims with possibilizing power, "directing itself to what might be rather than to what must be" (Casey 1976: 231). Imagination can even turn into fantasy if it deviates substantially from the real world (Weiss 2009). Or it can be at least a haven or illusion for people to escape—if only temporarily—from their predicaments or marginalization.

Imagination and fantasy have recently been treated in studies on minorities and Han people in China and Taiwan, becoming important concepts to reflect on the nation-state (Mueggler 2001), kinship (Sangren 2013), mobility (Chu 2010), and the reconstitution of contemporary rural or urban places (Huang 2016a; A. Lee 2015). Their theoretical tendencies are varied, ranging over works by Castoriadis (1987), Munn (1986), Taylor (2004), and scholars of psychoanalysis. This book, being concerned with social imaginary, is closer to and inspired by Mueggler and Huang. For example, it is unsurprising that the state is omnipresent in southwest China, but Mueggler's description of the potent use of rituals (instead of political institutions or policies) by the Lòlop'ò people there to envision the power of the state is insightful (2001: 198). I will show how people, not only in the southwestern mountains, but also on islands in the southeastern seas have configured new modes of action to divert or deflect the grasp of the state. This book also draws on Huang's (2016: 23) exploration of how social imaginings are invented to create new sociality in contemporary Taiwan. Equally, this book shares with Chu (2010: 5) an interest in probing the aspiring subjects, their desires, and their spatial-temporal extensions of transnational mobility. However, I focus more granularly on the imagining subjects themselves, interrogating their subjectification processes and varied uses of mediating technologies to constitute new social imaginaries. I believe these perspectives can bring us closer to the people in this society who always confront instability and face an uncertain future. Above all it is their *in-betweenness and rootlessness* which echo most insistently our own precarious state of living in the contemporary world, while their curiosity in exploring—and resourcefulness in forging—new paths and futures for themselves brings us hope.

The Ethnographic Setting

From north to south, the Matsu archipelago comprises Dongyin, Xiyin, Beigan, Nangan, Xiju and Dongju, among other islands. They run to the northeast of Fujian province, close to the estuary of the Min River and only sixteen nautical miles from Fuzhou (Map 0.1). Because the islands are mountainous and narrow, they were initially used mainly as a temporary waypoint for fishermen from Changle and Lianjiang. Later, dwellings were built around the inlets, until villages eventually formed along the hillsides. Fishermen sold their catch along the coast of Fujian, trading for necessities to bring back (J. Lin 1991). Each island, whether in terms of economy or other social factors, was therefore closely tied to the Fuzhou region. Their customs, cultures, and languages all bore resemblance to those of eastern Fujian.

In the past, each island had its own name (or even multiple names) that spoke to its own special characteristics. For example, the southernmost

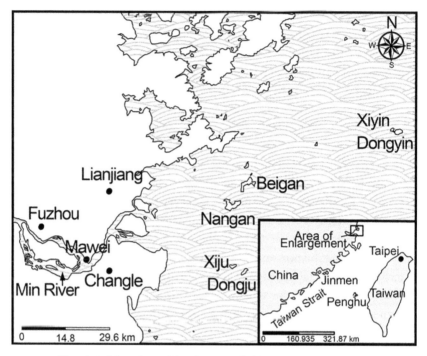

Map 0.1 Matsu's position between Fujian and Taiwan

group of islands was called White Dog (F. *pa ing*), because on misty days, from afar they looked like a crouching dog. The islands were divided east and west, and so became East Dog and West Dog, or lower and upper, so Lower Sands and Upper Sands. The two islands in the middle of the archipelago, Nangan and Beigan, were known as Matsu after the temple to the Goddess Mazu built there (Y. Yang 2014: 143). Located far to the north were Dongyin and Xiyin, whose interaction with the other four islands was fairly limited.

Beginning in the twelfth century, the islands gradually began to be mentioned in local gazetteers. As they were located well out to sea, descriptions were sparse, and details remained unknown. Cultivation of the islands was frequently prohibited or suppressed by adjacent coastal defense authorities, and so they oscillated between being temporary waypoints and abandoned wasteland. This lasted until 1790, when the Qianlong Emperor decreed cultivation in the southeast islands legal, and people from the coast of Fujian gradually began to make their way there. The present villages were mostly formed by the end of the nineteenth century. The people, however, continued to move freely between the islands and the mainland, and were not long-term residents of the archipelago.

In 1949, the armed forces of the Nationalist Government withdrew to the islands off the southeast coast of the mainland after suffering a series of losses to the Communists. The military arrived in Nangan and established the "Matsu Garrison Command Post" (*Matsu shoubeiqu zhihuibu*) and the "Matsu Administrative Office" (*Matsu xingzheng gongshu*) in order to administer Matsu's six islands and the four islands to the north. As those northern islands fell successively under communist control, the Nationalist Government ended up with a total of six islands, which later came to be known generally as "Matsu." The six islands were administratively named Lianjiang county, a name borrowed by the army from the nearby coastal mainland. The objective was to demonstrate that the Republic of China (ROC) still had control over mainland territory in addition to holding Taiwan. Even today, there is a "Lianjiang county" on both sides of the Taiwan Strait. In short, these islands were united by virtue of historical happenstance, as the result of the confrontation between the People's Republic of China (PRC) and the ROC military forces. This book applies the most commonly used term, "Matsu," to refer to these islands.

The arrival of the military utterly transformed life on the islands. The conflict between the PRC and the ROC turned Matsu into a frontline and severed its previously close contact with and reliance on the mainland. In an instant, the islanders were stranded at sea. With 114 nautical miles and more than a ten-hour marine voyage from Taiwan, Matsu was positioned as the sole island border in the distant north of Taiwan. In 1956, the Nationalist Government implemented a system of warzone administration in Matsu, and the islands fell completely under military control. Not only were ordinary Taiwanese prohibited from visiting the islands, but islanders could no longer come and go at will, and so Matsu became a military zone cut off from the rest of the world. Only with the democratization movement in Taiwan in the 1980s, when Matsu people also participated in demanding change, did military rule over the islands finally fade into the history books. However, although martial law has long since been lifted, even today Matsu remains vague in the minds of many Taiwanese, still muddied with past images of military rule and faraway frontiers.

Becoming a frontline brought tremendous restrictions to the lives of the fishermen of Matsu. The fishing economy took a beating and went into a steep decline. When Taiwan embarked on a path of industrialization in the 1970s and needed a vast new workforce, large numbers of Matsu people moved there to find employment. Many of them ended up in the industrial zone in Taoyuan, and in particular today's Bade City. There is still a "Matsu Street" there, with venders selling local products from Matsu. Most of the people who remained in Matsu engaged in some kind of commerce, selling products to the military in what is commonly known as "G. I. Joe business" (*a'bing'ge shengyi*). After martial law was lifted in 1992, the soldiers gradually left, and demand for these products and services waned. As relations improved between Taiwan and China, the two sides established the "Three Great Links" (*da santong*) in 2008, opening up bilateral post, trade, and transportation. Stripped of its military usefulness, Matsu today is facing the difficult question of where to go from here.

Ox Horn in Nangan Island

Matsu's population peaked in 1970 at 17,000 people. The decline of the fishing economy and subsequent emigration brought that number to around 5,500 by 1990. At present, there are more than 10,000 people registered in Matsu, but long-term residents number only between 5,000–6,000. I have conducted interviews with people across all of the islands, but my in-depth fieldwork was carried out in Ox Horn (F. *ngu oyh*) in Nangan.[4] This village is located in northeastern Nangan (Map 0.2) and was the island's primary village before 1960. This was mainly because the village faces the waters shared with Beigan, and the tides in both directions are quite rapid, making it an excellent place for fishermen to set up their nets (J. Liu 1996a). Indeed, many fishermen settled there in order to be close to their fishing grounds. The Fujian provincial government set up a salt warehouse there at the beginning of the twentieth century so that the fishermen could easily salt their catch.

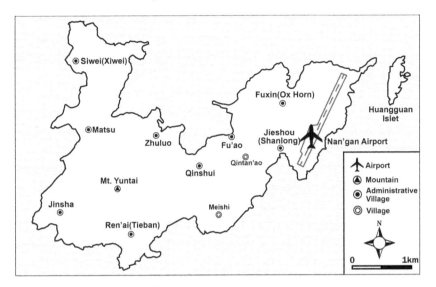

Map 0.2 Nangan Island

After the Nationalist Government took control of the islands, the village became politically important, as the warzone administration established its offices (later to become the Lianjiang county government), stationed security and law enforcement officers, and built a hospital and other facilities there. Yet since land in Ox Horn was limited, there were not sufficient opportunities for development, and the government organizations successively left the village to find larger sites on which they could expand. As the fishing economy floundered and waves of locals left for Taiwan, the village fell into decline. The history of Ox Horn demonstrates several important historical changes that Matsu as a whole underwent, as well as the issues the archipelago is currently facing, which is why I chose it as the main site for my field research. Another important site is Ox Horn's neighboring village, Shanlong (Jieshou), where the county government seat and the only marketplace on Nangan Island are located. Much of the information about the fishing economy in this book was collected in Dongyin, the northernmost island close to many rich fishing grounds. In the past, when the fishing season approached, many Matsu locals would gather there for large-scale fishing, and so many residents there were highly experienced fishermen and often excellent storytellers. I also conducted interviews in Taoyuan, Taiwan, and in some cities in mainland China where I followed my informants during fieldwork.

The place names of Nangan mentioned in this book are all displayed in Map 0.2. The islands and villages of Matsu often have two different names, one the locals use and one decreed by the military. If the army felt that the name of a place sounded "uncouth," they gave it a new name. The new ones generally connote military or governmental ideology; for example, Baiquan (White Dog) was renamed as Juguang (an allusion to a historical allegory about recovering national territory), Ox Horn as Fuxing (referring to the rejuvenation of China), Shanlong (a small piece of land by the mountains) as Jieshou (a reference to celebrating Chiang Kai-shek's birthday), Tieban (a plank of iron) as Ren'ai (meaning 'love for humanity,' a Confucian virtue), and so on. Locals became accustomed to the new names and often used both interchangeably. Because the names of the islands and their main Goddess are homophonic, I have for clarity decided to use "Matsu" for the name of the islands and "Mazu" for the name of the Goddess.

Jinmen, Matsu, and Beyond

Matsu was not the only archipelago on the military frontline. Jinmen, to its south, was the site of several important battles. It is better known generally, and also has been the subject of more scholarship. A range of research has been conducted by a succession of scholars, including on its kinship, architecture, and migration process (Chiang 2009, 2011), as well as on its economy and religion (Chi 2009, 2015). In recent years the historian Michael Szonyi has made very important contributions to the study of Jinmen's social history. His *Cold War Island* (2008) takes the perspective of geopolitics to analyze how the war between the PRC and the ROC and the US–Soviet Cold War had a sudden and profound effect on the local society. He explains how militarization (Enloe 2000; Lutz 2004) penetrated the families, religion, and economy: military values and interests, together with various modernization projects, turned frontline Jinmen into a "militarized utopian modernity" (Szonyi 2008: 6).

Szonyi's book offers an important basis for understanding Matsu's history. His analytic point—placing Jinmen in the geopolitical framework of the Cold War—gives us a much wider lens through which to examine local society. My book benefits greatly from it. As an anthropologist, however, I take a different approach: my research and fieldwork are focused on the islanders' experiences of this historical period from their *lived worlds*. Those who lived through military rule do not easily reveal their inner feelings and thoughts about that time. But through their living experiences—spatial movements, economic practices, and leisure activities—we can come closer to their lives during the military period.

This book also takes the different histories and ecologies of Matsu and Jinmen into consideration to explore how the same system of rules applied in two different places can give rise to alternate worlds and views. Put differently, I am concerned with the ways that local culture and society articulate with the military. For example, unlike Jinmen with its longstanding history of cultivation and well-developed society, Matsu in its early stages was merely a temporary stopover for fishermen. The rudimentary and very limited development on the islands meant that locals had conflicted feelings about military rule and its effects, since along with the strictures of authoritarian rule, the army also brought large-scale construction projects and widespread elementary education. These were advantages that the people living on these small islands had never experienced before. As described above, Matsu was never self-sufficient, and it relied on the mainland for supplies and education. Military rule brought oppression, but it also created new opportunities, engendering, if not a purely positive attitude toward the army, at least a more ambivalent love-hate relationship with it; this is very different from Jinmen.

This rather different picture of the military world in Matsu has to further take account of the culture of fishing. Consider, for example, gender relations: The social situations of women in Matsu during the fishing era, under the warzone period, and in the present day are markedly different from those of women in Jinmen. During the height of the fishing economy, men went out to sea to fish and make money, while women stayed behind and took care of the household. In a society in which marine accidents were common and residence was temporary, women had to take on the role of maintaining the household and often became the center of the house. Despite this, women had no actual income, and their overall status remained low in a patrilineal society. When the army arrived and a military economy was established, however, women had new opportunities to make money. Their economic contributions to the household often exceeded what their husbands could earn from fishing or doing low-level government work. Unlike the women in Jinmen, new economic practices during the military era transformed the women of Matsu, especially those who engaged in petty business with soldiers. They left the isolation of the house and formed their own sister teams; they began to participate in public affairs and gradually gained a space outside of the patrilineal society.

Another quality of the fishing society which characterized this period was its gambling culture. Gambling was a common pastime for islanders as they waited for the tide to turn, and it was an important way of cultivating bravery and daring in fishermen who faced unpredictable situations. It is in the practice of gambling that we most clearly see the Matsu people's characteristic willingness to take chances and wager against fortune. When the army took over, gambling was strictly banned, possibly to prevent unauthorized groups of people from gathering. Nevertheless, it persisted even as the military implemented increasingly harsh punishments. Various kinds of gaming became ever more widespread, reaching people in every walk of life in coordination with their new social and economic dynamics. This book will further explore how these gambling practices became an emotional release and a kind of imaginative evasion by which the islanders could endure, play with, and deflect the oppressive might of military power.

When martial law was finally abolished, all kinds of information channels were opened, and new media technology made its way into Matsu. Owing to its location at the farthest northern border of Taiwan, its scattered islands, and inconvenient transport links, interactions between the islands themselves had never been easy. The unique geography of the archipelago gave the new media technology a chance to thrive, and *Matsu Online*, with its instantaneous newsfeed, quickly swept across the islands. Its focused reporting on Matsu further fostered a new kind of emotional connection between the islands that the army had never encouraged, instead emphasizing the self-sustainability of each island so as to be able to fight independently in a war. Internet technology in Matsu gave rise to a new sense of place (Miller and Horst 2012: 27). This process was completely different from Jinmen where a single big island dominates, and which is also much better connected by air to Taiwan. Although a similar website, "Good Morning, Kinmen" (*Zao'an Jinmen*), followed the style of *Matsu Online*, it was never as influential. The peculiar effervescence of cultural practices and media technology in contemporary Matsu shows that it is a highly imaginative space which can no longer be understood only through a Cold War Framework. *Imagination is the key to this frontier society.*

Book Outline

The book is divided into three parts—namely, the history of the Matsu archipelago, new technologies of the imagination, and fantasias of the future. These cover the span from the early settlement of the islands to the period of military rule and lead up to the current era. Part I is the historical portion, with Chapter 1 introducing pre-1949 Matsu as a stateless and fragmented society. Lying at the frontier of the state, the islanders had strong links to the mainland. Chapter 2 discusses the complete transformation of the islands upon the establishment of the warzone administration in Matsu. This chapter focuses on the reformation of landscape and on space; that is, the ubiquity of military institutions, the imposed isolation of the islands, and the suffering involved in difficult sea journeys to Taiwan.

Chapter 3 analyzes the appearance of new social categories and the changes in gender relations in wartime Matsu. I show that the military's strictures on the fishing economy brought about its eventual collapse, while its guaranteed admission program gave rise to a new category of public servants and teachers who returned from Taiwan to work in return for free education received there. Those who remained on the islands engaged in petty business, catering to the needs of the army. The status of women was notably elevated as they began to have greater opportunities to earn money. The final chapter in Part I, Chapter 4, examines gambling practices within the context of the islands' fishing culture and the socioeconomic transformation in the military period to demonstrate that what started as a leisure activity of fishermen eventually became a pervasive daily pastime for Matsu residents from every walk of life.

Following the dismantling of the military government in 1992, new media technology arrived in Matsu. Part II explores how this technology enabled the creation of a new imaginary of Matsu. Chapter 5 discusses how the website *Matsu Online* quickly became an essential aspect of island life, with its finger on the pulse of society. Simultaneously, it surmounted the limitations of the archipelago's geography, connecting Matsu, Taiwan, and China together into a "new online community." Chapter 6 narrows the focus to individuals and explores how the advent of *Matsu Online* opened up possibilities for the development of individual imaginations. This chapter takes the wildly popular *Matsu Online* serial *The Wartime Childhood of Leimengdi* as its main case study to explore how online writing can become a process of subjectification by which individuals and social relationships are renewed. It lays important groundwork for the final section of the book, which discusses the transition from individual imaginations to social imaginary.

Part III, focusing on island fantasias of the future, addresses the different imaginaries towards which the Matsu subjects are aspiring. Chapter 7 takes three women born in the period 1950–80 as examples with which to analyze the rise of a new self-consciousness among women and the changing meanings of marriage and family. Women in present-day Matsu are still struggling to balance traditional motherhood and their careers. Their difficulties importantly reflect the challenges that contemporary Matsu society is grappling with.

Chapters 8 and 9 discuss how the educated middle-aged generation who returned from Taiwan deployed rituals, myths, and religious material practices to connect Matsu to a larger world. Chapter 8 looks at how Cao Yixiong—a member of the county legislature who had worked in Taiwan—introduced the Taiwanese idea of a "community building project" to turn Matsu into an "Eastern Fujian Culture Village," and later constructed a temple with the support of local residents. I show that the materializing process of temple building became a medium in which individual imaginations could negotiate and spread out into a social imaginary. Chapter 9 examines pilgrimages, the invented myth of "Goddess Mazu in Matsu," and the construction of a giant statue of the Goddess. I point out that these innovations in rituals, myths, and material practices are a series of imaginaries which attempt to rescale Matsu within a greater geopolitical framework in order to forge a bridge between the two contentious sides of the Strait.

The final chapter discusses the attempts of the county commissioner, Yang Shuiseng, to bring to Matsu an American gaming capitalist's global project, an "Asian Mediterranean." The vehement debates this project elicited—leading up to a public referendum—demonstrate that contemporary Matsu subjects have diverse visions of the future. This chapter pays particular attention to the young generation that grew up after the military period, whose understanding of Matsu and expectation of the future are entirely different from those of elderly fishermen or middle-aged generations. Finding an amicable resolution for these contending views of the future will present a challenge to the islands in the days ahead.

In the conclusion, I argue that imagining subjects are a vital basis for the social imaginary. Despite the fact that the projects "Eastern Fujian Culture Village," "Goddess Mazu in Matsu," and "Asian Mediterranean" seemingly all came to naught, the imagining subjects still remain potent and continue to pursue further dreams. The case of Matsu, an isolated archipelago in the Taiwan Strait, is thus not an exception. Its liminal existence epitomizes the experiences of Taiwan (Weller 2000) and of many other places which are caught between much bigger powers.

The Matsu archipelago, in many ways, also reminds us of the Trobriand islands. Though they have in common their minute size and relative geographical isolation, it is the Trobrianders' imaginative capacity and adventurous explorations of their imaginings that truly capture our attention. We are already familiar with the Trobrianders in the Pacific; we are still getting to know the Matsu people's daring adventures in the mercurial contemporary world.

Part I

History of the Matsu Archipelago

1   Forbidden Outpost

Coming and Going

The most comprehensive local gazetteer about the early history of Fujian, *Sanshan zhi* (1174–89), records that there are many islands in the northeast sea of Lianjiang County, among which are "the Upper and Lower Gantang in the sea."[1] Upper Gantang and Lower Gantang are the old names of Nangan and Beigan, the major islands of Matsu. A later record explains the origin of the name: "Gantang ... was named for its abundance of cogon grass (*maogan*)."[2] A stele standing in Dawang Temple, Tieban Village, Nangan, further reveals the ancients' footprints on the island. The inscription reads: "Lin Youcai happily donated twenty *guan* of Zhongtong paper notes." Zhongtong paper notes were issued during the reign of Kablai Khan (1260–87). By the early years of the thirteenth century, therefore, fishermen were already docking their boats in Nangan and building a temple there.

When Japanese pirates became rampant along the coast in the early Ming period, the government adopted a scorched-earth policy as its coastal defense strategy. In 1387 (Hongwu 20), all the islanders were moved back to the mainland, leaving the Matsu Islands deserted.[3] The storytellers' memories help us to track this large-scale movement of population. According to Chen Jinmei, a storyteller in Shanlong, Nangan, it was said that there once lived a family with the surname Sun and the village was thus once called "Sunlong." Later, when Japanese pirates went on the rampage, the Ming emperor, Zhu Yuanzhang, ordered all the people evacuated and had the whole village burnt down, turning it into a barren wasteland (J. Liu 1996b).

Despite an official edict that "not a single ship should sail the seas," coastal residents began to revisit Matsu for fishing or resettlement by the mid-Ming. At that time, there were already thirteen settlements in Nangan and Beigan. An important gazetteer, *Bamin tongzhi* (1490), records:

> The Upper Gantang Mountain in the sea has winding and twisting peaks and ridges, on which are six ports including Zhuhu and Huwei. The Lower Gantang Mountain protruding from the sea stands opposite the Upper Gantang Mountain; it has a steep, tall shape and has thereon seven ports including Baisha and Jingcheng. ... In Hongwu 20, to defend against Japanese pirates, all the people were moved [inland] near the city.[4]

Yet in the early Qing years, the residents of Matsu were once again ordered to move: To wipe out the anti-Qing forces led by Koxinga (Zheng Chenggong), the Qing government issued the Great Clearance Order. In 1661, the coastal residents in Fujian, Zhejiang and Guangdong were forced to move 30 *li* inland:[5]

> South Gantang and North Gantang are in the northeast seas of the county, with a distance of eighty *li* from each other; both are on strategic locations and have military posts. South Gantang belongs to Min County, and North Gantang to Lianjiang. Beacon towers and watchtowers have been established on North Gantang, where there are ... seven ports. ...In the early Ming the people were moved inland. The ban on dwelling in coastal areas was later lifted, and agricultural and fishing activities flourished. But when our country was newly established, the rebellious forces in the sea were yet to be pacified, so the people were moved inland again.[6]

After that year, Matsu was abandoned once again (S. Li 2006: 75). In 1683 (Kangxi 22), following the pacification of Taiwan, the Qing government gradually lifted the sea ban, allowing the coastal residents to return to their homeland. Nonetheless, it was still forbidden to move to the coastal islands, or to fish or build shelters there. Nangan and Beigan remained "deserted islands in the sea."[7] It wasn't until the reign of Qianlong (1735–96) that coastal residents gradually started to colonize the islands. Fishermen went there to "build shelters and to hang fishing nets" (*daliao guawang*), and the number of settlers steadily multiplied (131). This, however, disturbed the officials: "It is inevitable that some tricky fishermen would build shelters or erect poles to hang fishing nets. ... But it is reported that there are even people who live there permanently, who gather crowds to cultivate the land and the mountains, and who disobey expulsion orders."[8]

Faced with this trend, some officials in Zhejiang and Fujian (such as the Zhejiang Commissioner, Gu Xuechao, 1721–?) worried that the people on the outlying islands would become outlaws and thus suggested burning down the illegal thatch settlements that had been stealthily built over time. Others (such as the Viceroy of Zhejiang-Fujian, Gioroi Ulana, 1739–1795) feared that if all the people of the numerous islands along the coasts of Zhejiang and Fujian were expelled, they would be out of work and might even be forced to turn to banditry. Gioroi Ulana suggested that those people who were already incorporated in the *baojia* (household registration system) should not be expelled, while other scattered households and those living on forbidden lands should be returned to their domicile of origin and their shelters burned. As for fishermen sailing to the islands and building temporary shelters, the local officials should go and inspect them and issue licenses as appropriate.[9]

As habitation of the southeastern outlying islands had been debated for a long time, Emperor Qianlong finally decided to legalize it. The imperial decree in 1790 (Qianlong 55) proclaimed that the coastal residents had lived and worked in peace and contentment on the islands for a long time; if they were suddenly ordered to move, hundreds of thousands of people along the coasts might be put out of work, and so they were deserving of sympathy. Besides, if the local officials handled this matter improperly, they would disrupt people's lives and might even cause them to become vagrants or pirates, a most unsatisfactory outcome. The emperor thus ordered that people on the outlying islands should be allowed to live there without fear of expulsion, with the exception of areas classified as forbidden lands. As for the scattered households, most of them were impoverished, and it was wrong to dash the hopes of such people. In the end, the emperor decreed the following:

> The fishermen sail the seas to fish; it is improper to comprehensively forbid them from setting up temporary shelters on the islands. In addition, since there are only a few households, it is not difficult to perform an inspection. …Thus people shall be allowed to live on these islands, and their houses need not be burnt.[10]

From then on, it was no longer illegal to stay on the islands, and the number of people there gradually increased.

From the mid-Qing to the late Qing, a steady stream of coastal inhabitants of Lianjiang, Changle and other counties moved to Matsu. Yet the
residents still traveled back and forth between mainland China and the
islands. Previous studies on Taiwan have shown a close relationship
between temple construction and settlement formation (See 1973;
C. Hsu 1973). The temples in Nangan were mostly built during the
Daoguang years (1820–50) in the late Qing (H. Wang 2000); the Matsu
residents probably settled there in this period. By the early twentieth century, there were already more than 300 households in Tieban, Nangan.[11]

As isolated and peripheral islands, the historical literature about Matsu
is very limited, and descriptions are even rarer. However, the few extant
entries disclose again and again the fact that Matsu had historically been
a forbidden outpost. Located in the southeast seas of China, Matsu was
inevitably under the sway of the constantly changing frontier policies of
the government. The fishermen fluctuated between using the islands as
temporary shelters, settling there permanently and deserting the islands
when forced to do so.

Signposts in the Sea

As indicated above, historical records of Matsu are scarce. Other documents, such as nautical maps, mark the islands as signposts in the sea and
describe how they may serve as places to ride out the tide or to take
shelter from the wind before entering Fuzhou, the provincial capital.

Sitting at the mouth of Min River, Nangan, Beigan and Baiquan appear
in many ancient nautical charts; Dongyin, Nangan and Beigan are marked
in "Zheng He's Nautical Chart."[12] S. Li (2006: 46–7) further indicates
how Matsu was one of the stations along the sailing routes frequented by
both investiture ships (*fengzhou*) and tribute ships (*gongchuan*) during the
Ming and Qing periods. Investiture ships were sent from Fuzhou to
Ryukyu to confer kingship on its kings, while tribute ships carried tributes
back to the court. An early Qing record (1684) states:

> The two mountains of Gantang are very close to each other. ...Whenever a
> scout is sent to Tamsui, Keelung, Ryukyu or Japan, he always departs from
> there and returns to the port. Each time the Japanese pirates arrive at Gantang,
> they also put down anchor there to gather water.[13]

Historically, the Matsu Islands harbored ships destined for Fuzhou while they waited for the tide or took shelter from the wind. The role of Matsu as a safe harbor became more prominent when Western forces reached China in the late Qing. After its defeat in the Opium War of 1842, China ratified the Treaty of Nanking with Britain, stipulating the opening of five ports along the southeastern coast of China. To safely navigate the reef-ridden waters, the British Navy sent vessels in 1843 to map the islands and reefs along the coast of eastern China, and to determine their latitude and longitude. The results were published in *The China Sea Directory* (Reed and King 1867), offering an overview of the ports on different islands.

The British Navy provided more information about navigation in the sea of Fujian, including entries about Baiquan (now called Juguang), Nangan, and Beigan (S. Li 2006: 98). An Englishman named Collinson (1846: 231) indicated that if ships encountered the northeast monsoon before entering Min River, they could dock in the south of Baiquan Island to take shelter from the wind. The British warship HMS Cornwallis was recorded to have anchored there for five days due to a strong monsoon wind. Ships could obtain small amounts of fresh-water in Baiquan and hire pilots capable of navigating ships to the Min River during ebb tide. Two ports in Nangan could harbor ships during the northeast and southwest monsoon seasons, respectively, and fresh-water was also available in both ports. The south of Beigan also allowed for anchorage, and junks and small fishing boats traveled back and forth between Beigan and the Min River.

Later, in order to help ships identify routes through the reefs, Robert Hart, who served as the Inspector-General of the Chinese Imperial Maritime Customs Service, built two lighthouses on the south and north ends of the Matsu Islands in 1872 and 1904. The Dongju Lighthouse in the south directed boats to safely enter and exit Fuzhou and Mawei, while the Dongyin Lighthouse in the north directed them to sail in and out of Sandu'ao (see Map 1.1).

The two lighthouses stood as signposts to guide boats in the sea of Min. In this period, the Matsu Islands were influenced by the treaty port of Fuzhou: the islanders started to have access to Western ideas and goods. Today, houses including elements of Western styles (F. *huang ngiang nah*)

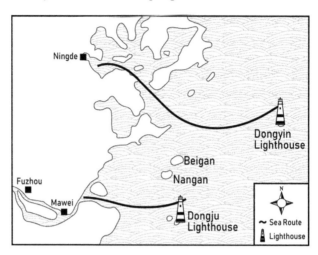

Map 1.1 The lighthouses in Matsu and the sea routes around them
(Map based on Wang, Wang, and He 2016: 61)

are still very popular in Matsu. These houses in a mixed style were
probably developed by artisans inspired by the foreign houses in Fujian.

Pirates and Bandits

As the Matsu Islands were located at the very border of the state, and
there was no formal governance over it, numerous pirates and bandits
rose to power one after another. For a long period, the islands along the
coast of southeastern China were infested with pirates. On Dongju Island
a stele commemorating the defeat of Japanese pirates by a general in the
late Ming period (1617) still stands. The notorious pirate Cai Qian
(1761–1809), who plundered Zhejiang, Fujian, and Taiwan during the
mid-Qing, was active on the Matsu Islands. Historical descriptions show
that Cai Qian often hid himself in the seas of North and South Gantang
(Beigan and Nangan today). According to a memorandum from Li
Diantu ([1738]–1812), the viceroy of Fujian, while the coastal navy was
gathering in Gantang to blockade the pirates, all of a sudden, "thirty-
something pirate ships sailed out from South Gantang; the navy bom-
barded and fired at them, chasing them in full force …all the way to the
outer sea of Baiquan."[14]

Cai Qian exacted taxes from the island fishermen and forced the people to supply freshwater. In addition, Cai built shacks in Beigan, and procured rice, food, and material for ropes to use on ships.[15] Even in the present day, many elders can still point out the traces Cai Qian left on Matsu. For example, the Matsu people call Cai Qian "the Sea Emperor" (F. *hai huongna*) (J. Liu 1996c); "Datielu" (lit. the blacksmithing furnace) in Tieban Village was said to be the site where Cai forged his weapons; and the crude cannon originally placed in the Goddess Mazu Temple in Tieban was said to be forged by him as well (Wang, Wang, and He 2016: 104). It is said that the four Goddess Mazu temples in Matsu were all built by him (J. Liu 1996c); indeed, the name of the islands originated from one of those temples (Y. Yang 2014: 143–4).

The relationship between the islanders and the pirates was in fact even more complicated. Previous studies on the pirates in southeastern China have shown that the pirates relied on the coastal residents in China or the islanders to supply the necessities of life (Antony 2003: 17; Murray 1987: 89). The story of the Wheat-Field-Plowing King (F. *Lemah Toyuong*) told by Chen Ruichen, an elder in Dongyin, reveals more about the ambivalent relationship between the islanders and the pirates:

When the pirate ships were docked in Bei'ao Bay, Cai Qian was suddenly agitated and could not sit or lie down. He stood up and strode to the ship's wheel. The sky above was completely cloudless, and the strong, powerful south winds blew directly at him; suddenly he spied on Bei'ao Hill a farmer and a large yellow ox plowing a field of immature green wheat shoots. Cai was greatly surprised by this scene and muttered to himself, "a farmer shouldn't be doing that to unripe wheat—how strange!" So he instantly sent out some men to investigate the matter, ordering them to report back to him as soon as possible.

The men sailed ashore on sampans, but when they climbed the hill, they saw neither the farmer nor any green wheat but spotted instead dozens of giant sails on the remote horizon in the direction of Matsu. It was not the fishing season, so there should not have been so many ships in the sea. The men glanced at one another, knowing from experience that something was wrong. They hurried back to the ship and reported what they saw to Cai Qian. Cai thought it very likely that the navy was coming …so he ordered all his ships to embark at once and flee downwind, escaping a possible disaster.

Because Cai Qian called himself "the Sea Emperor," Cai ordained the mysterious farmer as "the Wheat-Field-Plowing King" in gratitude for saving his life, and had his statue placed on the left side of Goddess Mazu in Dongyin Temple. (J. Liu 2003)

In fact, the fate of Matsu was intertwined with pirates and bandits not only in the Qing Dynasty but also well into the early twentieth century, when the newly formed Nationalist government set up in Beigan the first Gan-Xi Joint Security Office (administering Gantang and Xiyang Islands) in 1934. However, in this time of political instability, the Nationalist government was unable to control the numerous islands in the southeast seas. When the Sino-Japanese War broke out in 1937, the Japanese forces quickly came to these islands (although they did not occupy them). The Japanese warships patrolled the ocean, mainly with an eye to preparing an attack on southeastern mainland China. Meanwhile, the Nationalist government deployed troops on both banks of the mouth of Min River to defend the provincial capital of Fuzhou. During the turmoil of war, islands in the southeast seas, such as Matsu, became an ungoverned no-man's- land where many local despots rose to power one after another, transforming themselves into pirates. Japan bought off the local forces to fight the Chinese, calling them the "Fujian National Salvation Army" (*Fujian jiuguojun*). Though the pirates and bandits abided by the orders of the East Asia Development Board in Xiamen under the Japanese, they also cooperated covertly with the National Bureau of Investigation and Statistics, profiting from both sides of the conflict.[16] As for the pirates themselves, they constantly clashed with each other, seeking every opportunity to drive their opponents away. Up to the present day, legends continue to circulate about the pirates and about the many buildings they left on the islands, such as the pirate house in Beigan (see Fig. 1.1).

This house was built by a particularly menacing bandit in Beigan named Chen Zhongping during his heyday in the 1940s. Hiring masons from mainland China to construct it, Chen also had a secret tunnel dug under the floor to allow him escape when needed. Right before completion, however, with only the floor of the second level unfinished, Chen's "boss" Lin Yihe was killed by the Japanese and he was forced to become a fugitive. Chen did not have a chance to use the house even for a single day. He was later killed in Nangan (J. Liu 2004a).

When I first visited Beigan, I was amused to find my guest house hostess reciting in fluent Fuzhou dialect the following limerick composed by Chen:

Fig. 1.1 Pirate house
(Photo by the author)

My ancestors moved from Heshang to Beigan,	(*tsuluong ouhluong, tshiengky poyh kang*)
And lodged above Qinbi called himself Banshan.	(*khyngmiah suong'o, toho puangnang*)
In youth I worked in Yuansheng, buying fish,	(*tsoey' iu tshouhsing, nguongsing kautshiang*)
I lost all my money because of gambling.	(*ingui tujieng, suokho kangkang*)
Having no way out, to Nangan did I flee,	(*mouhhuah khotaih, tahlouh nangngang*)
Where the Yihe army granted a position to me,	(*ngiehuo uilui, hungngo tsokuang*)
raised to a director, to Beigan I transferred	(*kuangtso tsuoeing, teusuong poyhkang*)
Whoever hears my title Quanquan gets scared,	(*miangho kheingngeing. hungnoeyng tukiang*)
for if I beat you up, a single punch will strike your heart.	(*kungnau khatheih, suohthui kau ny singngang*)

I still clearly remember the rather realistic punch she threw in my direction to illustrate the last line!

This limerick was obviously intended to intimidate the local people, but it also briefly accounts for the origin of Chen Zhongping and his rise to power. His ancestors came from Changle, Fujian and settled in a place above the Qinbi Village in Beigan. As a young man, he worked in a store in Qiaozi, trading shrimp and other common low-cost fish. Having lost everything by gambling, he fled to Nangan to seek protection from Lin Yihe, a pirate chief. Later, Chen was assigned to Beigan as a boss, collecting protection money from passing fishing boats and merchant ships. All the people in Beigan were afraid of him, for if they dared to disobey him, they would suffer his wrath and even violence.

Other pirates also often compelled the locals to collect fees for them. For example, Chen Ruichen, the Dongyin elder, recalled his own experience:

> In the early 1940s, I was forced by the Peace Salvation Army to become the security head (*baozhang*) of the Dongyong Security Group. ...There were tithing heads (*jiazhang*) under security heads, and at that time the usual practice went as follows: lots written with words like beds, tables, chairs and quilts were put into a bamboo jar or an iron can; each tithing head drew a lot and "collected" the item specified on the lot from each household. (Liu and Qiu 2002 [2001]: 475–6)

During the Second World War, many pirates and bandits of this kind dominated the sea along the coast of Fujian. For example, Lin Yihe, who granted Chen Zhongping a position, was an important figure on the Matsu Islands.

The rise of Lin Yihe vividly illustrates how these islands remained "a place outside civilization" (*huawai zhi di*) during the early twentieth century, where local despots, the Japanese, and various Chinese forces collaborated, competed, and clashed with one another. As noted above, it wasn't until 1934 that a state institute called the Gan-Xi Joint Security Office was established in Matsu for the very first time, with Wang Xuanyou appointed as its director. Yet in less than two years, Wang was shot dead by Wu Yike, a bandit from Changle, China, who seized the office's guns. After that, Wu often extorted money and goods in Nangan and Beigan; he even robbed the house of Lin Yihe, by then an important local figure. One day the following year, when Wu sailed out to go plundering, Lin captured him and delivered him to the government of Lianjiang County in China. For his actions, Lin was awarded the position of "police captain" (*tanjing*) by the county government and made responsible for anti-smuggling operations at sea. Before long, however,

Lin himself was listed as wanted by the county government and forced to flee because gangsters in his employ had stolen legally confiscated opium. One day, when a village in Nangan was staging performances for deities, Lin Yihe broke into the Township Office and stole its guns, thereby formally becoming a pirate living on pillage and booty. Lin collected protection fees from fishermen and exacted taxes from passing ships (P. Zhang 2001 and J. Liu 2004b). He also opened an opium shop in Matsu, where opium was sold publicly (J. Lin 2006).

As previously mentioned, the Japanese bought off the local forces and named them the "Fujian Peace National Salvation Army" (*Fujian jiuguo-jun*); Lin Yihe was among their ranks. He was incorporated in 1939 and appointed "the commander of the first road army under the second army group" (*Di'er jituan diyi lujun siling*), while simultaneously cooperating with the National Bureau of Investigation and Statistics, thus playing both sides. At his peak, he built a munitions factory in Siwei Village, Nangan, and mustered his own private armed force. Later, an unfair division of spoils triggered a conflict between Lin Yihe and Lin Zhen, who was in charge of the army group in Dongju. In 1942, Lin Zhen introduced the forces of Zhang Yizhou from Nanri Island and, conspiring with the Japanese, lured Lin Yihe into the sea to drown him (P. Zhang 2001: 983). After defeating Lin Yihe, Zhang Yizhou renovated the Mazu Temple in Nangan in 1943 and erected a stele in front of the temple as a mark of his victory.

Taking over Lin Yihe's forces, Zhang Yizhou built his short-lived "Kingdom of the Min Sea (*minhai wangchao*)" which was headquartered in Nangan and stretched from Xiamen in the south to Zhejiang in the north (C. Zhang 1984: 94). Skillful in dealing with the Japanese, Zhang took good advantage of them:

> Whenever the Japanese special agents were sent ...to South Gantang, Zhang treated them to feasts and even provided opium and morphine to them. ...As for the Japanese on the warships in the sea around Dongju Island, when they reached Baiquan or South Gantang, Zhang also paid due respect to them, so the Japanese didn't have any worry in the Fujian seas. If the Japanese warships mooring offshore at the mouth of Min River requested freshwater, vegetables or other provisions, Zhang was always responsive, and he also often offered intelligence collected from the mainland to the Japanese. Meanwhile, he used ...steamships to smuggle goods banned for export during wartime, such

as food, tung oil and timber, to Xiamen and Shanghai …in exchange for cotton yarn, cloth and other materials. After transporting the materials back to the islands, he resold them to the mainland, earning a good return. (J. Lin 2007)

Zhang also realized that Matsu was on the route from Hong Kong to Shanghai and was frequented by many merchant ships. With roads often blocked during wartime, the sea routes became highly lucrative. Accordingly,

[Zhang] established a taxation bureau in South Gantang and set up branches on other important islands to collect cargo tax, fishing tax, license tax etc. … Every ship that passed through the sea near Gantang had to apply for a sailing license from the appropriate taxation bureau, and the fishing boats in the sea had to pay fishing taxes. (J. Lin 2007)

As the Japanese gradually retreated in 1945, Zhang quickly pivoted and opportunistically pledged support to the Nationalist government, transforming himself into part of its "Fujian Vanguard Army" (*Fujian xianqian jun*), though he was dismissed soon after his incorporation.

To conclude, we could say that in the early twentieth century Matsu was a stateless society located within a no-man's-land: ruthless bandits and pirates scrambled for power and profit using physical force and tactical ingenuity and surviving in the crevices between warring Japan and China. On these outlying islands they rose, fell, and vanished in the blink of an eye, fleeting as shadows. As the local saying goes: "He whose fist is strongest takes everything" (F. *Tie nëüng kungnaumo tuai, tie noeyng to sieh*). Indeed, the Matsu islanders seemed to take this for granted.

Islands Indivisible from the Mainland

The people who migrated from the coasts of China to Matsu mainly made their living by fishing. They usually chose an area near the sea as a base, and later extended the village inland toward the mountains (see Fig. 1.2).

Fishing was a man's job and the only source of family income. When men sailed out, they spent all day or sometimes many days at sea, and so the management of the household fell solely on women who were responsible for chores such as cultivating sweet potatoes, cutting firewood for fuel, feeding livestock, and taking care of children. Life on the sea was

Fig. 1.2 Ox Horn surrounds the inlet and spreads uphill
(Photo by Yang Suisheng, approximately 1986)

unpredictable and dangerous and the threat of disaster loomed large; shipwrecks were relatively common. When a fisherman did not return, the entire responsibility for the family fell on the shoulders of his widow. There is a saying in Matsu to the effect that "a wife (or a mother) is a bucket hoop (F. *Lauma/ nuongne sei thoeyngkhu*)." The analogy drawn between a bucket hoop that encircles the bucket to prevent the staves from falling apart and the role of a mother who holds the family together, protecting the children from destitution, is an apt one.[17] If only one family member is to survive most "would rather that the mother lives" (F. *gangnguong si nuongma, me a si nuongne*). Nonetheless, the hardships endured by widowed mothers and fatherless children were almost unbearable in these barren islands, and thus the Matsu people also practiced a special kind of marriage arrangement in which a man came into the family of a widow (F. *suongmuong*). His responsibility was to support the family and to take care of the children left by the deceased husband. This allowed the children to receive good care, instead of becoming "a burden as children-in-law" (*tuoyou ping*). The rewards flowed both ways: the man entering a widow's family earned respect for looking after her children, and the family's continuation was guaranteed.

As for the inter-household relationships, people who had lineage relations or came from the same place usually formed their own communities inside the village. Those who came to Matsu alone would ally with people with similar circumstances into multi-surname dwelling units. In Ox Horn, for example, there are five major neighborhood units, including Da'ao (F. *toey o*, Big Inlet), Niujiaopi (F. *ngu oyh biah*, Ox Horn Slope), Xibianshan (F. *se bieng nang*, Western Hill), Nanguan (F. *nang nguang*, Southerner's Place), and Liujianpai (F. *loeyh kang be*, Line of Six Houses). Not only do the residents of each of these units have diverse hometown origins, but they also worship their own separate deities. Before the communal temple was built in 2008 (discussed in Chapter 8), they organized separate ceremonies on festival days. Take, for example, the Lantern Festival (F. *pe mang*), which is the most important local celebration. Each unit observed it on a different day; thus the same festival was celebrated as many as eleven times in a village! Even though both banks of the inlet in Ox Horn had jointly built a temple for a deity named "Big Brother Chen" (F. *ting noey o*), each area still chose a different time (during the Dragon Boat Festival and the Mid-Autumn Festival, respectively) to hold the ceremony. In other words, although the villagers of Ox Horn lived together around the inlet, they were not integrated into a community in this period.

Inter-village interactions were limited too. The islanders usually sold fish directly to the mainland in exchange for daily necessities, but there were few inter-village exchanges inside the islands. The islanders seldom visited other villages except to see relatives, and the roads between villages were merely narrow trails overgrown with grass. The Matsu people called the act of going to another village "traversing a mountain" (F. *kuo lang*), a phrase which clearly illustrates the inconvenience of movement. A good number of Matsu people mentioned that "it was faster to row a boat" to a neighboring village.

During this period, the residents of the Matsu Islands formed an indivisible whole with their hometowns on the mainland. Indeed, the islanders usually replicated their hometown lineage relations on the islands. For example, of the Cao lineage members in Ox Horn, only the fourth and seventh branches lived in the village; the descendants of the eighth branch were isolated on the other side of the mountain, near the islet of Huangguanyu, lying to the east of Nangan. Not until their shabby thatched huts were burned in an accidental fire were they allowed by the other lineage members to move into Ox Horn. This spatial allocation in Ox Horn reflected the relationships of the Cao lineage in their homeland, Caozhu Village in Fujian. It is said that the founding ancestor of the Cao only had seven sons. The eighth branch comprised the descendants of a long-term farm laborer who was considered to be "of impure ancestry" by the other lineage members. When members of the fourth, seventh, and eighth branches moved to Ox Horn, the Cao people still isolated the descendants of the last branch away from the village as before. This spatial distribution reveals how the early society in Matsu duplicated social relations in the mainland.

Between the islands themselves, there were also linkages based on the relations radiating from the hometown. After moving to Matsu, lineage members still kept in close contact with one another even when they were on different islands. For example, the Caos in Ox Horn were the descendants of the seventh branch Cao lineage in Caozhu, Changle. Some of the members of the seventh branch had also moved to Fuzheng Village in Dongju. In earlier days, these Cao lineage members scattered across different islands even bought boats together. Some Ox Horn people said their parents would, on their deathbeds, urge them in particular to keep up close contact with their relatives on other islands.

Similarly, if lineage members moved to different villages on the same island, their relationships would be even closer. For example, there are two lineages with the surname Chen in Shanlong, the largest village in Nangan. Though both Chens came from Changle, China, one belonged to the Chen lineage of Wenshi (hereafter Wenshi Chen), and the other to the Chen lineage of Lingnan (hereafter Lingnan Chen). The ancestors of the Wenshi Chen originally came from Jiangtian, Changle; some of them later moved to Nangan, and they developed into an important group in Shanlong. There are fewer Lingnan Chen than Wenshi Chen in Shanlong itself, but this is not the case when we take the whole of Nangan Island into consideration: in addition to Shanlong, the Lingnan Chen moved to the villages of Tieban and Meishi. Indeed, if the Lingnan Chen united their members in all three villages, they would outnumber the Wenshi Chen and become the biggest group. Liu Jiaguo, a local historian of Matsu, has recorded a dispute in 1930 between the Wenshi Chen and Lingnan Chen which expanded to the other villages in Nangan, and eventually their hometown—Changle, Fujian:

> In Shanlong Village, Chen Guanbao of the Wenshi Chen had an argument with Chen Zhengzheng of Lingnan Chen. The family of Chen Guanbao ran a cargo business that made a lot of money. Chen Guanbao, well-fed and corpulent, gave Chen Zhengzheng a good beating. Later, one time when Chen Guanbao was passing by Meishi, he had the misfortune of falling into the hands of the Lingnan Chen. He was kidnapped to the mainland and was being transported to Lingnan to suffer some extralegal penalty. The group who escorted Chen Guanbao, however, was discovered by the Chens of Jiangtian (Jiangtian being the ancestral residence of the Wenshi Chen) at an inlet in Changle, and Chen Guanbao was released through mediation. After this incident, in order to empower the lineage members on the outlying islands, the Chens of Jiangtian even "opened the ancestral hall (F. *khui sydoung*)" and carried a palanquin to Lingnan. They demanded that the Lingnan Chen stop bullying the Wenshi Chen on the outlying islands; otherwise, they would "fight the whole village" (F. *piang tshoung*) of Lingnan regardless of cost. (J. Liu 1996b)[18]

This story shows how the Matsu Islands and the relevant mainland hometowns were an indivisible whole during this period. Though geographically separated by the ocean, they shared a strong social and cultural affinity. Indeed, the Matsu people say that in the past, traveling to Matsu was described as "going to the outer mountain (F. *kho ngie lang*)," while departing for the mainland was called "returning home (F. *tuong tshuo li*)." At that time, people on Matsu would try to return home to celebrate important festivals. Since the location of Ox Horn is very close to the mainland, the villagers always held festivals one day early so that the residents could return to their hometowns in time for the celebrations there. This special custom continues to the present day, but the residents of Ox Horn are now teased by their neighbors as "real foodies (F. *tshui ia ie*)," who just cannot resist feasting twice for the festival. Last but not least, when islanders reached the end of their lives, some hoped to be brought back to their hometown for a proper burial. As a result, there was a practice of the "waiting coffin (F. *ting nuo*)." The bereaved set up a shelter outside the village and temporarily placed the coffin on a wooden rack or on a stone to wait for the ship to take the coffin back to the mainland for burial.

Fig. 1.3 Ancestral tablets and photos in a house
(Photo by the author)

Conclusion: Stateless, Transient, and Fragmented Islands

When I first visited Matsu in 2007, I was surprised to find that unlike in Taiwan or southern China, there are no lineage halls on the islands. It wasn't until I visited an old house and heard an eighty-year-old woman's explanation that I understood the reason for this. The ancestral altar in this lady's old house looks very rough and rudimentary (Fig 1.3): when her family built the house, they simply dug a hole in the corner of a wall to place ancestral tablets or pictures. The tablets are often surrounded by a messy collection of objects and appear to lack the aura of sanctity that we commonly see in Taiwan.[19] I asked her why this was so. She replied that the Matsu people did not intend to stay on the island permanently; they lived simply and remained flexible in life, ready to return to the mainland at any time.

Indeed, people who relocated to Matsu in earlier times often moved back and forth between their hometowns and the islands according to the fishing season. As they did not necessarily plan for a long-term settlement, the relationships between the lineage members in Matsu were not as stable as those in their hometown. The lack of a lineage hall or relevant ceremonies further reduced the cohesion among the members on the islands. Cao Changbi, the editor of the genealogy of the Cao family in Ox Horn, spent more than two decades going back and forth across the Strait for his laborious investigations.[20] Cao told me that the greatest difficulty he encountered while compiling his book was a frequent lack of links between the lineage members: many people only vaguely know that they are descended from a common ancestor but are unable to trace genealogical relationships in detail. His difficulty gives further clues as to why there are no lineage halls on the islands. Since the islands for them were but "outer mountains," the Matsu people thought it unnecessary to build a lineage hall in a temporary residence. Neither did they hold any big celebrations on the islands or pilgrimages to China in the early days, since they could return to the mainland at any time.

In sum, Matsu in early times was not even an immigrant society but merely a stopover or temporary place to live, with people coming and going in a constant state of flux. Lying beyond the reaches of state power, the islands were almost deserted, a lawless place where "the strongest fist took everything." The island society during this period was characterized by transience and brokenness. All of that changed with the arrival of the army in 1949.

Memories of a Murder

One evening around dusk, the company commander of military base 99, located just above Ox Horn, caught sight of Guoxing—a soldier from Jinmen who had been transferred to the Matsu Distillery in the village—heading toward the house of his lover Xuemei. The company commander immediately grabbed his bayonet and strode toward the village.

Xuemei was an attractive woman. She had been dating the company commander for a while when she also began to get close to Guoxing, who frequently went to her house to chat and flirt. The commander had seen him heading there many times and suspected that the two were having an illicit affair. It was around five o'clock that evening, and the commander had already planned what he would do. Watching Guoxing go into her house, he armed himself and hurried straight there.

He barged into the house and attacked Guoxing with his bayonet in a rage. Although badly wounded, Guoxing managed to escape in the confusion. The commander did not bother to follow him. Instead, he turned his attention to Xuemei, forcing her into a corner and stabbing her dozens of times until she collapsed dead in a pool of blood.

Having murdered Xuemei, the commander left the house to find Guoxing. He did not give chase, but rather stood near the doorway of Xuemei's house and kept watch. He knew the layout of the village so well that there was nowhere Guoxing could escape him.

Bleeding and desperate, Guoxing fled down to the bay to try to find shelter with the soldiers at the Port Military Base, screaming, "Help me! Help me!" But the soldiers had no orders from above and did not know who he was, so they warned him away as he approached. When Guoxing saw that they had no intention of protecting him, he headed back across the village. He passed the central state school to the county hospital, looking for someone to help him. But since it was after five o'clock, the hospital was closed, and the military doctors and nurses had gone home.

Guoxing had no choice but to turn in another direction, likely heading toward the village administrative office. His shrill screams for help carried throughout the village, but no one dared to come out and aid him. The company commander heard him and headed toward his voice. A little past the rice storehouse, he caught up with Guoxing and repeatedly stabbed him in the back. Guoxing collapsed and died beside the fishing nets outside a villager's house. Then the company commander calmly left the village and returned to the military barracks without so much as a backward glance.

The day after these events occurred, the commander was arrested at military base 99. Because the circumstances involved not only the taking of two lives, but also the highest-ranking official on the island ever to be implicated in a crime, the news had risen through the lines of command to the very top. The judgment came quickly, and announcements of the time and place of the execution were posted all over the island.

Early on the day of the execution, the commander's hands were bound and a wooden tablet stating his crimes was fastened to his back. He was made to stand in the back of a military truck and was driven from village to village as a warning to the public. Finally, he was taken to the execution site near the entrance to Ox Horn. Many villagers, even those who were just primary school students at the time, witnessed the execution. "Although terrified, we were curious to see what would happen," they said. Their descriptions of the execution are particularly striking:

> Across from the execution site was a hill covered with military police. They all carried guns—it was scary!

> The military commander was pulled off the truck and made to kneel at the foot of the hill.

> They offered him some food. He didn't eat anything, but he drank the sorghum liquor they gave him.

> After that, the placard on his back was taken off and thrown to the ground. It was time for the execution.

> Six executioners lined up in a row with their guns pointed at his head. In fact,

only one of them was going to shoot, but they wanted a show of force.

Before he was killed, the company commander let out a shout, something like "Long live the Republic of China!" or some such patriotic motto.

Everyone fell so silent that it was as though we could hear each other's hearts beating.

Bang! Bang! Bang! There were three shots in a row, but the commander didn't fall. He wasn't dead! According to the custom, if three shots didn't kill the criminal, it meant he wasn't destined to die. But because the circumstances involved someone so high up, the higher-ups at the WZA had already made their wishes known: "He must die!" So they shot him once again.

I heard his last sigh...oh!...and he was gone.

Cao Daming, an Ox Horn villager who at the time was barely fifteen years old, later helped the deputy head of the village investigate the case and so could describe the events vividly even forty years later. Others remembered the case clearly because they had witnessed the execution. This event gives us an important perspective on the reign of the military in Matsu. How was military rule imposed on the islands? How were the people governed? In a place which had never been directly governed by a state power before, how did the locals conceptualize the military state?

The Advent of the Military State

When Chiang Kai-shek's army suffered successive losses against the CCP (Chinese Communist Party), his government withdrew to Taiwan in 1949, while the KMT (Kuomintang, Nationalist Party) armed forces retreated to the islands along the coast of southeastern China. In 1949, Chiang's army reached Matsu, and in 1950 they set up the Matsu Administrative Office (*Matsu xingzheng gongshu*) with jurisdiction over the archipelago of Matsu and the islands to the north. After the northern islands fell into enemy hands in 1953, the KMT government set up three county administrative offices in Fujian—Lianjiang, Changle, and Luoyuan—on the islands of Nangan, Xiju, and Dongyin, to symbolize that Chiang Kai-shek still governed Fujian province, and therefore more generally the rest of China.

Simultaneously, the KMT established the East China Sea Fleet (*Donghai budui*), which included fishermen from coastal Fujian, pirates (such as the aforementioned Zhang Yizhou and the former "National

Salvation Army") (*Donghai shilu bianzhuan weiyuanhui* 1998: 97), and
soldiers stationed at Xiju by the mouth of the Min River, who were posed
to launch guerrilla warfare at any moment. Since the KMT government
offered almost no provisions at that time, the soldiers behaved much like
the bandits of the past, plundering shipping vessels to survive (226–8).
With the outbreak of the Korean War in 1950, the United States established Western Enterprises Inc. (*Xifang gongsi*) in Taiwan in 1951, a
Western outfit that was designed to spy on the enemy and to carry out
guerrilla warfare in order to contain the People's Liberation Army's (PLA)
military strength and to prevent it from dispatching forces along the southeastern coasts to fight on the Korean peninsula. The company operated
under the auspices of the CIA and established a liaison station in Xiju,
collaborating with the East China Sea Fleet in attacks on coastal China
(Holober 1999). The company closed down when the hostilities ended,
and the East China Sea Fleet was absorbed into the KMT armed forces
in 1955. Although the USA Military Assistance and Advisory Group still
maintained a base in Nangang, they withdrew completely in the 1970s.[1]

After repeated losses in the series of battles between the KMT and the
CCP on the southeastern islands, the KMT government was left holding
control over only two island areas, Jinmen and Matsu. With no end in
sight to the standoff between the KMT and the CCP, Chiang Kai-shek
implemented military rule over the frontlines of Jinmen and Matsu in
1956. The Warzone Administration (hereafter WZA) was a centralized
military administration, subordinating civilian affairs to the military command. It took centralized orders from the highest military commanding
officer on the islands, unifying the whole society and the lives of citizens
under military rule (*Guofangbu shizheng bianyiju* 1996: 96, 109). It was
originally employed during the war to govern occupied territories and
newly recaptured territories, and it was designed to control manpower
and resources within military zones for the benefit of the military (8,
101). Since Jinmen and Matsu were on the frontlines of the conflict
between China and Taiwan throughout the 1950s, Chiang Kai-shek
chose these two areas as a "testing ground" for military administration.

From the point of view of the government, over the short run the implementation of the WZA in Jinmen and Matsu could provide a protective
screen across the Taiwan Strait. In the long run, it was hoped that political,

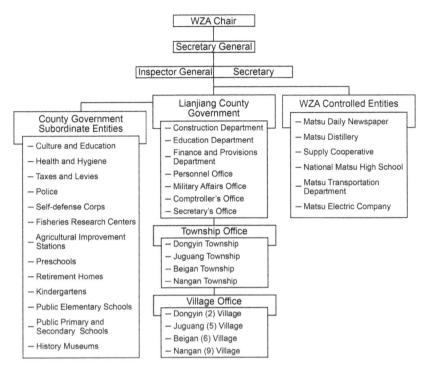

Fig. 2.1 Matsu Warzone Administration Organization
(*Fujiansheng Lianjiangxianzhi bianzuan weiyuanhui* 1986: 192)

economic and cultural development of these warzone areas would be carried out under military control. With the ideal "to administer, instruct, enrich, and secure" (*guan, jiao, wei, yang*) (190), the military army aimed to transform Jinmen and Matsu into "a model county for the Three People's Principles" (*sanmin zhuyi mofan xian*) in the Republic of China.

The WZA was led by the committee chair, held by the islands' highest commanding officer, with a secretary-general under him, held by the director of the Office of Political Warfare. The Warzone Administration Committee (WZAC) consisted of five to seven members and had jurisdiction over the Liangjiang county government. On the premise that the military would govern civil affairs, the WZAC was responsible for governmental policies and supervision, while the county government was responsible for the planning and implementation of those policies (Fig. 2.1).

In addition to WZA organs, the military had other ways of managing the villages. Each village head was selected by the WZA, and a deputy village head (also known as a political instructor) was sent by the military to supervise and oversee village affairs. The military also had a hand in the lives of individuals: locals were armed and organized into civil defense units. Every man between the ages of 18 and 45 and every woman between the ages of 16 and 35 had to participate in four weeks of training twice a year.[2]

From the above description, we can see that the WZA produced a system in which the military had full command of the local people and their resources. It was, first and foremost, a systematic administrative system commanded by the military. Second, it reorganized the people into civil defense units to assist in the war effort. Third, it controlled the resources of the islands with the establishment of the "Supply Cooperative" (1953) and the Matsu Distillery (1956), which brought the consumption and circulation of goods under government management. Finally, the military state also published a local newspaper, *Matsu Daily* (starting in 1957), to promulgate government orders and enforce ideological control. Overall, the WZA or military governance represented a kind of militarized modernism (Moon 2005; Szonyi 2008): power plants, water reservoirs, hospitals, and schools were set up on each island. Many modernizing projects of farming, forestry, fishery, and animal husbandry were implemented to make the best use of the people and resources within the warzone.

The establishment of this particular administration had its own historical basis and objectives. Szonyi's (2008) research on Jinmen builds on the geopolitics of the Cold War and greatly clarifies the significance of Jinmen and Matsu with respect to America, Taiwan, and China. When the Korean War broke out, the American president Harry Truman declared a "neutralization of the Straits of Formosa" in order to cool hostilities between China and Taiwan. In 1958, America and Taiwan signed the "ROC-US Mutual Defense Treaty" to work together to prevent the spread of communism, but the treaty did not extend to Jinmen and Matsu. In 1979, when the US and China established diplomatic relations, America abrogated its mutual defense treaty with Taiwan. Although America agreed to sign the "Taiwan Relations Act" to help Taiwan to protect itself and to consolidate its East Asian line of defense in the Cold War, the position of Jinmen and Matsu was left unclear.

For Chiang Kai-shek, Jinmen and Matsu had great significance. Located in the southwest and northwest parts of the Taiwan Strait, they could block Taiwan's access to Xiamen, Fuzhou, and Sandu'ao (*Guofangbu shizheng bianyiju* 1996: 193). The islands were also of military importance in other ways. They allowed outposts of soldiers to carry out intelligence gathering and guerrilla warfare, as well as preparation for PRC counterattacks. Because they were so close to mainland China and had once belonged to Fujian province, their very existence as such could be claimed as evidence that Chiang Kai-shek was still in control of "China" (and not just of Taiwan). Chiang Kai-shek also believed that the strategic importance of Jinmen and Matsu could actually ensure America's continuing support for Taiwan (Szonyi 2008: 43). It was for these reasons that Chiang tried to construct an image of Jinmen and Matsu as symbols of a global fight against communism.

In China, Mao Zedong considered seizing Jinmen and Matsu. However,

> ...by September [1958] Mao was confirmed in his decision that it would be counterproductive for Jinmen to fall to the PLA. The ROC presence on Jinmen was a reminder that both regimes agreed there was only "One China" that would one day be reunified. If Jinmen were to fall, it might be a first step toward the permanent separation of the two regimes, toward "Two Chinas." (Szonyi 2008: 71)

Therefore, from 1958 to 1979, when diplomatic relations were established between China and the US, the People's Liberation Army engaged in a special "one day on, one day off" (*danda shuang buda*) battle tactic, which allowed the defending forces in Jinmen and Matsu a chance to resupply. This also served to remind the US and Taiwan that both Taiwan and the islands of Jinmen and Matsu belonged to China (76).

"One Island, One Life"

How did the implementation of military rule, and in particular, the WZA, influence Matsu? As previously described, Szonyi's research on Jinmen, another frontline island of Taiwan, demonstrated how militarization (Lutz 2001, 2004) infiltrated every aspect of Jinmen, and how the local society—whether in terms of the labor force, material goods, minds and bodies—was gradually molded to serve military goals. To understand the effects of military rule on Matsu, it is therefore important to note that it had a very different history from Jinmen before the army arrived. A brief reminder of Matsu's transient and fragmented past, discussed in detail in Chapter 1, will aid in our discussion.

Matsu before 1949 was a forbidden outpost and a stateless society. The first official administration over the area was established only in 1934; even so, the responsible officer sent to the island was killed by bandits in less than two years. Matsu was quite lawless in the early part of the twentieth century and hostage to violent clashes between pirates, bandits, and warring international forces. Before the arrival of Chiang Kai-shek's army, there were few links between the villages of the Matsu archipelago; rather, each was connected to Fujian separately. The people at that time were often temporary residents during the fishing season: they described the islands as merely their "outer mountains," while their real "homes" were on the mainland. Not only were they ready to return "home" at any time, many important rites were performed on the mainland. For this reason, inter-village interactions were limited, and even within each village, different neighborhoods often remained independent from one another.

The establishment of the military administration in Matsu was thus unprecedented and totally transformed the islands. On the one hand, modernizing projects including power plants, reservoirs, fishery and agricultural improvement centers were initiated to augment local production capacities; and a new Matsu currency and the Regulation of Goods Department directed the flow of money and goods. On the other hand, intensive surveillance, including household registration and regulation of people's movements, as well as normalization, such as schooling and other ideological controls, were implemented at the level of the individual. The islands were thus brought totally and abruptly under military control.

The Matsu archipelago, however, is spread along a stretch of 54 km of ocean. During a war, contact between the islands could be easily cut off. Even more important than developing the labor and resources of Matsu was the need to foster a spirit of independence so that each island could

Fig. 2.2 A carved slogan erected beside a Matsu transportation hub:
"One island, One Life"
(Photo by the author)

carry on the war effort on its own. When the army arrived, they quickly
constructed ring roads on all the islands; military trucks served as means
of public transport, running between villages to encourage interactions
between locals. Important intersections were festooned with spirited
slogans, such as "One island, one life—the army and the people are
one family," to indoctrinate the population and to promote a sense of
solidarity (Fig. 2.2). The army also published an island newspaper,
Matsu Daily. A shared daily rhythm thus appeared; an idea of simultaneity, provinciality, and even a common fate among the islands had
emerged. A new consciousness on each island, and also on the archipelago writ large, had arisen: Matsu had become an imagined community
(Anderson 1991[1983]).

   The army's large-scale modernization projects, from the paving of
roads and island-wide forestation, to compulsory education, were jar-
ringly new for the people who had long lived on the peripheral margins of
the state. Since the Matsu Islands had always served as a temporary
residence, the first facilities were rudimentary and shabby. The massive
improvements of infrastructure, and the ubiquitous schools in particular,
met with the people's approval, to the extent that to this day they are

grateful even today for the army's contributions to these once-barren lands. Locals and soldiers gradually formed a sense of being "one community." Although this concept was initially imposed by the army, it penetrated deep into the island's social texture and the people's minds.[3] During this time, the islanders identified "Matsu" as a place of great military importance, "a springboard against communism" (*fangong tiaoban*), and "a protective shield across the Taiwan Strait" (*taihai baolei*), a notion which legitimized military control and justified the many sacrifices made by its people.

A Trail of Blood

Even so, it cannot be denied that the military state was an imposed power, one that was armed with physical and disciplinary force. How did the people of Matsu experience this abrupt intrusion? How exactly did this power weigh on individuals? The memories of the murder love triangle recounted above provides further clues.

The people of Matsu called the soldiers "*lang a liang*," meaning "two different voices" in the local dialect, emphasizing the difference of their origins and languages from those of the islanders. The two men involved in the love triangle—the company commander, and Guoxing, who had been transferred there from Jinmen to work in the Matsu Distillery— were both outsiders. The new administration, the WZA, brought in such outsiders and set up institutions that had never before existed in these outlying islands. When locals recounted the event, they usually empha- sized how Guoxing turned to different state institutions for help after he was injured: the port authorities, the county hospital, and the village administrative office (Fig. 2.3). This reveals how a once isolated world had by this time become a military state. The institutions Guoxing or the commander passed, such as the military intelligence post and the rice storehouse, had been set up as part of the war effort. These buildings obtruded everywhere in the village as physical manifestations of the intrusion of the military state in every aspect of life.

The crime of passion also demonstrates how these state institutions were frequently inhumane and unconcerned with the plight of the local people. When Guoxing ran, dripping with blood, to the port authority to seek help, the soldiers made no attempt to assist him. He could only flee

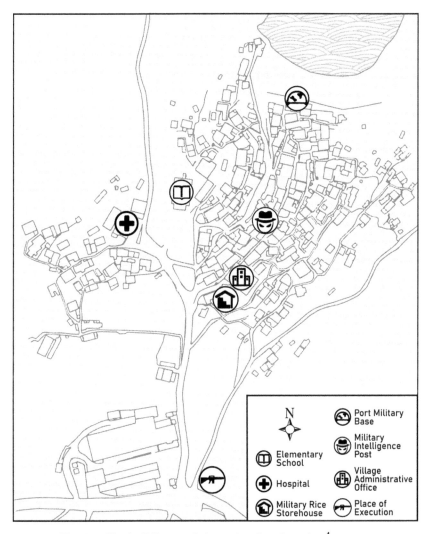

Fig. 2.3 The buildings and sites related to the crime[4]

in a panic to the next place of possible aid, namely the army hospital. But since the military personnel there were regular nine-to-five workers, they had already gone home.

This story was narrated to me in detail by Cao Daming, who was fourteen or fifteen years old at the time of the murder. A child of a poor family, he began to work as a messenger boy for the local village office not long after he finished primary school. Encountering this tragic event at an impressionable age, he remembered it vividly, particularly the long trail of blood. The deputy village head was charged with investigating the causes of the murder and reporting back to the army. Cao accompanied him to examine the sites and timeline of the violent acts. That message boy is now over sixty, but he spoke of the events as though they had happened yesterday, becoming agitated and even beginning to stutter. When asked about his speech impediment, he answered that when he was a young boy, his family lived next to a room used for interrogation by the army, which often held "communist spies." Curious, he would sometimes creep up to the room's windows with his two brothers to watch the prisoners being tortured for information. He was still young and innocent at that time, and he and his brothers would imitate how the spies talked as they underwent water torture or were beaten:

I – I – I don't know!
I – I – I really didn't do it!
It – it – it really wasn't me!

Even today, he and his brothers still have a slight stutter. The scars left by military rule have not healed.

I heard this story not long after arriving in the village. Startled, I decided to scrutinize how military rule had changed the lived world of the islanders.

Circumscribed Spaces

What followed the imposition of military rule was a general sealing off of the islands. The people of Matsu used to be able to move about freely, but soon each island was encircled by military bases. The coastline of Nangan, for example, had ninety-five coastal military bases and checkpoints keeping watch over the open sea (Fig. 2.4).

Each inlet and all of the coastlines had layer upon layer of military defenses. Inlets were fortified with anti-landing spikes and shards of glass, and both sides of promontories were dotted with hillside military blockhouses. This fortification of village inlets (Cheng 2010: 74) not only cut the islands off from one another, but also cut the local people off from the ocean. The sea-going Matsu people, who liked to collect shellfish

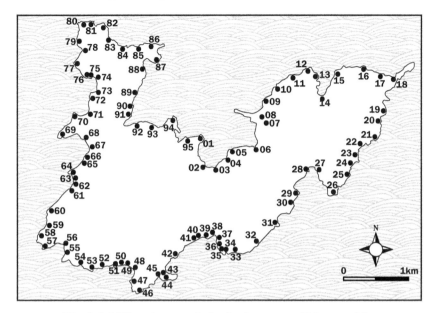

Fig. 2.4 Military bases and checkpoints around Nangan, Matsu
(Revised from Zhongguo keji daxue 2007; Y. Chen 2010)

during low tide, now had to pass through layers of wire fencing and
landmine zones in order to get to the shore where they then risked being
driven away by soldiers. For years, the people of Matsu born during
military rule grew up as strangers to the sea. Here's how Xie Zhaohua,
a local doctor, describes his experience as a child:

> To me, the sea was always foreign. Though I could see it each morning when
> I left the house, I always kept my distance from it. It was foreign not because
> I couldn't see it, but because there was no way to get close to it. Our teachers
> told us again and again not to approach the shores, especially areas surrounded
> by wire fencing, which meant that they were "dangerous landmine zones."
> Those were forbidden areas, secret places, just like the many military
> encampments hidden in the mountains. (Z. Xie 2016: 29)

In this passage, Xie Zhaohua's allusion to the "many military encampments hidden in the mountains" is worth examining. The memories of
old residents as well as photographs from the period show that in earlier
days, trees were very sparse on the islands and hillsides were covered with
thick cogon grass. According to records from 1956, "the whole island

had only about twenty banyan and other trees, and the bare hills were covered in pale sand" (Fujiansheng lianjiangxianzhi bianzuan weiyuanhui 1986: 471). Thick vegetation, however, could also provide camouflage for military encampments and helped to prevent enemy fire from reaching its target; moreover, military activity could be carried out in secret behind the tree cover. Given this necessity for concealment, the WZA began to carry out continuous "Matsu forestation" projects, implementing measures of "rewards and punishment to promote forestation" (Weihu shumiao 1961). The military at one point even decided that sheep were an impediment to forestation, and promulgated an edict ordering the "elimination of sheep" (Tan lühua 1962). Not content with forbidding the grazing of sheep, the army announced that any sheep found grazing outside the allowed areas could be killed by any person (Y. Li 1998: 49; B. Yang 2014: 271–2). Liu Hongwen's article "Sheep," describes an incident that occurred at the time between a group of Matsu school children and a sheep:

> In those years, you would always see a few sheep around the islands, perching high up on towering ocean cliffs. ...Some said that these were sheep that had been driven into the wild after the forestation projects and the prohibition on grazing. Others said that they belonged to noncommissioned officers who were raising them on the sly.... At that time, I was in elementary school, and each day I had to walk with some of my classmates down a mountain path to get to the school. ...One day not long after we had left our village...we suddenly saw a frail-looking sheep on the mountainside to our left. It was nibbling at the grass and staring at us forlornly. One of us started shouting "baaaa baaaa"...and it lifted its head to look at us. We...gave the sheep a nickname, "White Whiskers." Every day we hoped to see White Whiskers again. The bolder ones among us would even pull on White Whiskers' beard and rub his belly. ...Forming a relationship with White Whiskers became the most exciting event of our schooling.
>
> One day we came home from school, and the atmosphere in the village seemed strange. The adults were all silent and mysterious...as though they were hiding something. Then...I went around to the back door of my uncle Jinquan's house, and my eyes fell on the already-skinned body of a sheep...hanging bare and naked from the doorframe. ...It was White Whiskers. In that difficult time of deprivation, especially in a poor remote village on an outer island, a meal of stewed mutton was a very rare pleasure. That night, the whole village was happy, and everyone got a share of the meat and organs. My family got a small portion of a leg. ...I had no appetite. All I could think about was why White Whiskers had come down from the mountain. He had trusted us so much that he'd lost his wariness around the villagers. And when the villagers caught sight of him... (H. Liu 2016: 144–7)

After the sheep disappeared, the forestation of Matsu proceeded apace. Today Matsu is completely green, and each island has more than eighty percent forest cover (B. Yang 2014: 272). However, this also divided the island's high-altitude areas from its low-altitude areas; the difference between the military encampments concealed in the mountain forests and the exposed villages along the inlets was thrown into stark relief. The history of the development of the villages of Matsu cannot be separated from the fishing economy. The villagers were fishermen and built their houses first around the inlets and then expanded out toward the mountain cliffs. Outside of the villages, the mountains were covered in trees, concealing military bases, blockhouses and encampments. From above, the soldiers stationed in the woods could maintain a clear sense of what was happening in the villages.

Foucault's (1977) concept of panopticon can help us understand the power dynamics of this spatial arrangement: the Matsu villagers below could not see the soldiers hidden in the mountain forests, but the soldiers above could tell at a glance what was happening in the villagers' lives, even knowing the comings and goings of any given individual. If we return to the crime of passion and examine it in terms of its location—Ox Horn—we find that there were three nearby encampments placed above the village, from which each household could be seen clearly. In other words, the company commander need only look down from his encampment to apprehend what was going on with his lover and his rival and prepare to ambush them. After Guoxing was stabbed and fled, the company commander knew Ox Horn so well that he could infer the route Guoxing would take to try to escape and felt no need to pursue him. He need only wait at a major intersection for his rival to return exhausted and weakened. The company commander's gaze in this incident thereby represents the state's panoptical power. The state could observe every villager, while also remaining invisible to the villagers. As an agent of the state's panoptical nature, the company commander both created and enacted the state's potential to see and to know.

If Foucault's concept of the "panoptical" can help us understand the spatial structure of the military rule over these islands, then the execution following the love triangle murders shows us an example of state cere-mony. Geertz (1980: 123) says that the state draws its force from imaginative energies. From this perspective, it is clear why the state decided to publicly execute the company commander. Indeed, the set up was a carefully staged state ceremony: the company commander forced to wear a placard inscribed with his crimes and paraded around the village, the execution grounds filled with somber military police, the six pointed rifles, and the WZA's order to shoot to the death. Its goal was to display, defend, and reaffirm the state's power. Ironically, only the patriotic slogan shouted by the company commander before his death revealed the real executioner behind the scenes.

Sailing through Liminality

As one can imagine, with the islands closed off from the outside world, border-crossing became very difficult. During the military reign, strict controls were imposed on movements between Matsu and Taiwan. The application process to leave was very tedious:

> To board a ship, you had to have papers, formally called a "Republic of China Taiwan-Jinmen-Matsu Area Travel Permit." First you went to a studio to get a headshot taken, then you had to fill out the forms, find a guarantor, and take everything to the village office. Your paperwork was checked at the local police headquarters before finally being sent on to the local command post. Every detail was inspected at each stage, and each step carefully controlled. …Then you had to wait…and when the papers were issued…you had to somehow get a berth on the ship. Sometimes there was space and sometimes there wasn't. It all depended on what kind of connections you had. (H. Liu 2016: 47)

Even after all of the aggravating paperwork, traveling by supply ship was a painful experience shared by nearly all the islanders. At that time, no civil vessels made the trip between Taiwan and Matsu, so Matsu residents heading to Taiwan had to take supply ships. A resident of Dongyin recalls that in the early days, a supply ship could take as long as a week to reach Taiwan: after leaving Dongyin, the ship first went to the administrative center in Nangan, and then headed back north to Beigan before proceeding to Dongju and Xiju. Only after it had circled all of the islands did it finally make its way to Taiwan. Although this detour was later shortened, one still considered oneself fortunate if one could make it to Taiwan within two days.

A long tedious journey was one thing, but what they encountered on the ship was really torturous:

> On the day of the trip, we rose at dawn…it was drizzling, and people squatted in rows all along the beach, patiently waiting to be called onboard. The military police shuttled back and forth, checking our papers, ransacking our luggage… they went through everything and left behind a mess.
>
> Finally, we were given the signal to board, and the crowd swarmed toward the mouth of the huge beast [ship], and found berths in the gloomy cabins that were filthy with cement, dust, rice bran, engine oil, and putrefied fruit. Many were left without a berth, and had to find a spot in a corner where they could spread out a mat or put down a piece of cardboard. This was where they would rock back and forth for eighteen hours.
>
> The summer was easier, since people could be aboveboard on the deck… occasionally a wave would come up and slap their faces, and soon their eyes, faces, and arms would be covered in a thin layer of sea salt. Even the breezes were salty. …In the winter, the ocean wind was piercingly cold, and enormous waves would beat the deck while everyone hid in the hull and retched as the children wailed and the filth got worse and worse. (H. Liu 2016: 47–9)

It was just as agonizing to come back to Matsu from Taiwan. Migrants returning to Matsu first had to register at the Jinmen-Matsu Guesthouse (*Jinma binguan*) in Keelung and then wait. Sometime in the afternoon, if the guesthouse posted a sign saying "Departures Today," everyone would prepare to board with relief. If no sign was put up, they would have to return the next day. The Jinmen-Matsu Guesthouse was provided for soldiers to have a place to stay on those days when the weather was too poor for the ships to sail. In general, ordinary citizens had to return to their residences each day until they could leave. For young people in particular, who had very little money to begin with, going back and forth a few times would easily exhaust their funds. Cao Daming recounts how he waited once for seven or eight days until he ran out of money and decided to sleep in an empty freight truck parked near the Jinmen-Matsu Guesthouse with his teenage friends. He woke up to realize that the truck was driving south. It turned out to be a vegetable truck from a nearby market, and the driver had stopped to rest before leaving early the next morning to pick up more produce. When the driver realized he had stowaways, he scolded them and shooed them off. The penniless young men could only put their heads together and try to figure out a way to get back to Keelung.

The passage between Matsu and Taiwan was like a liminal period, in which both the body and spirit were tested and transformed. As Turner has stated: "[D]uring the liminal period, neophytes are alternately forced and encouraged to think about their society, their cosmos, and the powers that generate and sustain them. Liminality may be...described as a stage of *reflection*" (Turner 1967: 105, original italics). This kind of reflection happened not only during the journey on the ship, but also became deeply ingrained in people's memories. The local leaders examined in Part III frequently begin with their painful experiences of such trips when explaining the impetus behind their desire to change Matsu.

Conclusion: Imagined Community vs. Individual Suffering

In 1949, the army abruptly arrived in Matsu and indelibly changed the fate of the islands. This chapter analyzes how military rule transformed the lives of the local people from the perspective of space. I have demonstrated that once the Matsu archipelago became a frontline in the war, the close connections that had previously existed between the islands and the mainland were severed. The WZA carried out large-scale construction projects, propagated public education to modernize the islands, and also employed print media and local currency to create pan-island connections. As a result, "Matsu" became a newly imagined community, with a new social imaginary as a "fortress in the Taiwan Strait" and a "springboard for anticommunism." This imaginary gradually became the identity of the Matsu people.

If we examine the lives of individuals more closely, however, we see a different picture. The state came from afar and penetrated every aspect of the islands immediately and deeply: all kinds of military institutions (such as port bases, intelligence posts, and rice storehouses) mushroomed, and became integrated into the living spaces of locals. In the hills above the villages were secret military barracks, with their constantly surveilling eyes: the oversight and control of the state was ubiquitous. Anyone wanting to enter or leave the islands had to brave the torture of travel by sea. The crime of passion, Cao Daming's stutter, the schoolchildren who lost their beloved sheep, and the sense of being close to the sea but estranged from it—all these examples demonstrate how the power of the state permeated people's bodies, minds, emotions, and knowledge, clashing with them and creating conflicts and trauma.

The impact on individuals and society when a place becomes a frontline is complex and intricate. In Chapter 3, I will explore this issue further from the perspectives of the fishing economy and gender relations.

3   To Stay or to Leave?

In descriptions of the love triangle murders, Xuemei's husband never puts in an appearance. When I asked about him, the answers I got from residents of Ox Horn were always vague and ran along the lines of: "He was a fisherman"; "The fishing in Matsu wasn't good, so he moved to Keelung (Taiwan)." Is the absence and silence of this fisherman husband connected in any way to the difficulties of the military period in Matsu?

Restricted Fishing and Imagination

Beginning with the establishment of the WZA, the proportion of the population involved in the fishing economy steadily declined (J. Wang 2000: 165–6), with many fishing villages emptied out by emigration to Taiwan. Most of the Matsu people who moved to Taiwan came from fishing villages such as Beigan's Qinbi and Qiaozi, Nangan's Ox Horn and Jinsha, and Juguang's Fuzheng and Tian'ao (S. Cao 1978). Indeed, the implementation of military rule had a tremendous effect on the fishing economy, such that fishermen could no longer make a living. After Matsu was militarized, the unrestricted movement of fishermen on the seas was deemed a threat to national security; fishermen were seen as "internal enemies" and potential leakers of military secrets. The state started to implement a series of stringent rules and inspections to reduce any potential threat.[1] The procedure was as follows: anyone wanting to work in the fishing economy was required to apply to the village administrative office. Each applicant needed to supply three guarantors and was required to pass a clearance check before he could receive a fishing license.[2] A licensed fisherman had to register with the village administrative office the day before he wanted to go fishing and receive a day permit. Before he set out, the fisherman had to show his fishing license and permit to the port authorities and pass an inspection before the guards would return his oars (for sampans) or motor starter (for motorboats). Every fishing trip had to have at least three people, and the boat was required to return with the same personnel onboard (Z. Chen 2013: 80). These layers of onerous restrictions served to control fishing on and off the water.

Military officials worried that once at sea, Matsu fishermen could come into contact with fishermen from enemy territory and leak military secrets, so they established fishing boundaries that could not be crossed. In addition to being assigned a serial number, fishing vessels were required to fly an official flag so as to be more easily monitored. If fishermen crossed over a boundary or were suspected of fishing outside the allowed zone, upon return they would be restricted from going out again for at least a week, face interrogation and sometimes torture, be subject to jail time, and could even be banned from the water for extended periods. When any boat returned to harbor, the port authorities would inspect it for contraband and again impound the oars or motor.

Given the enormous maritime area, however, there were necessarily sporadic gaps in military control and surveillance. Matsu fishermen had a keen sense of where they could go at sea to avoid the eyes of soldiers, and where they could have contact with fishermen from the other side of the Strait: "Sometimes, when the weather was good, we'd run into them and hide someplace we couldn't be seen to chat. But when we came back, we wouldn't dare talk about it…otherwise we'd be locked up!"[3]

Matsu and mainland fishermen behaved like old friends when together, conversing congenially, joking and laughing with each other. They shared a mutual understanding, and did not participate in the enmity between the KMT and the CCP:

> The policy of shelling only on odd-numbered days [Chapter 2] was more about propaganda than it was about harming people…And we'd shelled them before too. We fishermen didn't have any issues with each other. We'd bump into them and chat like friends, but we wouldn't say anything about it when we went home. We'd talk about ordinary stuff, never about the shelling or anything like that. They'd also tell us how their families were, how their lives were going, how well they were eating…They told us, "Your army is really

strict with you out on the sea." The Chinese fishermen could go out to sea for several days without fear and return whenever they liked, but we had to come back at the end of each day. They'd also say, "If you can get away, we'll take you out for a few days of fun." The war was being waged by the governments, while we'd just treat each other like friends.[4]

Sometimes, however, the friendliness of the mainland fishermen would cause problems for the Matsu fishermen.

The soldiers were afraid we'd have contact with fishermen from China, but they couldn't watch us all the time! Once when I went out, they brought a bag of peanuts and we ate them together on the boat. There was so little time to eat! When we came back, we dumped them all overboard! It'd be illegal to bring them back with us. They brought a big bag to give to us, but we said we'd just take a handful. They didn't know we couldn't bring it back with us, and they told us to just leave it on the boat and have some whenever we wanted it. But if it were found, we'd be in serious trouble. Fishing is nothing but suffering![5]

In this unique space on the water, the fishermen could temporarily escape military control and imagine they were still connected with the other side. On the ocean they found freedom and friendship, and shared small pleasures, but this space and imagination was always hidden, momentary, and evanescent. "Fishing is nothing but suffering!" (F. *thoai ia siuai*) was a cry heard from fishermen throughout the wartime period.

Indeed, if a vessel was even suspected of coming into contact with an enemy boat, military officials could easily impound the boat for days, but not going out to sea had a huge effect on the fishermen's livelihood. In an interview with me, a fisherman from Tieban sorrowfully recounted:

My brother was suspected of having contact with the other side and was punished by not being allowed to go out for a week. In order to make a living, after a few days he secretly set off from the other end of the harbor. He never came back.

Matsu Daily even recorded an order from the WZA chair demanding that fishermen gather at the Temple of Goddess Mazu to take an oath:

Yesterday at the Tianhou Temple, the fishermen of Nangan took an oath not to circumvent regulations. The vows were overseen by the WZA chair and were taken by 310 people. ...At the meeting, Wu Muken, the executive manager of the Fishing Association, took a public oath on behalf of his members, and led everyone in pronouncing this oath: I swear to Goddess

Mazu that I will respect the rules and regulations of the fishing zone, not leak secrets, and have no contact with enemy boats or anyone else at sea. If I violate this vow, I will submit to the punishments of both military law and Goddess Mazu: may I never bring home another catch, may my boat overturn, and may I die at sea.[6]

For 300 people whose entire livelihoods depended on fishing to condemn themselves before Goddess Mazu to never bringing home any fish or to dying in a disaster shows that there was considerable coercion behind the taking of this oath. There can be no doubt that it was made under duress.

Clock-in Clock-out Fishermen

Among the multiple layers of rules controlling the time that fishermen could spend at sea, it was the restriction of permitted hours of fishing which dealt the greatest blow to their livelihoods. Military authorities did not allow fishing at night: in the summer, boats could set out at 6 am and had to return by 7 pm; in the winter, the hours were from 4:30 am to 6:30 pm. However, many factors, including the variety of fish, the tides, weather, and routes were difficult to control and affected the timing of the boats. Delay in returning was the most frequent problem for fishermen. One of them said:

> The rules dictated what time you had to be back in port. The truth is that they were worried about us going to the mainland. If you came back one hour late, they'd keep you from going out for a week. They didn't even care about tides. Sometimes I'd come back at six, but could only enter [the harbor] at eight, because of the tide. They didn't know anything about tides, they'd just interrogate you, "Where'd you get off to…"[7]

Fishermen from Ox Horn alluded to similar problems. The former village head told me: "It was often impossible to come back on time. If we got delayed, we'd give our biggest catch of the day to the harbor guard and beg him to let us back in."

Controlling the hours of access to the harbors had the serious effect of limiting the number of times fishermen—in particular, the local shrimpers—could put their nets in the water. Cao Yaping's (2017) research meticulously describes the close relationship between the fluctuations of the tides and the shrimp industry. The tidal range between the

high water of high tide and the ebbing of low tide was particularly extreme
in the ocean surrounding Matsu, and fishermen frequently used fixed nets
to capture their most important catch, namely shrimp. Each day brought
two cycles of high and low tides, and fishermen would calculate the timing
before going out to gather shrimp. As one fisherman explained:

> [We'd] go out at the peak of high tide and the lowest point of low tide. ...We'd
> stop for an hour at each. Stopping for an hour when the tidal waters weren't
> moving made things much easier. The fixed nets needed to take advantage of
> that quiet moment on the sea, and we'd have to put the nets out and bring
> them back in within an hour.[8]

The fishermen said that when the tides weren't moving, the nets would
naturally float to the ocean surface, and that was when it was easiest to
collect shrimp. If they didn't pull the nets in promptly, the shrimp would
suffocate and rot in the sun. But with the military restrictions in place,
fishermen could only go out during the daytime. Where they used to
bring in the nets four times a day, they now could only bring them in
twice, seriously limiting their working time at sea. When I interviewed
the highly experienced Tieban fisherman Chen Qizao, he told me that
the rules restricted their time considerably. Fishermen often didn't have
time to bring their nets in properly, and when the water was high, the nets
would easily tear, causing significant losses.

The army disallowing fishing at night not only reduced the daytime
catch, it also presented an even bigger obstacle for fishermen who spe-
cialized in the kinds of fish, such as ribbonfish, that were caught at night.
Some of these fishermen had no choice but to switch their speciality and
invest in new fishing equipment. Fisherman Cao Qijie said: "Ribbonfish
can only be caught at night...but later because of communist bandits...
we couldn't go out at night, and the fishermen all started to switch to
shrimp fishing, which meant they had to buy new equipment. Most of us
had to go into further debt when we hadn't even paid off our old debts."[9]

The purchase of fishing equipment and tackle presented another
important dilemma for fishermen. In the past, the materials that fishermen needed to make their equipment, such as bamboo fiber and rice
straw for rope, bamboo stalks, and wood, were all purchased on the
mainland. A few months before the fishing season, they would begin to
make their equipment: fishing rope, stakes, buoys, fishing nets, and so

Fig. 3.1 Picture of a shrimping net (with stakes, buoy, and net)
(Drawn by Chen Zhilong and Wu Shuhui)

on. Approximately two months before the start of the season, fishermen would drive stakes into the seabed, which they used to anchor their nets when the fish arrived. (Z. Chen 2013: 50–3, 85–6) (Fig. 3.1).

In the past, maintenance of the boats and equipment relied on the mainland, but after relations between China and Taiwan were severed, fishermen could only turn to Taiwan. Taiwan is much farther from Matsu than the mainland, and conditions in the Taiwan Strait are dangerous and highly unpredictable; thus fishing supplies rarely arrived on time. After the WZA came into effect in 1956, fishermen faced serious difficulties for two successive years while there was no regularly scheduled movement of cargo ships between Taiwan and Matsu (J. Lin 2013a). By that time, fishermen had already taken out large loans that they had no way of repaying. *Matsu Daily* recorded similar struggles that recurred year after year:

> This year the needed shrimping equipment has not reached the islands, preventing fishermen from putting out their nets.[10]

Due to a delay in delivery of fishing supplies, fishermen have suffered more than 3 million [Taiwan dollars] in losses.[11]

[Fishing] materials are scarce, transport is difficult, and because of related delays, fishermen frequently suffer significant losses.[12]

The shrimp season has begun two months early...but fishermen do not yet have their equipment.[13]

This year, bamboo has been slow to arrive, affecting the timing of the net staking.[14]

In addition to the lack of supplies, the export and sale of fish also became an issue. In the past, Matsu fishermen could efficiently ship their goods to Fuzhou. With the imposition of military rule, transportation and labor expenses rose precipitously; there was also insufficient cold storage. As a result, fishermen could only sell their catch to soldiers on the island or to dried fish vendors. Even in times of a bumper harvest, the market was extremely limited. Fishermen were forced to borrow from the government or depend on unreliable government aid year after year. Flipping through *Matsu Daily*, it becomes clear that poverty among fishermen in the 1960s and 1970s was widespread.

The WZA Chair has indicated that loans will be granted to the fishing industry and distributed among needy fishermen in the area.[15]

The WZA Chair has indicated that loans will be granted to needy fishermen before the lunar new year, in amounts between 500 and 1000 yuan per net.[16]

Before the lunar new year, the WZA Chair distributed a total of 130,000 *jin* of rice to fishermen, in loans of 100 *jin* per shrimping net, which can be returned interest-free after the fishing season.[17]

In the lean times before the shrimp season, loans of 36,000 *jin* of rice were given out.[18]

The shrimp season has ended with a total haul of 700,000 *jin*...with an average of nearly 500 *jin* per net. After expenses for equipment are deducted, fishermen face difficult times.[19]

With losses in the fishing industry over the two past years, fishing villages are on the brink of collapse.[20]

Uncertain supply lines, the harsh new rules imposed on the fishing economy, and the limited opportunities to sell their catch sent Matsu fishing villages spiraling into poverty, forcing them to rely on government aid. And what about the fishermen themselves and their families?

A construction contractor in Ox Horn provided the most poignant image of their suffering:

> My dad died when I was ten. But I still remember seeing him smoking in bed late at night, looking dejected. At that time there were a lot of restrictions on fishing: what time you had to leave, what time you had to come back—and none of it corresponded with the tides. And every time he saw the guards with their loaded guns, he'd feel even worse.

When I returned from Matsu to Taipei in 2008, I went to see Guan Quanfu, who was born in 1920 (and passed away in 2016). People in Matsu told me that he had a lot of experience in the fishing economy. As chairman of the Fishing Association around 1960, he would be a useful source of information. Guan Quanfu had long since moved to Taipei, and when he heard that I wanted to ask him questions about the fishing economy, he immediately exclaimed: "The government...didn't understand anything!" I asked him why, and he answered:

> Without the government, we could fish freely. When the army arrived, it nearly killed us. Before they came, people in Matsu did fishing and many ships came from Lianjiang on the mainland to buy the better fish. The leftover fish would be bought by other villagers to be sold to the northern part of Fujian. At that time, small fish were preserved with salt and alum, and tasted really salty and bitter, but it kept them from turning soft and going bad. We weren't used to eating it, but the "northern natives" liked to eat that kind of fish. They lived in a place with so much fog, their faces "looked blue." If they didn't have that salty bitter fish to eat, they wouldn't be able to take it. They would come to Fu'an and trade bundles of wood [for the fish]. People on Matsu made cooking fires with cogon grass and leaves, which burned quickly. Wood would burn longer.

Curious, I asked him where the salt and alum came from. He replied:

> It came from the north. We used our own boats to go purchase it or trade for it. If we didn't have any rice, we could trade sweet potatoes for it. When the army arrived, they made us leave and come back at certain times, so how could we fish? The fish are most plentiful at night!

Mr. Guan described a more lucrative system of exchange between fishermen on the southern islands and those living in the mountains of Fujian (indigenous peoples). This system was completely disrupted when the army arrived, and in order to survive, many islanders had no choice but to leave the islands.

"Carrying all their Possessions on a Pole to Taiwan"

Toward the end of the 1960s, Matsu people began to emigrate to Taiwan in large numbers. According to statistics, the population of Matsu was highest in 1970, at around 17,000 people. From that point on, people began to leave, and the population reached a low of 5,500 people around 1990 when military rule was abolished (Qiu and He 2014:16–18). Over twenty years, emigration reduced the population of Matsu by two-thirds. Why did so many people leave? Liu Hongwen's (2017) *The History of the Emigration of Matsu Villagers to Taoyuan* informs us that whether it was an individual or a family that moved, the reason was the same: "There's no way to live on Matsu; there's no hope there" (F. *mo leinguah, mo hiuong*). This was why so many "carried all their possessions on a pole to Taiwan" (F. *suoh ba piengtang tang suoh kaui kho teiuang*).

There were many reasons why people from Matsu left for Taiwan. Although Matsu did not experience any actual battles, it was under constant threat. In the twenty-one years between 1958 and 1979, the "one day on, one day off" shelling from China led to many injuries and deaths and kept people in a state of constant terror. For Hu Shuiguan, who now lives in Bade, Taoyuan, the scars run deep. He lost his left leg in a bombing of the Matsu movie theater (located at the army recreation center) in 1969, and watched his youngest son die in front of him. His eldest son Hu Zongwei was sitting in another part of the theater and escaped this catastrophe. Hu Zongwei recounts:

> After my father got injured, he fell into despair because of the death of my little brother. Since the shelling happened [at an entertainment facility], it wasn't covered under the ordinances of the Ministry of Defense regulating pensions given for work injuries. Not only did he not receive any compensation, he also lost his job as the village office assistant because of his disability. He tried to eke out a living by opening a little grocery store and learned photography so he could open a studio. But he always lived under the shadow of the bombing, getting nervous on odd-numbered days, and becoming terrified at the sound of artillery shells overhead. In 1969, my father couldn't take the unending torment any more and decided to move the family across the sea to Taiwan.[21]

Born in the same village as Hu Shuiguan, Zhang Yiyu was a construction worker who also worried about his family's safety. After watching family after family leave, he moved his own to Taiwan as well.

The other reason people left was the shrinking fishing economy. As described, under the WZA fishing had become an increasingly arduous way of earning a living. In order to survive, many fishermen moved to Taiwan. As Chen Hanguang puts it:

> In 1968, I saw how difficult it was to make a living by fishing. I agreed to sell off my equipment and nets for NT$3,000, but the buyer ran away after paying me only NT$1,000. I took that money and set off on the long, uncertain road to Taiwan.[22]

Chen Deyu, who tried to modernize his fishing technique by buying a modern pair-trawler with a government loan, also ended up moving to Taiwan. He recounts:

> Around 1983, the government offered loans to fishermen to buy motorized pair-trawlers. Together with twelve other fishermen, we bought two boats…and began to use them to fish. We worked together for more than a year, but our partnership still dissolved. It wasn't because our catch was insufficient, but because of an imbalance between supply and demand. When we had a good catch, we couldn't manage to sell it all, even at a low price. We didn't have cold storage at that time, and the local market was limited. The fresh fish couldn't make it to Taiwan.[23]

In the early 1960s as the fishing economy contracted, people began to move to Keelung, the major port in northern Taiwan, to work as fishermen. Others moved to Taipei County (today's New Taipei City) and largely ended up working as street vendors and laborers. The area that received the most immigrants was Bade in Taoyuan (74). Why was it able to accept such a large number of immigrants?

The Emigrants' New Home

Looking at the area as a whole, Taoyuan County is a key industrial and manufacturing center in northern Taiwan. Several industrial zones are clustered there, and people from across the island came to find work during the early stages of Taiwan's industrialization (see also W. Lin 2015: 107–10). Later, foreign laborers were also drawn to the area, such that today the neighborhood around the railway station in Taoyuan is replete with Southeast Asian stores, creating a multinational mix of businesses and people (Z. Wang 2006: 105).

Today's Bade City in Taoyuan County was once known as Bakuaicuo (lit. "Eight Houses") and became Bade only in 1949. It was once a

Map 3.1 Bade in Taoyuan County

farming area, but with the industrialization of Taiwan in the 1970s, the government began establishing industrial zones in Taoyuan (L. Lin 2007: 112), and many factories were set up in Bade since there was a considerable amount of land there. By 1976, industry had already surpassed agriculture as the primary economic activity in Bade. As of 1988, nearly 60 percent of the people there were employed in this sector, of which the three main industries were the manufacturing of machinery, electronic components, and textiles (Z. Liao 2008: 110–1). These flourishing industries meant ample employment opportunities, allowing more people to move to the area. The result of this rapid increase in population was that Bade was upgraded directly from a township (*xiang*) to a city (*shi*) in 1995, skipping the intermediate stage of town (*zhen*) entirely (W. Lin 2015: 109) (Map 3.1).

The opportunities provided by Bade's busy industrial area encouraged many Matsu people to settle there. Some came because of family members, some based on the recommendation of neighbors or friends. They found work making textiles or clothing, or took all sorts of positions in steel mills, plastics plants, and tableware factories. The boss of the Lianfu Clothing Factory was a man from Fuzhou, and many of the immigrants from Matsu ended up taking jobs there after they heard his familiar Fuzhou dialect.

However, owing to the differences between the languages and cultures of Matsu and Taiwan, the people who settled in Taoyuan had a hard time adjusting at first. The Fuzhou dialect being their mother tongue, those from Matsu usually spoke heavily accented Mandarin. They did not speak or were largely unable to understand the Hokkien dialect popular in Taiwan, and so were alienated from the mainstream culture. When they spoke in their dialect to each other, however, they would speak volubly (from their habit of speaking loudly in their native island valleys), and their loud incomprehensible voices could give Taoyuan locals the impression of arrogance and aggression. Zhang Xiangfu, who worked in the Lianfu factory from the early 1970s until his retirement, told me:

> At that time, the Bade hoodlums looked down on us and would throw their beer bottles into our factory. Sometimes they'd take sticks and watermelon knives and charge into the factory to find a Matsu person to beat up. The factory had to hire a local guard to sit in front of the entrance every day. When we went to the factory or got off our shifts, we'd always go in a group. We'd try our best to stick together.

Gradually, Matsu immigrants gathered in an area near the factories called Danan. A street there is named "Matsu Street," with many stores selling traditional Matsu products. More such stores, selling all sorts of goods from Matsu, are located near the main market in Danan.

In general, however, those who emigrated to Taiwan are happy with their decision, despite the hardships they faced. For example, Liu Meizhu, an early immigrant says:

> At that time, there were lots of people from Matsu working for the Lianfu Company. We worked long days, from 8 am to 9 pm, almost every single day. When we first arrived in Taiwan, we were grateful to Lianfu for giving us a chance to work. My mother said that with a job cutting threads in the Lianfu factory, you had air conditioning and could sit as you worked, and sometimes you could even chat a bit. Back in Matsu you had to work out in the wind and rain or under the scorching sun, and in the winter the cold would get into your bones, and you had to fight the others for water. ...It was much easier working for Lianfu. Above all, if you worked your regular job, and did some overtime, you could earn at least NT$10,000 yuan a month. If you had three people in

the family earning that much, that was NT$30,000–40,000 a month in income. You could save more than NT$20,000 each month, and in two years you'd have the money to buy yourself a little single-story house.[24]

Beside the regular salaries, the people of Matsu often mentioned that the rice in Taiwan wasn't the rationed rice they were used to, and that it tasted much better. Fowl was also cheaper and tastier than at home. The bright lights, new electronics, sturdy pavement, shiny tiles, and so on, all made them feel as though their lives had improved both spiritually and materially (H. Liu 2017: 83).

Yet they still missed Matsu. They invited their deities to Danan, set up branch statues, and finally built the Longshan Temple (1970) and the Mintai Temple (1974). Every year, they held traditional Matsu festivities for the Lantern Festival, and established the Matsu Association to maintain their connections with their hometowns. In 2018, they even went so far as to build in Bade an exact duplicate of a Longshan temple from Ox Horn in Matsu.

Guaranteed Admission Program

As the fishing economy declined and fishermen emigrated, a new social category began to appear in Matsu: teachers and civil servants. Before 1949, education in Matsu relied primarily upon private teaching. Teachers were employed from the mainland to teach the traditional classics. At that time, most of the population was impoverished, and only those from relatively well-off families could afford to go to school, with a fraction of those wealthier students going on to middle or high schools (Y. Chen 1999). Take Ox Horn as an example: the well-to-do Chen Lianzhu studied on the mainland and thus spoke Mandarin well. Under the WZA, he was a cultural and linguistic bridge between the military and the locals, and later he became the chairman of the Matsu Association of Commerce (S. Li et al. 2014).

When the army came to Matsu and discovered widespread illiteracy on the islands, they aimed for an ideal situation of "one village, one school" (*yi cun yi xuexiao*) and established elementary schools across the islands (J. Lin 2013b). At that time, Matsu had no middle schools; once children finished elementary school, the best students were sent to Jinmen to continue their studies. With the implementation of the WZA in 1956, the first middle school on Matsu was built in 1957 and was intended to help improve the general educational level. The school was immediately faced with a shortage of teachers and its graduates with a lack of opportunities for further study. Of the very few teachers on the islands, most were soldiers from the mainland. When older Matsu people speak of their teachers, they frequently say: "The teachers at that time were all soldiers, they taught both Chinese and English." To address the shortage of teachers, the WZA established the guaranteed admission program.

The guaranteed admission program was designed to help Matsu students go to Taiwan to study, guaranteeing them a tuition-free place without having to participate in the national test. The first year of Matsu middle-school graduates in 1960 numbered forty-eight, of whom twenty were sent to junior normal universities, as well as farming, fishery, business, and nursing schools.[25] When they finished their studies, they were required to return to Matsu to serve as elementary school teachers or to work in county government organizations for at least two years. With the opening of Matsu's first high school in 1968, a series of students were sent to Taiwan via the guaranteed admission program. There was also another program designed to improve the quality of teaching. The returning teachers could apply and go to Taiwan again to study in normal universities (Guan 2008), after which they could qualify to teach in middle or high schools.

Overall, these programs gradually produced a new category of educated people in Matsu, which superseded traditional family and lineage influences, and the dominance of those who had studied on the mainland. These people had a tremendous impact on Matsu, particularly after the dismantlement of the WZA, as will be discussed in detail in Part III of this book. Still, even during the WZA rule, we can see the effect of their return to villages and their assumption of teaching posts or positions in local government. Students of farming or maritime vocational schools could work in farming or fishing associations, or for agricultural development centers. Graduates of business schools could return to work in local government accounting bureaus. In this way, a new social category of teachers and government employees gradually arose in Matsu.

Even those who had only graduated from local elementary schools also began to have opportunities to work in local government organizations. They frequently worked at the lowest levels, responsible for the general administration of various offices with meager but secure wages. However, they could take the ad hoc civil service examination (*quanding kaoshi*) designed by the WZA to obtain further qualifications and slowly climb up the career ladder.

The Rise of the "Boss Lady"

By 1970, many from Matsu had moved to Taiwan, but some decided to remain behind. I asked those who remained why they stayed, and they replied along the following lines:

> I didn't have any relatives in Taiwan, and I didn't have the money to move. On Matsu I could grow vegetables and run a small business.

Indeed, at that time many Matsu people knew no one in Taiwan and had no practical way of moving there. At home, at least they could grow and sell vegetables, or sell fish and shellfish to soldiers. They describe this way of earning a living—doing "G. I. Joe business" (*a'bing'ge shengyi*) (Szonyi 2008: 134)—as "supporting a family with one scale" (F. *suoh ba tsheing yong lo suoh tshuo noeyng*). Many businesses, such as snack and drinkstands, small grocery stores, billiard rooms, barbers, laundry services, public bathhouses, tailoring for uniforms, etc., arose to serve the needs of soldiers.

These businesses were frequently run by wives (Fig. 3.2). A woman from Shanlong who once ran a snack stand told me:

> At that time, we had to take care of our elderly parents and children, but my husband only made NT$700 or 800 a month. It wasn't enough to live on.

Not only did the wives of low earners and fishermen begin working, it was also common to see wives of high-level government workers opening stores that catered to soldiers. For example, while the former county commissioner Cao Changshun was the principal of Jieshou middle school, his wife ran a shop selling stationery and Western medicine in Shanlong. Further, the wife of the chair of the County Council sold breakfast in the market for decades before retiring only a few years ago.

Fig. 3.2 Women at a market selling shellfish they have gathered
(Photo by Su Shengxiong, 1986)

Almost every woman participated in these businesses. A woman from Ox Horn who grew vegetables and went each day to Shanlong to sell them recounts:

> My husband was a fisherman and he often lost money on it. So I grew whatever I could sell. That was the only way our family could survive.

Matsu was traditionally a fishing society, in which the men went out to fish and the women stayed at home to look after the family. They grew sweet potatoes, took care of animals, gathered firewood in the mountains, and did all kinds of household labor. Their husbands would frequently not return for days at a time (especially when they had gone to the mainland), and accidents at sea were common, so the wives or mothers of fishermen were often solely responsible for their households. As I mentioned earlier, Matsu has a saying: "A wife/mother is the hoop around the bucket" (F. *lauma/nuongne sei thoeyngkhu*)—in other words, the wife or mother is the force binding the whole family together.

Nevertheless, it is indisputable that the status of women is low in most fishing societies. In the past, Matsu women primarily provided household labor, and since they could not go out to sea to fish like men, they were not able to make money for the family. Earning money being "a man's work," many elders said that men would apply this very rude phrase to curse their "disobedient" wives for their inability to earn even a cent: "Even if women pissed oil, men would still have to carry it to market!" (F. *tsynoeyng niu na pienglau iu, toungmuonoeyng tang kho ma*)

These traditional gender relations changed demonstrably under the WZA with the influx of soldiers and their consumer demands. Fisherman Liu Mujin says:

> Men rarely went to sell things at market. The soldiers wanted to buy from women. They'd only do business with them.
>
> Women could carry things in to sell at the barracks. If a man approached the barracks carrying something, the soldiers would block his way. But they wouldn't stop women. Once they sang out a peddler's cry, the soldiers would all come out to buy.

As we can see, in the military economy, women could go to the market early in the morning and sell vegetables or fish. Later in the day, they could go to the barracks to sell things or take the soldiers' dirty clothes home to wash. They could also work in shops, or even open their own. Under the WZA, women not only took care of their households but also conducted business. They interacted with the soldiers and became an important source of income for their families.

Younger women even became a conduit to military goods for their families. People often said that coveted tickets for ships headed to Taiwan could be easily procured if a family had a daughter. H. Liu's article (2016) of "Carrying Swill" describes how the older sister of his childhood companion drew the attention of military officers because of her good looks. At that time, most families on Matsu raised pigs, and everyone wanted to fatten them up by getting swill from the military camps. Not only did his pretty sister obtain swill for them, her whole family had steamed buns and meat to eat because of her connection to the soldiers. Eventually, she reluctantly married an officer around the same age as her father.

Young or pretty women could easily attract the attention of the soldiers or become objects of unwanted attention or even assault. Previous studies have shown how women become targets of sexual violence during times of war (Das 2008; Kelly 2000; Sanford, Stefatos, and Salvi eds. 2016, to name only a few). For this reason, Xuemei, of the love triangle murders I described in Chapter 2, is rarely criticized by villagers. In fact, they usually sympathize with her for the difficulties she faced as an indigent fisherman's wife. As Cao Daming commented while showing me the murder trail, "she may have been a bit open to other men, but what other options did she have?"

Despite the difficulties they faced, women under the WZA came to have new opportunities: they participated in the market economy, and gradually identified themselves with their businesses. The "boss lady" (*laoban niang*) was undoubtedly a significant female identity that came to prominence during the war era. For example, in the army there was a popular song called "My Home is on the mainland" (*wode jia zai dalu shang*) which described the homesickness felt by those soldiers who had followed the KMT government to Taiwan in 1949. The original lyrics began:

> My home is on the mainland, (*wode jia zai dalu shang*)
> where the mountains are high, and the water flows afar, (*gaoshan gao, liushui zhang*)
> and the seasons change from one to the next. (*yinian siji buyiyang*)

In Matsu, these lyrics were changed by the soldiers to:

> Boss lady, let me tell you, (*laobanniang wo genni jiang*)
> my heart is in the billiard room, (*wode xin zai zhuangqiuchang*)
> if I don't see you every day, it starts to itch. (*yitian bu jiandao ni, wo jiu xin yangyang*)

"Boss Lady and Her Business" became a way for soldiers to sing about their feelings and attachments, above and beyond their longing for the motherland.

Women who worked outside of the home at this time also began to form their own business associations, such as the "Thirteen Golden Hairpins" (*shisan jinchai*) of the Shanlong market. The Thirteen Golden Hairpins was by no means the earliest market organization—the "Fourteen Brothers and Sisters" (*shisi xiongmei*) already existed—but it was the energy of these new women members that first attracted greater attention, and soon such sister groups began to gain popularity across Matsu.

The members of the Thirteen Golden Hairpins were women who sold vegetables, fish, dried goods, and frozen foods inside the Shanlong market, and ran breakfast stands, bakeries, and small groceries outside the market. In the beginning there were thirteen women, but the number gradually increased to fifteen. They set out together as businesswomen from a young age, grew up, and married all around the same time. Maintaining frequent interactions, they gradually became a solid community. I asked them at what point they had sworn sisterhood with each other, and they said: "We've been together from the beginning. It was probably thirty or forty years ago, at some festival when we put on two feasts together, that we formally declared ourselves sisters."[26]

They saw each other every day at the market, and whenever one had an important event such as a wedding or funeral, they would all join in to help. After their economic situation stabilized, they learned dance together, sang karaoke, played cards, and even now, in their old age, still travel together. One local man said:

> In the past, if women sang or danced, they'd be called loose or flirtatious (F. *ia hyo ia tshiang*). But the Fifteen Golden Hairpin women learned how to sing and dance.

As their old dance teacher pointed out:

> The Fifteen Golden Hairpin women might have learned how to sing and dance, but when a temple festival came around, they would all make food, beat the clappers, and help carry the goddess's palanquin. At other times, they would help clean up the village. They "took the lead" (F. *tsau thau leing*) in such things.

The local temple recognized their impact and named the head of their organization to an honorary post at the temple, circumventing a vote by the all-male temple council. The WZA chair also took notice of their importance, and would formally invite them to dine with him, even including them in his New Year's celebrations.

These women always speak of their work spiritedly. For instance, the "squad leader" (*banzhang*) of the Fifteen Golden Hairpins told me proudly:

> Men can only do one thing at a time, but women can take care of a lot simultaneously.

When I asked them why it was that women had to undergo the most hardship, the second Hairpin, whom people called *erjie* (second eldest sister), spoke passionately:

A woman's work is her "career (*shiye*)"; it's her source of support and her responsibility. Sometimes a husband doesn't make much and has to rely on his wife. Matsu people have a saying: "The big stones make the wall, and the small ones fill in the holes" (F. *tuai luoh lieh tshuo, sa suoh tai*). ...You have to see the old houses on Matsu to understand. The stones here are all oddly shaped instead of having smooth surfaces. So when you built a house, you couldn't just use big stones; you had to fill in the holes with smaller stones in order to keep the walls from just falling down. The small stones are key!

The second Hairpin clearly pointed out that a woman's business during the military period was her "career," having importance both for herself and for her family. She also used the metaphor of the small stones to suggest that although women might be physically smaller than men, they held an important part of the responsibility for keeping their families going. Her self-confidence is obvious. Matsu women like the compliment of being called "capable" (F. *ia puong nëü*), indicating that they are competent, skillful, and able. To call a wife or a mother "capable" is to praise her ability to run a household: able to give orders, delegate work, and turn a profit. Nearly every Matsu woman was a skillful budgeter and could adjust her business to meet the needs of the soldiers. Any money they made was invested in local money-loan associations. When it reached a certain amount, it would be used to purchase property for their children in Taiwan (or also Fuzhou after martial law was lifted). As their economic contribution increased, so too did their status.

Influenced by the Fifteen Golden Hairpins, women across Matsu began to organize. Not only did the women on the snack street in Matsu Village (located on the western side of Nangan Island) organize into the "Twelve Sisters" (*shier jiemei*), but the women of Ox Horn also formed the "Sorority of Twelve." The mothers of Ox Horn danced together, played the clappers in rituals, and got involved in local matters. In fact, I once went with them to clean up the seashore, and saw how they helped collect ocean detritus. The Sorority of Twelve, however, was in some ways distinct from the Golden Hairpins of Shanlong or the Twelve Sisters of Matsu (village). Most of the Sorority worked not at their own businesses but in government kitchens or at the Matsu distillery, either as laborers or as service workers. The reason for this was likely connected to the love triangle crime described in Chapter 2. After the murders took place, Ox Horn was declared a "restricted zone" (*jinqu*), and the roads into the village were stationed with guards who prevented soldiers from entering. The decline of the fishing economy was already a blow to this fishing village, and things worsened once it was declared a restricted zone. The stores of the earlier business area, Da'ao (Big Inlet), had to shut, and many of those who wanted to do business opened shops in the market at Shanlong, the neighboring village. The former village head told me that when the government decided to establish a market on the island, the people of Ox Horn pushed hard to be chosen as the site. But because the village did not have enough space, the market went to Shanlong instead. The laborious and menial jobs, taken of necessity by the Sorority of Twelve, demonstrate the deterioration of this village's economy.

In Shanlong in 2009, I met Cao Xiaofen, the "boss lady" of a florist's shop (I shall discuss her further in Chapter 7). Like many women on Matsu, after graduating from elementary school, she worked as a clerk at a bookstore in Shanlong and ended up marrying a man from the area. Her husband's family raised chickens and ran a restaurant, and she was kept very busy each day helping with the work. As the G. I. Joe business became increasingly competitive, she left Matsu in 1976 to work in a clothing factory in Bade, Taiwan. When her husband took ill, he went to Taiwan for treatment; she took care of him and engaged in some minor business to support her family. After her husband died, she had the chance to study floriculture, which she enjoyed, but unfortunately her son fell ill. After many years of toil, she herself was diagnosed with cancer. With the help of her family back in Matsu, she returned home to recover. Having gone from Matsu to Taiwan and back again, she shared her observations with me:

> When I returned to Shanlong a decade ago, I realized that the women here had changed! They sing and dance and play cards—they're more active than the women in Taiwan!

Returning to Matsu helped her recover from her illness, and inspired by her friends, she opened a flower shop with a café and taught floriculture. The media reported that she had "returned to her hometown to finally live for herself" (J. Liu 2004c). Even today, we can see vigorous boss ladies arriving at the markets early to buy ingredients for their restaurants catering to Matsu's burgeoning tourism. There are also some female graduates from high school or college who have formed cultural organizations and participate actively in Matsu society nowadays.

Conclusion: Men and Women during the War Period

During the WZA period, the fishing economy in Matsu confronted severe challenges. As Taiwan began the process of industrialization in the 1970s and required a greater labor force, many Matsu locals moved there—mostly to Taoyuan—to work in factories. Those who stayed behind on the islands shifted their forms of livelihood to offering services and goods to the military. The guaranteed admission program and obligation to return home to work also introduced a new social category of government employees and teachers to Matsu. They would come to exert a tremendous influence on the future of Matsu, as I will discuss in Chapters 8–10.

Under the WZA, women also faced circumstances utterly different from those seen in the past. In the fishing society, men had made the primary contribution to the family finances by going out to sea, while women, who maintained the household, held a lower social status and were offered few educational opportunities. The military economy, however, opened up new possibilities for women. The G. I. Joe businesses, as Szonyi (2008:140) pointed out, were part of the militarization of the war period; female labor in Matsu was mobilized, as it was in Jinmen, to provide goods and services to soldiers. However, the changes the women of Matsu experienced differed from those in Jinmen. On the one hand, the new role of women, as in Jinmen, did not subvert traditional patrilineal ideology: the members of the Fifteen Hairpins were mothers first and foremost. They did not try to usurp the position of their husbands as head of the household, nor did they show great enthusiasm for temple politics. On the other hand, their role as boss ladies and their brisk business with the army gave them different possibilities outside of the patrilineal authority. The Fifteen Hairpins not only challenged the traditional Matsu view that singing and dancing were for "loose women," their collective power even induced the elders and military leaders within the patrilineal society to acknowledge their contributions. Finally, they were given their own honorary posts in the temple without being subject to a vote by the all-male temple council. These differences from the women in Jinmen are related to the islands' differing histories: the lineage organizations on Matsu were never as strong as on Jinmen, given Matsu's long history as a temporary stopover for fishermen.

In many ways, the development of the women of Matsu was more along the lines of the Taiwanese or mainland model of the "female entrepreneur." Gates (1996, 1999) describes how petty capitalism offered women, both in Taiwan and in the mainland, more autonomy and social power. Simon (2004) also points out that in Taiwan, boss ladies often stressed that their businesses endowed them with free space in which to live. Not only could they contribute to the family income, they could also go beyond their household and develop new connections with the larger society. Under the WZA, the lives of the women of Matsu were in important ways different from the earlier days.

4   Gambling with the Military State

In many places, gambling is taken as a sign of moral decline. Persistent gambling can lead to addiction or a loss of self-control and has the potential to engender serious social problems. This chapter examines gambling from the perspective of Matsu's ethnography. I locate the Matsu people's gambling habits in the context of the island's ecology and society, showing that early on gambling was embedded in the fishermen's lives. It was elaborated during the WZA era to coordinate with the oppressive and tedious rhythm of a society tightly controlled by the army. I argue that gambling in warzone Matsu was not only a cultural metaphor (Geertz 1973) or a form of social resistance (Scott 1985), but also an emotional outlet and imaginative practice by which the islanders escaped, ridiculed, and even and contended with the military state.

Gambling and Fishing

Gambling has been a part of Chinese life for a very long time, both in China itself and in Chinese emigrant societies (Watson 1975; Basu 1991). Matsu is no exception. Before 1949, the men in Matsu had a tradition of drinking and gambling. Whether after an exhausting day out at sea, or while waiting for the tide, drinking and gambling were diverting ways to pass the time and constituted the main form of male entertainment on the islands. Gambling, unlike the labor of women in the domestic space, was a communal activity. As they drank and gambled, men exchanged fishing information and current social news, and created, demonstrated, and reaffirmed their social connections. A man who did not drink or gamble showed that he had neither money nor power. As a Matsu saying reveals:

> No whoring, no gambling: ancestors are dishonored (F. *Me phiu, me tu, ta louh kung tsu*).

Yet fishing and gambling are in fact mutually implicated at an even deeper level. The senior boat captains I interviewed, who have closely observed the fisherman lifestyle, all pointed to the fact that fishing is inherently a form of gambling. Fishermen are different from farmers who work the land; out at sea, they must confront a host of unpredictable factors, such as ocean currents, wind direction, weather, and so on, all of which can change on a dime. Fishermen not only have to be highly adaptable; they must also be resolute and fearless in the face of danger. Gambling involves a high degree of luck and a "winner take all" mentality that is closely complementary to the fishing experience. For this reason, gambling was more than just entertainment; it was also a training ground (Chu 2010: 267), and a way of cultivating bravery and daring in fishermen.

When a comparison is made with agriculture, the connections between gambling and fishing become even clearer. Engaging in farming requires land, and it relies upon a farmer's patience during lengthy periods of cultivation before crops can be harvested. Preservation of property and harvest from year to year is the main method of building wealth in an agricultural society, which lacks the possibility of sudden windfalls. Fishing societies operate very differently. Fish multiply in the sea without having to be cultivated, and catching them depends not only on skill, but also on luck. When the opportunity arises, one must quickly "grab as much as one can" in order to have any chance of an "unexpected windfall." Gambling, therefore, is inherent in the fishing livelihood.

Indeed, on such far-flung islands where one had to struggle with the sea for an unpredictable livelihood, life was more dangerous than in an agricultural society. Anyone who was not brave enough to take substantial risks was unlikely to achieve a breakthrough. This notion is reflected in the Matsu saying:

> Better to give birth to a prodigal son than a fool.
> (F. *tsai iong pei ngiang, me tsai iong ngoung ngiang*)

Although a prodigal son may admittedly squander away the family fortune, his risk-taking behavior also demonstrates that he can tolerate danger, think quickly, and seize an opportunity when it arises. In contrast, a "foolish son" only consumes a family's assets and is often caught off guard by unexpected events.

However, since uncontrolled gambling can clearly be ruinous to the family, the Matsu people also emphasize:

> In either whoring or gambling, you have to take your own measure. (F. *phiu phiu tu tu, tsy a tho tsu*)

This expression indicates that in both gambling and in illicit sexual relations, one must first be certain of one's own limits. Again, the point is not to forbid gambling, but rather to achieve a balance so as not to destroy oneself. In sum, gambling represented the adventurous or even audacious character of the islanders. It was not only the main entertainment or social activity for fishermen; the luck, skill, and inherent spirit of risk that it entails also capture what men needed to equip themselves when facing the perils of the capricious ocean.

"Gambling is the Origin of All Vices"

Perhaps owing to worries about people gathering together and causing trouble, or concern about fostering addiction, the army detested gambling from the start. Nearly every year, *Matsu Daily* reported on the ban on gambling and the arrest of gamblers. A 1959 article already announced strict punishments for gambling:

> Any civil servant who gambles will be dismissed from his position, and is banned from taking up a government post in the future. Military officials will be dealt with severely under military law.[1]

In order to rid Matsu of gambling, the WZA held endless meetings to discuss the problem of "how to eradicate gambling."[2] A 1969 decree entitled "Implementation of a complete gambling ban," stated that government employees and teachers caught gambling would not only be dismissed, but also that their work unit supervisor would be given a first level demerit. If common people were caught gambling, businessmen would be forced to close their businesses, while fishermen would be kept off the sea for a period of a week to a month. Others would be punished according to the specific circumstances with forced labor, jail time, or fines. Often, the newspaper would publish the names of offenders along with statistics about their professions. For example, a 1972 *Matsu Daily* article recounts that police had apprehended:

> Fifty-six participants in a gambling ring, including two government officials, twenty-six businessmen, fifteen fishermen, three visitors, and ten women.[3]

What is worth noting in this report is the appearance of government officials and women as gamblers, a subject that I will revisit in the next section.

Nearly every year the police would publicly burn gambling paraphernalia, and the WZA chair would be at the scene to personally supervise and express how seriously the authorities viewed the issue.[4] The authorities' attitude reveals the state's deep anxiety about losing control over gatherings of locals. Despite their intense efforts, however, the official ban on gambling had only a limited effect.[5] As *Matsu Daily* reported:

> Yesterday at 2:30 PM, county police and other officials participated in a burning of gambling equipment at the Shanlong harbor. …Although officials have put a strict ban in place…evil still persists in the face of good, and addicted offenders have continued their old ways, in disregard of the law.[6]

In this situation, authorities could only implement increasingly harsh laws. For instance, the importation and sale of books about gambling and articles that could be used for purposes of gambling (such as mahjong tiles, Chinese dominos, dice, and four-colored cards) were tightly controlled:

> 1. Importation regulations: Gambling paraphernalia imported through the regular channels will be confiscated without exception, and the offender's work unit and name will be recorded and investigated.
> 2. Sales regulations: The county government forbids all stores within its jurisdiction to sell any gambling paraphernalia.[7]

The WZA also regularly announced new rules and increasingly severe punishments. By the end, anyone who worked for the government—including all office workers, maintenance workers, service workers, and other employees—would be fired immediately if found to be engaging in gambling activities.[8] A year later (1983), there was even an announcement that people who were apprehended three times for providing venues for gambling to soldiers would be expelled from the islands and not allowed to come back. The newspaper denounced the behavior forcefully: "Gambling is the origin of all vices."[9]

As officials engaged in this cat-and-mouse struggle against local custom, however, gambling became a kind of shared knowledge between officials and locals. While officials thought of every means possible to enforce a ban against gambling, they also used it as a kind of larger metaphor. For example, in an interview that the WZA chair granted a Taiwanese reporter, he told the following story:

> Confucius went on a journey but didn't bring enough money. So he played a game of mahjong with Shakyamuni, Jesus, and Mohammed, hoping to win enough to cover his expenses. But Confucius's luck was bad, and he kept losing. Finally, his luck turned, and he got a good hand that included the four directions [and a red tile], so all he needed was another red tile [to make a pair] to win. But then he had a second spell of bad luck, and after several rounds he still hadn't obtained the needed red tile. The moment he decided to just play the red tile he had in his hand, he received another red tile, but by that time it was too late to win. Confucius was very disheartened. Zilu [Confucius's student] said: "Having received the four directions, he hoped for another red tile, but as soon as he played his first red tile, of course he lost!" The WZA chair recounted this story, and then added the conclusion: That red tile with a "中" in it represents the "Republic of China." It's like a trump card. You can see from this how important the place of China is in the world.[10]

In the story, Confucius is unlucky, and he does not manage to win any money. When his luck finally changes, he is able to collect tiles for the "four directions," along with a "red tile." If he can collect a second red tile, he will win. Unexpectedly, in a moment of carelessness, Confucius gives up his red tile and ruins his potentially winning hand. To educate people, the WZA chair used the "red tile" as a metaphor for the Republic of China, demonstrating that mahjong had already become a form of shared knowledge for the government and locals, as well as a medium for communication.

Lightening the Drudgery of Military Rule

In contravention of the government ban, gambling during the military period extended to all walks of life, and its significances multiplied.

Killing Tedium

"The harder they tried to catch us, the more we gambled" (*zhuade yuejin, dude yuexiong*), many Matsu residents said. Moreover, while in the past it was mainly fishermen who engaged in gambling, the practice now spread beyond any specific group. Even government officials and teachers began to participate during the WZA period. *Matsu Daily*'s reports of repeated government orders regarding civil workers show how much of an issue it was. Workers at the Matsu Distillery, the Regulation of Goods Department, and the publishing office of *Matsu Daily* were caught gambling and named in the newspaper. Yet despite constant government threats, as well as severe punishments including dismissal, people continued to gamble. A man who worked for the Matsu Electric Company recounted the situation at the time:

> Back then, we never put away our office mahjong table.[11] When the lunch break began, everyone would rush to the table to get a spot. In order to keep a seat, some even skipped lunch completely.
>
> "Why were people so crazy about gambling?" I pressed.
>
> I don't know. It felt like that was the only way we could get through the day.

It seemed as if only by playing mahjong could one alleviate the boredom of civil service under military rule and make life bearable.

By examining the Supply Cooperative, we can go a step further in understanding the connection between the drudgery of life under military rule and gambling. The Supply Cooperative was a special work unit under the WZA that managed the circulation of supplies within the islands. Its head, deputy head, and section chiefs were all appointed by the military authority, while Matsu locals were employed in subordinate positions as ordinary personnel. Thus, the Supply Cooperative was partly a military entity: at the beginning of each day, workers raised the national flag and did morning exercises before beginning work. Even today, at the old site of the Supply Cooperative, one can see the flagpole towering over the middle of the complex (Fig. 4.1).

The Supply Cooperative was responsible for regulating all the important supplies on the islands. Aside from rice, which was controlled directly by the military, all of the goods necessary for daily life such as wheat,

Fig. 4.1 The main building of the Supply Cooperative
(Photo by the author)

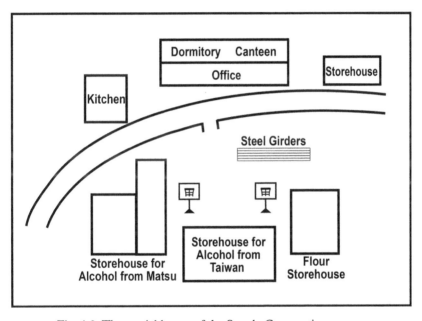

Fig. 4.2 The spatial layout of the Supply Cooperative

sugar, different kinds of alcohol, and construction materials like steel bars and concrete had to be purchased from the Cooperative. One might say that the Supply Cooperative was an enormous warehouse (Fig. 4.2).

Work at the Supply Cooperative took place nearly around the clock. In addition to keeping regular working hours, the warehouse also had to be

Table 4.1 *Daily Schedule of the Supply Cooperative*

Time	Activities
7:30 AM	Breakfast
8:00 AM	Flag Raising and Morning Exercises
8:30-12 PM	Work
12:00-1:30 PM	Lunch and Rest
1:30-3:30 PM	Work
3:30 PM	Outdoor Exercise
5:30 PM	Dinner
6:00 PM	End of the Shift, or Additional Nightshift

guarded at all times. If supply ships from Taiwan arrived, there had to be workers to go to the docks to receive and unload the goods. Consequently, workers took turns working the night shift, and slept inside. Each worker was expected to work at least one night-shift per week, and often more. The Supply Cooperative had its own kitchen, which prepared three meals a day for the personnel, and staff members slept in the office building. Table 4.1 shows how the staff spent their days and nights.

Personnel at the Supply Cooperative were required to arrive before 7:30 am to eat breakfast together, raise the flag, do morning exercises, and work until the afternoon. After dinner, some workers could go home, but many had to stay on for a nightshift. In order to break up the tedium, the head of the Cooperative included half an hour of rest in the day, usually for outdoor exercise such as basketball games (see the two basketball nets in Fig. 4.2).

Still, this dull, monotonous lifestyle was alleviated by many secret opportunities for different forms of gambling. For example, during the noontime rest, some workers would place small bets over cards or chess. At 3:30 pm, they would make bets over basketball games. There were more chances in the evenings, when they could play mahjong together. The air-raid shelter behind the Cooperative was a paradise for workers. They would run an electrical wire into it and hang lights to help pass the endless night. After an intense night of playing mahjong, however, they would often find the electrical line cut the next morning—a warning from

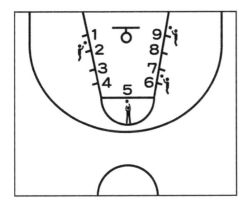

Fig. 4.3 "Betting on Basketball"

an unhappy commander. The next night they might resist the temptation to play and go back early to sleep.

How the workers turned the officially approved pastime of "basketball playing" into "basketball betting" right under their commanders' eyes is fascinating. Figure 4.3 shows how it was was done. The painted restricted area had nine positions; once everyone got into position they would dribble a few times, and then with meaningful glances, they would start to bet. Frequently four people would play together, sometimes with each person taking ten shots per turn and the highest points determining the winner. The more common way of playing was for each player to take turns making single shots. If the ball did not go in the basket, the person would remain in place. If it did go in, the person would advance from position 1 to 2 to 3 to 4, and so on. The person who made it to position 9 would win, and the rest of the players would pay up according to their position, owing 100, 200, or 300 Taiwanese dollars. The monotony of life in the Supply Cooperative was brightened by these different forms of gambling.

Gambling Goes to the Graveyard!

Occasionally, when the government crackdown was especially severe, workers would no longer be able to gamble in their offices. When that happened, people would find hidden spots on the island or deserted pigpens where they could gamble unobserved. For example, a graveyard upon a hillside near Ox Horn became a gathering place for gamblers. The ground that had been leveled for the cemetery was a convenient place to lay out their games. It is said that every day at noon, the area would be packed with government workers on their daily break, throwing dice until they had to return to work at 1:30 pm. The dense mountain vegetation helped conceal their activities and kept them from being discovered. Gamblers would also post lookouts. If a civil or military policeman caught wind of what they were doing, they could immediately flee into the forest.

In fact, the police themselves also gambled. In order to understand how this occurred, I talked to several people who had been police officers during the WZA period. One older man who had been a police officer from 1953–61 mentioned that a coworker whom he liked very much had been fired after he was caught playing mahjong. He said that he himself had been enticed into playing cards while patrolling the streets of Shanlong and had received a demerit at work. It seems that even police officers had difficulty avoiding the temptations of these games. I finally met a respectable older gentleman in Ox Horn who said he had never gambled. Still, he told me that when he worked as a police officer in the 1970s, someone notified him about a group of people gambling on a hill near Ox Horn. He went to arrest the culprits but was shocked to find that his own mother was one of the gamblers. Panicking on seeing her son approach, she fell while attempting to flee. Distressed and embarrassed, he hurried over to help her up and told her, "Don't run, you can take your time." Subsequently, someone else reported that people had gathered in Fu'ao and Shanlong to gamble; when he went there, he ended up arresting two of his own uncles. Frustrated at having to keep arresting his relatives, he applied to be transferred to work in the Household Registration Bureau.

Under the Table, Inside Tunnels

It wasn't just government employees who gambled; given half a chance, ordinary citizens also took part. People especially enjoyed gambling during civil defense training. As they told me without any qualms:

> An official would be up on stage with spit flying as he held forth about how to take care of our firearms and how to defend ourselves against communist spies, and we'd all be sitting there playing Chinese poker, dealing the cards under the table.

Military exercises presented even more opportunities to gamble. The long, meandering tunnels on the islands, where they would not be seen by their commanding officers, were a haven for gamblers. As one informant told me:

> We could gamble even if we had only ten or twenty minutes. If we were pressed for time, we'd deal two cards and go by straight value. If we had a little more time, we'd deal four cards and go by pairs. There's always a lot of flexibility in gambling.

Those in the teaching profession were no exception. Some teachers would hide in a corner of a school library to gamble. They would arrange to meet ahead of time, and if they heard footsteps approaching, they would immediately cover the mahjong tiles with a cloth, and slump against the table, pretending to nap over their books. A storage house located at the edge of the school campus was also a good site, as it was rarely frequented and filled with plenty of objects to obstruct the view of anyone who happened to pass by.

Women and Dice

During military rule, women involved in selling goods and services to the soldiers would also often gamble, particularly those who opened shops to do G. I. Joe business and those who collected shellfish on the seashore to sell. Once they had their own income, they sought opportunities for a little gambling in the middle of their busy days. They often preferred to play dice, since it produced a quick winner and would not take too much time out of their tight schedules. Their body language was particularly telling as they cast the dice, especially those with low dealer's points if they thought they had a chance to win. They first mumble some words to the dice, put them against their face and say as they rub them: "When a monkey washes its face there's money to be made" (F. *kau se mieng ou tsieng theing*). Then they blow on the dice, clutching them to their chest and rubbing them together. When they are finally ready to toss, they cry excitedly: "Four five six! Four five six!" encouraging the dice to land high. In response, the dealer shouts: "One two three! One two three!" hoping to end in a draw. The atmosphere would often get quite fervent and heated, for they knew if they were caught they would be punished by having to sweep the streets, clean out gutters, or even transport human fertilizer; nonetheless, they still sought out their secret games and after a short while would hurry back to work or to home to cook and take care of their families. Gambling was a part of their daily routine.

"They Just Cannot Catch Us!"

"But didn't the government control gambling strictly and constantly burn the equipment?" I asked. "What did you do if you didn't have anything to use to gamble?" One of older policemen mentioned earlier told me:

> Fishermen would sometimes hide mahjong pieces in the bottom of their fish baskets, and sometimes they'd bring them back mixed in with the fish! With so many fishermen, how could we check them all?

Other interlocutors spoke over each other excitedly:

> There were lots of ways to get hold of mahjong tiles. When we went to Taiwan for sports games or shows, each of us would bring back a few tiles. And when we got back to Matsu, we'd put them all together to make a complete set.

> You could also hide them in bamboo! You just hollow out the joints in the bamboo and bring them back that way.

> Matsu has no natural gas, so it had to be imported from Taiwan. Some people would saw a gas canister in half, stuff it with mahjong tiles, chess pieces, and playing cards, and then solder it back together. Once painted, it was indistinguishable from the other canisters in the pile.

Gambling in these descriptions became an audacious practice by which people imagined themselves escaping the clutches of the state, creating their own rhizomorphic space (Deleuze and Guattari 1987) and time beyond the control of the military. In the fishing period, Matsu islanders gambled with the ocean; now, they were gambling with the state. They endured and contended with military rule in terms of their gambling culture.

Yellow Croaker and Dominos

Gambling also developed into a kind of ceremonial practice in the military period, particularly during the yellow croaker fishing season in Dongyin. Yellow croaker is a lucrative species found along coastal China, with its fishing grounds spreading south towards the open sea; it is prized for its meat, which is as tender as tofu. They migrate in schools, and Dongyin was on their reproductive migratory route, thereby forming an important fishing ground. Yellow croaker came from the southeast to the Dongyin area from April to June each year, making up the main fishing season for this variety in Matsu (Z. Chen 2013:102). Since the 1980s, however, the species has mostly disappeared from the area because of over-fishing.

Before its depletion, the fishermen of Dongyin had a long tradition of catching yellow croaker. Local elders said that earlier in the spring fishing season, fishermen from costal China would come to fish and sell their catch to the mainland. After the separation of the PRC and the ROC, the fishermen of Dongyin were limited to selling their catch to the soldiers on the islands. When supply exceeded demand, they could only resort to drying the surplus fish. In the late 1960s, some Taiwanese ships with cold storage sensed a business opportunity and began to come to Dongyin to purchase fresh fish. Finally, the Matsu Fishing Association came to a negotiated agreement with the shipping companies, according to which they had to place competing bids and guarantee that the winner would buy the entire catch at a set price, irrespective of how much fish was caught. Thus, when the fishing season was good, fishermen could make quite a bit of money. At that time, when the fishing industry operated on cash transactions, catching yellow croaker could mean a welcome windfall. Beginning in 1968, fishermen from across the islands of Matsu came to Dongyin in pursuit of this fish. Before leaving, they had to undergo three days of ideological training in which they learned about the "savagery of the communist bandits" (*gongfei baoxing*) before being allowed to prepare for their journey. When they set out, officials would come down to the wharf to send them off, setting off firecrackers to wish them a successful return.[12]

Fishermen said that yellow croaker would rise close to the surface during high tide, and so were relatively easy to catch. The high tides on the first and fifteenth days of the lunar calendar were the most anticipated fishing days for yellow croaker. During the breeding season, the air bladders of the fish vibrate and let off sounds that attract members of the opposite sex. In a particularly crowded school, the noise can sound like boiling water or wind blowing through pines (J. Liu and Qiu 2002).

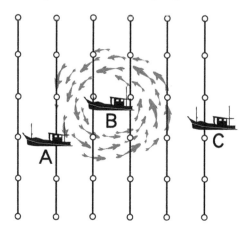

Fig. 4.4 A sketch of fishing boats trying to net yellow croaker

When there were few fish detectors to locate the fish, fishermen would often rely on the sound of the school to estimate its size. There is a common saying which is used to mock overly talkative people in Matsu. It alludes to the way in which the fish give themselves away with their own noises: "the Dongyin yellow croaker is betrayed by its own mouth" (F. *toeyng' ing uonghua khoeyh tshui hai*).

Just because the croaker made revealing noises did not mean that every fishing expedition was successful, however. Even if a captain was skilled at determining the location of the fish from their sound, there was also the question of unpredictable weather and tides, along with other unforeseen factors, so that even the most experienced captain could not guarantee a catch. All the boats went out at the same time and cast their nets in the same vicinity, yet some returned with a good catch, while others barely broke even. One highly experienced captain from Dongyin told me that when the yellow croaker gathered and made a lot of noise, many boats would arrive in the area. But where exactly the fish were at any moment was difficult to discern, and so catching them was a matter of luck (see also Q. Chen 2009; Yan 1977). He drew a picture to explain (Fig. 4.4). Boat B is the most fortunate, since its net is cast right in the midst of the school of fish, and so it returns with a full catch; boat A is a bit too far to the left, but it likely still makes a decent catch; but boat C is too far too the right to have much hope of catching anything.

Indeed, the Dongyin fishermen say that whenever they caught yellow croaker, it was like "hitting the jackpot," and "the excitement of the chase was just like gambling." During a successful fishing expedition, "the fish floated on the surface of the water like chunks of ice you could walk on" (Q. Chen 2009).[13] Chen Qizao, a fisherman from Tieban, Nangan, described a big catch:

> When luck was on your side, you could bring in 20,000 *jin* in one net, so much that you couldn't even fit it all on the boat and you had to shorten the net and let some fish go free! The Taiwanese merchant ships could only carry 200 metric tons of fish, and once they weighed off that much on their scale, the rest got dumped back into the sea![14]

The Dongyin boat captain mentioned above also told me that once when he went out in a pair trawler to fish for yellow croaker, he caught 40 tons of fish. "I spent a whole day raising the fish out of the water, that's how much there was!" He decided to steer the boat directly to Keelung Harbor in Taiwan to sell the fish and made NT$4,000,000 in one go. He continued:

CAPTAIN: That night, the crew celebrated by going out "drinking with girls." At that time [around 1980], it cost NT$100 to hire an escort. You know how much the crew gave her?
AUTHOR: How much?
CAPTAIN: NT$10,000!

Knowing how extravagantly a yellow croaker catch was celebrated in Taiwan, it is unsurprising that when the fishermen returned to shore they held big gambling parties. Either to test their luck once more or to celebrate a good catch, the fishermen who caught croaker usually gambled heroically. They bet extravagant amounts and were indifferent to loss: the real purpose behind their gambling was display, and to show off rather than to consolidate their earnings.

During the yellow croaker season, fishermen liked to play Chinese dominoes (the locals call it *pi peou*), which was usually played during the Lantern Festival, the biggest festival on the islands. The ceremonial atmosphere of the croaker catch is therefore significant. During the game, the dealer hands out four tiles to each player, and the players lay them out in two pairs to compare their values with the dealer in fast-paced rounds. Although there are only four players in any given game, others could also place stakes on any of them being the winner. During the catch season, the tables would be crowded with onlookers. There were at least three layers of participants at each table: the people actually playing the game formed the closest ring, the second ring was made up of those taking stakes in the game, and the third ring was observers standing on stools, all forming a noisy excited crowd. There was no limit on bets: a lot of money was quickly won and lost in each game, and the atmosphere was heated and charged with excitement.

The games of Chinese dominoes during the croaker season could be seen as a ritualistic activity. Precisely because of this ceremonial nature, the military tended to look the other way and not shut the games down. But because of the high stakes, fishermen would sometimes gamble away an entire season's hard-earned income. At the time, there was a popular saying:

You cry when you catch croaker, and you cry when you don't.
(F. *uong' ua huah ya thie, mo huah ya thie*)

The expression describes the difficulty of catching yellow croaker, and the misery of easily losing it all at the gambling table.

By the time the season was over, many had lost nearly all of their earnings (Q. Chen 2009). A man from Ox Horn, the son of a fisherman, told me that when he was young his father spent two months in Dongyin each yellow croaker season, yet he always came back with empty pockets. I asked him why his father continued to participate if he didn't earn any money from it, and he told me: "That's just part of being a fisherman, he couldn't not go." Owing to depletion, the yellow croaker faded into the annals of history after 1985, but elders still remember the season and their Chinese domino games as though it were yesterday.

Conclusion: Gambling with the State

Anthropologists have discussed the significance of gambling from different perspectives. Earlier it was considered a metaphor for other aspects of social life (Geertz 1973). More recently, it has been analyzed as a form of symbolic resistance to the state (Papataxiarchis 1999) or as a way of engaging with uncertainty (Davis 2006; Malaby 2003). Gambling in

Chinese society, especially mahjong, has also received considerable attention. Scholars have elucidated the cultural content of mahjong: notions such as fate, luck, and skill, and how they form analogies and affinities to other aspects of society. For example, mahjong bears a likeness to business adventures among the Chinese migrants in India (Basu 1991), while in Taiwan, mahjong "agonistics" and the vibrant political culture were mutually reinforcing (Festa 2007). In the twenty-first century, gambling is still very popular in the Chinese countryside: it is a way for the villagers to engage with the authoritarian state and with neoliberalism (Bosco et al. 2009), or for Fuzhounese migrants' wives it is a way to escape loneliness (Chu 2010). It is also, however, a means of contending with the boundaries between old and young, rural and urban, local sociality and state discourse for the people in Enshi, Hubei province (Steinmüller 2011).

My analysis, different from previous scholars, examines the changing significances of gambling practices: that is, I discuss how gambling in Matsu developed from a leisure activity for men in the fishing society to an everyday practice of the general population during the military's reign. During the WZA period, gambling was no longer limited to a particular time, space, or group of people (Basu 1991), but extended to all levels of society (from the WZA chair and government functionaries to the lowest rungs of society) and involved both men and women. It could vary from the public dominoes played by fishermen to people hiding cards under the table at civil defense training, and from the ritualistic to the ordinary. That is, it became "a way of life" in Watson's words (1975: 168). Various forms of gambling corresponded to the life rhythms of different people. Lengthy games of mahjong livened up the dull routines of low-level government workers under the WZA. Rapid dice games could offer a brief respite to women during their hectic days engaging in G. I. Joe business. The excitement and betting involved in Chinese dominoes mimics and re-enacts the risks and festivity of the precious fishing season. These different forms of gambling responded to the social dynamics across all professions during military rule.

However, the reasons gambling proliferated go well beyond its analogies with other social aspects or its role in negotiating the boundaries between the governed and the ruling state, as other scholars have argued.

During the years of tedious drudgery that the islanders were expected to endure under the WZA, gambling was a way to give vent to the boredom of routine and to relieve the tedium under an otherwise stifling military rule. Gambling was thus an emotional outlet—a stage for enacting humor, ridicule, and anger, and an imaginative practice with which to evade the iron control of the military.[15]

Nevertheless, the people of Matsu were still forced to the extremes of the islands—clammy tunnels, bleak graveyards, and deserted pigpens— to find room to breathe. As we can surmise, their rise against military rule was imminent.

Part II

New Technologies of Imagination

5   Digital Matsu

In the 1980s, many Matsu people were greatly encouraged by the burgeoning Taiwanese democracy movement.[1] Like the Taiwanese opposition, they used publications, demonstrations, and elections (Rigger 1999: 113) to convey their dissatisfaction with military rule. The Matsu opposition movement did not end with elections, however. Dissidents sustained their efforts, and in the twenty-first century introduced new media technologies to Matsu, eventually resulting in reforms that went beyond politics. This chapter discusses how these technologies have generated *a new imaginary of Matsu* which is different from that of the military period. I show how an internet community has taken shape, in which Matsu people can break up the tightly-knit social networks on the islands to develop new online selves. While it is certainly the case that different netizens have varied ways of using internet media, within this community a special intimacy with and affect for "Matsu" are engendered and assimilated, and social actions are initiated. Internet technologies have transformed Matsu from peripheral fishing islands and a military frontline into a place with its own unique values.

The Matsu Democracy Movement

The government's guaranteed admission program laid the foundation for the Matsu Democracy Movement. As I indicated in Chapter 3, this program sent Matsu's top students to study in Taiwan. Many of them were inspired by democratic ideas there and later led the protests for democracy in Matsu. Cao Yuanzheng is one of the pioneers in this movement among the wave of students. During his studies at a normal university in Taiwan, he was motivated by democratic ideas and came to understand the injustices brought about by the WZA in Matsu (Y. Cao 2012). In 1983, he raised funds to establish a magazine, called *Matsu Light* (*Matsu zhi guan*), and began criticizing the WZA; he proposed holding popular elections, allowing for tourism, ending restrictions on citizens leaving the islands, and abolishing military rule, along with other important reforms. Cao later invited Liu Jiaguo, a frequent contributor to *Matsu Light*, to be the editor of the journal, and the two began to propagate democratic ideals through their publication.

Liu, who hails from Dongyin, had been sent to Taitung High School in Taiwan after elementary education, again via the guaranteed admission program. He recalled that after spending more than ten hours in turbulent waters on a ship without any problem, he got motion sickness the moment he boarded a train in Taiwan. After graduating from high school, he studied history at Soochow University in Taipei before returning to his hometown. He initially taught in a middle school before being attracted by the commercial opportunities of G. I. Joe business. Noting that Taiwanese trends were also popular in Dongyin, he opened the first café there in 1979. It was very successful, and two years later he brought the Taiwanese fad of karaoke to Dongyin. Having made quite a bit of money, he decided to expand his business and open a branch on the main island, Nangan. In 1983 he started a karaoke bar there called "Happy Island," which was an instant success. The bar was quite a shock for Matsu citizens accustomed to the boredom of military rule. Many people—from ordinary citizens to soldiers and high-ranking military officers—became entranced by the seductive musical world of karaoke (S. Lin 2013). Within a year, five or six similar bars had opened in Nangan. Military officials soon decided that they could not allow the trend to continue, and they began to target Liu's business.

In an interview, Liu noted that at first the county government (controlled by the military) increased his taxes tenfold, from NT$2,000 to NT$25,000 per month, making it nearly impossible for his business to survive. Liu then allied himself with other business owners to negotiate with the government and came to an agreement to pay NT$5,000 monthly. Despite this, the karaoke business remained strong, so WZA officials dispatched military police to stand guard in the doorway of the bars. This successfully prevented soldiers from going in, and his business was totally crushed. Liu said:

> When that happened, I suddenly realized that there was an institution in Matsu called the "Warzone Administration." Before that, I just felt that the hierarchical segregation between citizens and the army on the ship to Taiwan was very unfair and that the civilian militias brought us a lot of inconvenience, but this event lit the fuse that made me start to oppose the military.

After his karaoke business collapsed, Liu spent a brief period trying to run his grocery store business again before going to Taiwan to edit *Matsu Light*. As stated earlier, the journal, under the management of Cao Yuanzheng, had already begun criticizing the situation in Matsu, but because at that time it received financial support from the Matsu government, its commentary was restrained. After Liu joined the magazine, they began to raise money independently, which released them from government control and allowed them to actively promote democracy and free speech. Liu also learned how to write articles, conduct interviews, edit, and raise money, along with other skills involved in running a magazine, from the much more seasoned reporter Cao Yuanzhang, and this laid the foundation that would later help him manage the magazine on his own (J. Liu 2006b).

Liu's experience of the military's interference in his karaoke business may be dramatic, but such stories were by no means unusual in Matsu. As Part I of this book describes, for a long time ordinary people in Matsu were subject to strict controls imposed by the WZA. In addition to regulated travel between Matsu and Taiwan, and an enforced curfew after 9 pm each night, people's daily lives were also severely constrained. The military often used the G. I. Joe businesses to pressure ordinary people. Many residents said that if they disobeyed the army, the authorities would threaten them by not allowing soldiers to frequent their businesses. Those who had returned after studying in Taiwan felt this especially keenly:

> When we came back from Taiwan, if we kept our hair long or wore the bellbottoms that were popular in Taiwan, the police would warn us that we were "destroying customs of decency" (*pohuai shanliang fengsu*).
>
> If we got into a fight with a soldier, they'd summarily throw us in jail for at least three days without even bothering to figure out what had happened.

Later, motorcycles came to Matsu, but there were so many rules about them. Even wearing slippers on a motorcycle would get you a fine of three hundred Taiwanese dollars.

It is unsurprising that when martial law was lifted in Taiwan in 1987 but was kept in place in Jinmen and Matsu, long-suppressed popular resentment began to erupt. Young people from Dongyin and Matsu signed petition after petition demanding the removal of the military government (J. Liu 1988). In Taiwan, Cao Yuanzhang led Liu Jiaguo and other Matsu youngsters to the streets to fight for democracy. Joining forces with protestors from Jinmen, more than 300 people went to Taipei for the "823 Jinmen-Matsu March." They gave a full account of their situation to the Legislative Yuan (the primary legislative body in Taiwan), trying to bring an end to the WZA, to gain direct telephone access, to eliminate border exit controls, to improve public transportation, to demand a return of private lands held by the military, to lift the ban on internal travel, to hold county elections, to found a county legislative assembly, and so on. The government did respond in some ways, for example by allowing elections and establishing a county legislature. Liu Jiaguo was elected to be a county councilor (Cao Yuanzhang was later elected as a legislator). In 1991, however, President Lee Tenghui declared the termination of "the Period of Mobilization for the Suppression of the Communist Rebellion" (*dongyuan kanluan shiqi*), and on the same day, the Ministry of Defense issued the "Proclamation of Temporary Martial Law in Jinmen-Matsu" (*jinma linshi jieyan ling*), commencing the second period of martial law in Jinmen and Matsu. Despite intense pressure from military officials, Liu Jiaguo still went to Taiwan along with two other representatives. They organized the "507 Anti-Martial Law" protest with Jinmen representatives, students and the migrants from Matsu and Jinmen living in Taiwan. A sit-in outside the main entrance of the Legislative Yuan building began on May 7 and lasted for eleven nights. The protestors left only when the Ministry of Defense agreed to end the second period of martial law in Jinmen and Matsu. On November 7 of that same year, the Ministry of Defense announced the lifting of martial law in Jinmen and Matsu, and the dismantlement of the WZA. Only then did military control over Jinmen and Matsu truly come to an end, and democracy was implemented in the region.

Matsu Report

After the WZA was abolished in 1992, Cao Yuanzhang felt that his responsibilities from that era had come to an end, and he decided to close down *Matsu Light* and stand for election. In contrast, Liu Jiaguo, after having participated in protests, was keenly conscious of the important role of the media in holding the government to account and influencing society. He felt that although the WZA had finally been dismantled, Matsu's major media outlet, *Matsu Daily*, was still firmly controlled by the county government without a counterbalancing power to monitor its activities. For this reason, he founded *Matsu Report*, and proceeded with his "post WZA era" social reformation (S. Lin 2013). Worried about potential pressure from officials about what to publish, he decided not to solicit funds from the government. Instead, he raised money entirely through contributions from like-minded people. He also discovered that he was not adept at catering to the whims of voters and decided not to stand for election again, throwing himself completely into editing his biweekly broadsheet.

Given all this, *Matsu Report* held a unique position in Matsu from the very beginning. It was widely read. As one resident amusingly put it:

> Everyone looked forward to the biweekly *Matsu Report*. People would often wrap their oily fried crullers in *Matsu Daily*, but if you did that with *Matsu Report*, someone would scold you! (S. Lin 2013)

Moreover, many people said: "I would read every single word of *Matsu Report*." Every time a new edition arrived, it would quickly sell out:

> Every time a new edition came out, there would always be the same scene: one crowd was grabbing up *Matsu Report*, another was scrambling to read it, and the third was hotly discussing whatever topics were in the paper [Fig. 5.1]... Every edition of the paper would be read carefully, and all of the issues in it would be widely debated. The topics were varied, covering politics, local opinion, profiles, articles about art and literature, and so on. [For nearly] fourteen years, *Matsu Report* brought news and the arts to the people of Matsu, and led to many transformations in the government and the social atmosphere. (ibid.)

With so much enthusiasm for it, *Matsu Report* was published for fourteen years. By the time financial difficulties finally forced it to close

Fig. 5.1 A brand new issue of *Matsu Report* being distributed to
passengers waiting at Fu'ao Wharf for a ship to Taiwan
(Photo by Liu Jiaguo 1993)

its doors in 2006, Liu Jiaguo had already created the vibrant and lively
forum of *Matsu Online*.

The Birth of *Matsu Online*

The genesis of *Matsu Online* was connected to Liu's critical stance toward
the government. Around 1997, Matsu's Bureau of Education created a
bulletin board system (BBS), and anyone who wanted to register to use it
had to be a professional educator. Others, like Liu, could only use the site as
a "guest." Liu was then banned from using the site after posting comments
criticizing the county government. On being silenced by the government in
this way, Liu sought out other conduits. Unfamiliar with how websites were
operated, he took advantage of the online network "Hahahou" created by
Chunghwa Telecom, and established a discussion board called "Free Talk."
By January 1999, Liu had set up a travel website, "Travels Deep in Dongyin"
(*Dongyin shendu zhilu*). Two years later, *Matsu Online* formally came online
on May 20, 2001. Liu recalls: "The first time we reached 500 visitors we held

a big celebration!" By November 9, 2004, the total number of hits had reached one million, and by August 2009, that number had soared to five million. During an interview around that time, I asked Liu:

So how many hits have you had at this point?

The webmaster responded: "We've stopped counting. We're pretty confident in ourselves now!"

Indeed, at that point *Matsu Online* was reaching a "plateau" and the number of visitors and hits was only slowly increasing. In January 2012, there were 4,000–8,000 daily visits to the site. In April 2016, there were already 10,000 visitors. Indeed, visitors from more than 100 countries around the world had already visited *Matsu Online*. Although other websites were subsequently set up, such as *Matsu Cloud Platform* (*Matsu Yuntai Liaowangwang*) and *Matsu Voices* (*Matsu zhi Sheng*), their popularity could not compete with *Matsu Online*. For instance, a local wrote the following:

When I was wondering whether or not a flight was going to take off as scheduled, my nearly seventy-year-old mother suggested that I check *Matsu Online*. I asked my brother: "Has anything important happened lately in Matsu?" He replied: "Can't you check for yourself on *Matsu Online*?" My sister complained that tickets to Matsu were too expensive, and my dad told her: "Write that up on *Matsu Online*." One of my students asked me, "I heard from your assistant that you recently wrote a wonderful article about former legislator Cao Yuanzhang, could you please email it to me so I can read it?" I said: "You can read it on *Matsu Online*!" (S. Lin 2013)

These dialogues (featuring the writer's elderly parents, her siblings, and her student) show how Liu Jiaguo's longstanding opposition activism and his experience using print media to affect popular opinion in fact laid the foundation for the widespread acceptance of *Matsu Online*. Below I will examine the website layout, management, and participation by netizens to explore how *Matsu Online* outpaced print media in the digital age and gradually grew from a website devoted to political machinations into a part of daily life in Matsu.

Digital Matsu

The layout of *Matsu Online* is based on a commercially available program for online forums. It has been successively adjusted many times over the

Fig. 5.2 The main page of *Matsu Online*

years, and it continues to change today. The interface and online content discussed here comes mainly from data collected over two years from November 2010 to October 2012, supplemented with my field research in the islands. This was also the period of peak usage for *Matsu Online*—with limited use of smartphone and application software (such as Facebook) in the islands at the time, the website's significance was epochal. The structure of the site's main page can be divided into the center, top, two sides, and four lower sections (Fig. 5.2). Each block has its own features and orientation to satisfy netizens' demand for variety. Through close analysis, we can see how the people of Matsu also live together in an online community.

The Central Section

The central section of *Matsu Online* is the liveliest, with daily updates of "Matsu News," the community discussion forum "Free Talk," and stories about life on Matsu in "Life & Culture" and "Video & Image," and so on. These sections are the most popular on the website. The webmaster and associate webmasters search the major Taiwanese newspapers for news about Matsu and publish it in the "Matsu News" section. These daily updates not only attract netizens to consistently check the site for the newest information, they also make the website seem current and relevant.

By reading *Matsu Online*, people can quickly learn about the latest trends in Matsu and become aware of the latest news about the area.

Unlike "Matsu News," the information in "Free Talk" comes from posts made by netizens themselves. The content on "Free Talk" is multifarious and enticing, and can be largely divided into two categories: politics and local life. Most of the political topics are complaints against local government agencies, such as satirically expressed criticism that government responses are well behind the times: "Matsu government efficiency is terrific! Really terrific!" (CTC 2011). Local topics might include something like: "What happened to the promises of the Taiwan Power Company?" (Shiyuan 2011). Netizens post about all sorts of issues in their daily lives, and air their indignation, while others can "respond" and express their own opinions.

Indeed, "Free Talk" itself, as the webmaster emphasized, is designed to attract the participation of netizens; its entries are organized sequentially by what has received the latest comment, with the newest placed at the top of the list. However, if a topic receives a lot of commentary, it leaps to the top as an important entry. For example, when netizens like a particular article, they can use the "clap" function to express their support. When an article has received more than fifteen "claps," the website software automatically adds a thumbs-up icon (👍) in front of that article's title, indicating that it has received a lot of attention. At the same time, whenever a 👍 appears, the article gets bumped up to the top of the "Free Talk" section. In this way, "Free Talk" continually stimulates reader participation.

Moving down the page, one comes to the "Life & Culture" section, which is oriented more toward interesting stories and self-expression. Here, netizens post about all kinds of events in their lives, such as "The paths I've taken—for my schoolmates who graduated around '75" (Mojieke 2011). The webmaster sometimes adds articles about the natural landscape of Matsu. For example, he posted a poem written by a local called "Autumn glimpsed from the pathways of Ox Horn, Nangan, Matsu" (admin 2011a), and posted an article entitled "A red-throated loon, which hasn't been seen here or in Taiwan for 40 years, has been spotted in Dongyin" (admin 2011c). This section, by mixing local information with landscape and culture, avoids being presented as diary entries or as formal "cultural" representation.

Next is the "Video & Image" section, where netizens can enjoy images and accounts of various events. Most of them are about the life-cycle rituals of Matsu people, such as the "long-awaited wedding photos of Sun Xiaohao and Wang Jingyi" (admin 2011b), which gives people who did not attend the wedding a chance to see the ceremony. Similarly, this section is also for people to mourn the dead. In the post "My father Cao Dianzhang" (Ruiyun 2011), Cao Ruiyun describes how much she misses her late father, and at the end includes an obituary. Below, Chen Qingzhi, Yang Suisheng, Xiaoxiao Cao, and Lanlang Qingtian, among others, all left comments. In addition, teachers also post photos and videos from school events. For example, in December 2010, Banli Elementary held quite a few activities, and added many photos to this section for everyone to enjoy.[2] Parents can use this online venue to see their children's participation; thus, it functions as a "virtual contact book" for parents and the school. Overall, these photos and videos allow netizens to participate in each other's life rituals and important events in the virtual world. It connects people in Matsu to those who moved to Taiwan, and them to the wider world, thus forming a new virtual community.

Continuing down the page are the sections "Activity Info" and "Matsu Board." Here we see a unique aspect of *Matsu Online*. Aside from the ordinary netizens, businesses, and local community organizations posting in these sections, all levels of government agencies, the army, and the media, also registered here to promulgate government policy and answer citizens' questions. It is truly astonishing how many government agencies have registered on *Matsu Online*. From the largest county-level "Lianjiang County Government" to subordinate units, and even the national court and the military (registered under "General Government Section Heads")— all have registered accounts (Fig. 5.3). It has become a kind of bulletin board for all levels of government organizations. Even *Matsu Daily*, the media outlet of the Lianjiang County government, has an account on *Matsu Online*, registered on August 22, 2005, and makes online corrections to mistakes that have appeared in print. Undoubtedly, *Matsu Online* has become embedded in the daily life of Matsu and is indispensable to understanding Matsu society in this period.

Lastly, the "Business Info" section collects different merchants selling all kinds of products. Many online shopping sites charge extra shipping

Fig. 5.3 All levels of government sections in Matsu have their own
accounts on *Matsu Online*

fees to mail goods to Matsu, so *Matsu Online* offers a platform for
shoppers to find one another in order to split the fees. If they buy in
bulk, they may also receive discounts. *Matsu Online* has thereby become a
helper for people living in Matsu.

The Top Section

The top section of the main page of *Matsu Online* displays links labeled
"Travel Matsu," "Soldiers' Girls," "Discussion Boards," "Message

Board," "Weather," "Search," "Top Posts," "Private Messaging," "Cached Pages," and "Simplified Chinese." Of these, the travel information page "Travel Matsu" and the personal connections page "Soldiers' Girls" are the most important, so I will begin with them.

Clicking on "Travel Matsu" directs the user to another website with fairly comprehensive information for visitors about lodging, food, and transportation. On the right side, one can find blogs labeled "Happenings" and "Recommended Posts." The "Happenings" blog consists mainly of messages posted by the webmaster, announcing current activities and events to interested online readers. At the bottom of the page, the "Recommendations" section shares links to blogs and discussion boards, and it offers readers a chance to see what visitors to Matsu have written about their experiences. In today's digital age, many people explore a destination online before they travel, and "Travel Matsu" offers a platform where travelers can find information about Matsu before they go there.

The "Soldiers' Girls" page was formed by a group of young women in Taiwan, whose boyfriends served as soldiers in Matsu, who referred to themselves as "soldiers' girls" (*a'bing mei*). With its history as a wartime frontline, many young men are sent to Matsu for military service. Given the islands' remoteness, many do not want to win the notorious "Jinmen-Matsu prize" (*jin ma jiang*) and be packed off to the islands. The main issue is the inconvenience of transportation to and from the islands: the distance separates the soldiers from their loved ones, and sometimes also nips burgeoning young romances in the bud. The forum "Soldiers' Girls" was formed as a way to deal with potential "mutiny." The main page is divided into sections: "Cool News," "Discussion Boards," "Personal Stories," and "Pictures." Postings on the site mostly involve these women's personal stories, or inquiries into how to visit Matsu to see a boyfriend. In the "Pictures" section, many of these "soldiers' girls" share photos of themselves with their soldier boyfriends. Whether the relationship is serious or not, the photos attract a lot of attention. The girls are of a similar age, have shared experiences, and they invariably encourage one another, producing a warm and supportive atmosphere.

The other links to the right offer personalized functions, allowing each netizen to look for whatever information he or she needs, and to use the site according to individual interests.

The Side Columns

The left column consists largely of travel information, in particular up-to-date information about the takeoff and landing times of flights, and whether ships have set sail or not. This information is of essential importance for Matsu islanders, who rely heavily on ocean and air travel to connect them to Taiwan and China. *Matsu Online* is thus an indispensable resource for residents and visitors. Further down the column, one finds detailed information about each individual island of Matsu. This is useful not only for residents of the islands, but also for potential travelers to Matsu, who can find a convenient source of answers to their questions. If travelers do not find everything they need, they can use the links at the top of the main page under "Travel Matsu" to search further. In this way, *Matsu Online* has become an important window onto Matsu for the outside world.

The right-hand column demonstrates the emphasis that *Matsu Online* places on culture: the webmaster adds links related to culture and history here, encouraging visitors to browse them. Under "Recommended Posts," "Xia Shuhua-Leimengdi Stories" are prominently placed (to be discussed in Chapter 6). There is also "a series on Literature and History from *Matsu Report*," in which the webmaster offers links to articles he published in *Matsu Report* from 1996 to 2004. At the very bottom are links to all manner of blogs that have to do with Matsu culture, presenting glimpses of the islands from different perspectives.

Developments and Changes in Layout

Initially grounded in a concern for Matsu's future, *Matsu Online* was at first designed to facilitate political discussions, and "Free Talk" was its only discussion board. However, given the webmaster's educational background in history and his longstanding interest in culture, he quickly established the section on "Life & Culture." "Matsu News"—updates of news about Matsu from Taiwan and China—was later added to supplement the media's neglect of this place. Under Liu Jiaguo's sound management, *Matsu Online's* readership gradually increased, and governmental offices and other social associations began to post advertisements to inform citizens of their services. *Matsu Online* became even more like a community website when "Matsu Board" was finally set up for people to find information easily. As successful management attracted businesses, the section on "Business Info" was subsequently added. When Facebook started to become popular in Taiwan, *Matsu Online* set up a link to it in December 2012 in order to facilitate the sharing of posts between the two forums. The development of the layout of *Matsu Online* shows how it has become ingrained into the texture of life in Matsu. In the twenty-first century, the people of Matsu live not only in their local communities, but also in the online world.

Nevertheless, a number of subsequent developments caused a decline in some of its functions. For instance, the "Soldiers' Girls" section gradually lost users because of the progressive scaling back of military forces before finally becoming inactive. With the ubiquitous spread of Facebook, netizens now prefer to use their personal pages there to share their opinions with friends without being maliciously attacked or bullied by anonymous criticism on a public site. The popularity of "Free Talk" also took a nosedive. Faced with the "self-media" era, Liu Jiaguo recognized that *Matsu Online* needed to change its format. In 2017, *Matsu Online* underwent a major overhaul—it transformed from a critique-based media format to a service-oriented website, and also launched a mobile version for cellphones. Website management was directed toward up-to-the-minute news about Matsu, gradually turning the site into a tool-based medium. In 2016 the site began offering a live feed from the harbor, and then from the airport in 2017, to provide more on-demand information for users.

The Online Self

Matsu Online is a Web 2.0 site, so it can be both read and added to by visitors to the site. Everyone can be an online author, adding information or opinions at will. The website's copyright statement specifies that information is published both by website personnel and by online community participants. Apart from expressing their personal opinions about Matsu, netizens also post all sorts of articles related to it. On a website of this kind, users play an important role: information is provided by everyone, and this diverse community of people is itself a source of what appears on the site.

During this process, however, website managers do play the role of arbiters. In the event that something inappropriate is posted, the site offers a "Report" button, with which readers can explain to the webmaster why an item should be reviewed. If posted material involves "a personal attack or insult, or spreads rumors, it will be deleted," the webmaster said. If the content continues to be posted, the site deals with it by blocking the originating IP address. However, the most common way for people to communicate with the webmaster is to make a phone call to request a deletion of a post that may be harmful or tendentious. For example, when I was in Matsu doing fieldwork, someone added pictures from a school reunion to the "Activity Info" section. A woman called the webmaster to ask him to remove a photo of herself with a male classmate whose arm was around her shoulder. She said she worried that the photo might cause troubles for her marriage were it not to be removed. The webmaster immediately deleted the photo. Clearly, the fact that it is responsive to the needs of the online community is one reason that *Matsu Online* has established itself firmly as a part of Matsu life. A successful virtual community is based on "its ability to manage different subjects, create its own style and norms, and continue to attract active participants" (Zhai 2000: 236).

Anyone can read the information on *Matsu Online*, but content can be posted only by those who have registered as users with the website. There are five levels of registered user: new, beginner (more than 20 postings), mid-level (more than 100 postings), senior (more than 250 postings), and expert (more than 400 postings). Above, I mentioned the "clap" and "recommend" functions on *Matsu Online*. Once a post receives more than fifteen claps, it is marked with a 🐾, which indicates that it has elicited significant discussion. This icon means that the post has garnered a certain number of readers, and that the discussion has been relatively active. The number of claps received results in points for the user, which in turn contributes to the ascent from a "beginner" to "mid-level" user, and from a "senior" to an "expert" user. For every clap, a member receives one point. When a post or picture reaches a certain number of points, the user is promoted as follows: 30 points to make beginner user; 90 points to become a mid-level user; 180 points to become a senior user; and 360 points to become an expert user (admin 2005). It is obvious that the posts of expert users are given the highest profile. One might wonder whether this way of organizing users generates a kind of "hierarchy" between different users. However, it is important to point out that this ranking is based on the efforts of individual users and the support of netizens, which is quite different from traditional place-based or kinship systems.

Evidently, these encouragement mechanisms and the different levels of user are mainly designed to encourage interactions between netizens and to increase traffic on the site, but they can also efficiently gauge the attitudes of users. The response of any given netizen alone may not be taken seriously, but in the online world, netizens' responses can quickly gather power. These opinions may diverge from the judgments of the political leaders, but grassroots efforts sometimes do influence final outcomes. Already in 2007, during my early fieldwork, a local government official put it this way:

> Government officials in Matsu aren't the same as officials in Taiwan. When we get up in the morning, the first thing we do is look at *Matsu Online*, to see whether anything has happened that we need to deal with right away.

In the real world, the status of individuals in Matsu is well defined, and their behavior is constrained by social custom and expectations, especially in the relatively restrictive environment of island life. On *Matsu Online*, one does not need to use a real name, and all that is needed to open an account is an email address. When their identity is blurred, people can not only freely exhibit themselves in ways they may not be able to in their ordinary lives (Turkle 1997 [1995]), but also participate publicly while remaining concealed. The demarcation between public and private becomes less and less clear, and traditional values and norms exert less of a hold over people. With social controls weakened, netizens have more courage to express their hidden, more extreme, or more emotional selves. This is shown in the way in which netizens choose their online names. Some examples of names include "Casting off my millstone," "Little Li's mom…and her knife," and even "Making my millions as a legislator," which satirizes, ridicules, and criticizes the corruption of government officials.

Not having to reveal their real names offers netizens a new space in which to express themselves. The language on *Matsu Online* often includes acerbic or surrealistically humorous expressions invented by netizens, through which they can more fully articulate their opinions. They openly challenge standards of speech and break the traditional authority of hegemonic discourse. *Matsu Online* allows people to engage in "self-imagining as an everyday social project" (Appadurai 1996: 4).

Matsu Online in Local Society

The most dynamic conversations on *Matsu Online* are about political issues. *Matsu Daily* was founded by the military government against the backdrop of Matsu as a military frontline, and had long been subject to military control. After the lifting of martial law, the newspaper was transferred to the county government, and its head is now appointed by the county commissioner. Given this lack of neutrality, locals often ridicule it as the "Doormat-su Daily" (*mapi bao*). When *Matsu Online* started, it offered a platform to challenge this media-governmental entity. Particularly on "Free Talk," netizens express trenchant criticism of governmental policies, and keep an eye on all manner of governmental actions. *Matsu Online* became a social space, with connotations of Habermas's (1989[1962]) "public sphere."

One minor controversy, involving a calendar that was initiated on "Free Talk," demonstrates how online critiques can influence the government. In 2010 the county government celebrated the centennial of the ROC and designed a special calendar for 2011. They chose pictures that were not militarily dogmatic, but very local in flavor, mainly scenes of Matsu's war heritage, ecology, and culture from different angles. The 365 photos were intended to provide an overview of a rich and varied Matsu. After 7,500 copies of the centennial calendar were printed and sent to homes, a *Matsu Online* user posted a piece called "Would you dare hang this calendar on your wall?"

> In the mail today I got the centennial calendar that the Lianjiang county government sent to everyone here on Matsu, and immediately…I opened it up to see the images inside, and the first thing I saw was an ad for Matsu Distillery products …and I thought, don't all advertisements for alcohol have to be printed with a warning? How come the government ignored this policy? (LOLO 2011)

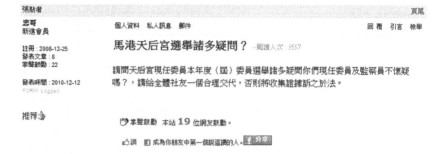

Fig. 5.4 A netizen challenges the Tianhou Temple election

The following day, netizen "Changle" responded: "Officials should be more careful about showing how little concern they have for the law, or all their good policies will end in failure." Adding fuel to the fire, a netizen added: "Why hasn't the appropriate authority in the Lianjiang government showed up to explain or apologize? … Obviously the government's crisis response needs work." Three days later, the county commissioner himself held a meeting to assuage public anger and levied a fine of NT$100,000 against the bureau that had published the calendar.

Governmental organizations are not the sole target; civic organizations can also come under fire. An election for the committee of an important Matsu temple, the Tianhou Temple, is a case in point. On December 12, netizen Zhongge (2010) wrote a post pointing out many problems with the election. It rapidly attracted attention and soon received a "recommended" icon (Fig. 5.4).

Another netizen called Mashan then claimed that the election was rife with issues, such as the facts that some voters had not showed up to cast votes, and that Tianhou Temple workers had taken the ballots to their homes. Other members of the temple did not know they were supposed to vote, yet ballots were cast for them. At the end of his post, he called for the relevant authorities to come forward and explain the situation. Another user, Hannibal B., further cast aspersions on Tianhou Temple by pointing to Taiwan's temples and the overall negative atmosphere that surrounded them. The suggestion was that many temples around Taiwan were inappropriately involved with political power and local factions. He expressed his hope that the temples around Matsu would not be similarly polluted but would instead serve as local spiritual centers. However, on December 13, the user "Little Li's mom...and her knife" raised even more issues, including the fact that the Temple committee was giving gifts of clothing, engaging in public relations activities, "exploiting the Goddess to make money," and so on. He or she felt the committee elections were deeply flawed and demanded that the elected members go before the Tianhou Goddess and cast divinatory blocks in order to show that they were truly chosen by the deities.

On December 14, 2010 Liangshanding wrote a post titled "Were the Mazu Temple Committee Elections in Mangang Suitable, Fair, and Legal?" in which he vehemently condemned the election. After this string of online criticisms, on December 16 the temple committee chair finally posted an announcement of his resignation from the Tianhou Temple committee (Zeng 2010). This kind of event may seem familiar to us now, but it had never happened before in Matsu, which had long been governed by the army. Now netizens who are strangers in their ordinary lives can join together to compel a responsible party to make amends. The above events took only five short days. The internet-enabled rapidity with which opinions are collected and disseminated on *Matsu Online* has transformed Matsu society at large.

Online Intimacy and Place Identity

Even more surprisingly, one of the first anonymous netizens ("Eric") to criticize the temple committee posted again a month later, and revealed his real name, Feng Quanzhong, apologizing to the former committee head, and admitting his own mistakes:

> Based only on my own personal guesswork...I made criticisms without seeking confirmation from the people involved, and did harm to the former chair and others, which led to them being unfairly censured by other people. (Q. Feng 2011)

I asked Feng why he had done this. He said that he had come to feel that this type of criticism was "too direct," and that his apology "benefited the

Fig. 5.5 A seller provides a phone number in an ad on *Matsu Online*

community" (at that time, Feng was the secretary of the Community Association of Matsu). He continued in an ironic tone:

> I used the name "Eric" to help my cousin post a rental ad on *Matsu Online,* and I gave my own phone number. Someone used that to figure out that I was "Eric." He went and found my boss…and my boss "suggested" that it "would be best" if I apologized.

Feng's public apology reveals that his online behavior was discovered and threatened by the traditional local power; in Matsu the distance between the physical and virtual worlds seems to have been difficult to maintain.[3] But why did it happen? For example, why did Feng give his own phone number on the "Business Info" section of the website? This is rarely seen on other mainstream websites. On most online auction sites, buyers and sellers bid online, and only after the transaction do they exchange their personal information. This offers some safeguards when two strangers do business. However, in Matsu it is common for people to give their own phone numbers in their postings on *Matsu Online*: often, at the bottom of many ads, users' personal contact information appears, making their identities at least partially public before any deal has been made (Fig. 5.5).

Locals consider this completely normal and have no problem with it. When I asked about it, they looked puzzled and responded: "Anyone who uses *Matsu Online* must have some connection to Matsu!" Put another way, they trust that the users of *Matsu Online* are part of the island community in some way; giving out their contact information is a way of showing their intimacy with each other (Herzfeld 1996). This practice, tinted as it is with public intimacy, is premised on the users' imagination of the offline Matsu community at large and is important to the formation of place identity.

Matsu, Taiwan, and China Simultaneously

The development of *Matsu Online* has expanded the island's reach by forging instantaneous links to other places and offering the island society a new basis for its social actions. Under the WZA, the government tried its hardest to bring each island individually into the war effort, rather than uniting them. "One island, one life" was the island imaginary of the military. After the WZA was dismantled, Matsu began to develop more links to the outside world. The appearance of *Matsu Online* further disrupted the isolation of each island and interconnected Matsu, Taiwan, and China. The up-to-the-minute reports on the 2008 Shanlong fire shows how *Matsu Online* was able to instantaneously link Matsu, Taiwan, and China.

At 8:40 pm on January 20, 2008, a fire erupted in Shanlong, Nangan. The associate webmaster of *Matsu Online*, who was in Taiwan at the time, quickly posted the news at 8:50 pm. The information was updated every half-hour until the fire was finally controlled twelve hours later. During that time, netizens in Taiwan continually asked for more information about the fire: "Can you tell us what's going on with the fire? Please report" (Zhonghe Ahfang 2008). The webmaster then discovered that important officials, such as the Lianjiang county commissioner and associate commissioner, were in China on official business, and he criticized them for leaving Matsu to fend for itself as they once again toadied to Chinese officials (admin 2008). A stream of criticism forced the officials to return to Matsu the following day.

Moreover, after these events, netizens offered different types of information on *Matsu Online*, hoping to build a realistic picture of the circumstances. For example, someone posted a picture of a building destroyed by the fire, showing the utter devastation (Biancheng Huashi 2008), while another user wrote to describe what he himself had witnessed as the fire raged (Aide 2008). As a small archipelago on Taiwan's northern most border with a tiny population, Matsu is rarely reported on by the Taiwanese media. When the fire started, netizens posted information on *Matsu Online* as rapidly as reports from Satellite News Gathering, thus helping the people of Matsu build a picture of what was happening at any given moment. If an imagined community is marked by its simultaneity (Anderson 1991 [1983]: 24; Taylor 2004: 157), then the community of Matsu today has stretched across Taiwan and China, and has been reconfigured in the online world.

Social Movement On-and-Offline

It is not only online that netizens come together to discuss; they also initiate and participate in concrete actions in the real world. The 2011 "823 March" that took place on Ketagalan Boulevard in front of the Presidential Office is a case in point.

Land issues in Matsu have long been a vexing problem. As stateless islands till the mid-twentieth century, land regulation of Matsu relied mostly on personal agreements. The military government at the beginning did not establish any land administration bureau to handle land registration.[4] The army could simply commandeer local land to build barracks and construct fortifications without gaining the consent of the local people.[5] Some locals were merely offered a verbal agreement: "The land will revert to you after counteractions against the mainland are over."[6] Only in 1972 did the Lianjiang County government establish a civil administrative bureau to deal with land affairs, and finally issued the first land deeds. Still, at that time, the bureau only registered land within villages, which accounted for a mere tenth of the territory in Matsu. After the military rule, the government finally established a land management bureau in 1993, which surveyed all of the land and registered it. Unfortunately, these surveys were riddled with inaccuracies, and caused much public anger. Moreover, under the law, anyone who wished to register a piece of land needed to produce proof of "occupancy" from before the first land deeds of 1972. This so-called occupancy had to involve "cultivation of the land." Early usage of land in Matsu, however, was not always connected to cultivation, but for example could be a family "firewood patch" (F. *tshia liang*), where plants were allowed to grow naturally and were then cut and gathered whenever fuel was needed. Officials frequently considered such plots of land to be "uncultivated," and therefore did not allow their return to the Matsu people. As for the land on which Matsu locals dried small shrimp in the sun, officials were even more convinced that such places "were areas without any effort at cultivation," and so were not to be returned either. These "ownerless" areas of land finally became "state-owned," and were thereby legally expropriated by the state. These land issues are a problem handed down from the period of military rule that have been frustratingly difficult to resolve.

Those people who did not obtain their land from the state frequently expressed outrage online over the immoral seizures of land by the government, eliciting many responses (Lin and Wang 2012: 127–33). Since the issue represents a continuing source of communal pain for Matsu, in recent years it has become an important issue which every candidate for county commissioner's position must address. For example, in 2006, after candidate Wu Shizi (2006) lost the election for county commissioner, he published a statement to remind the government that "Resolving the land problem depends solely upon whether government leaders 'really care.'" In 2009, the independent candidate for county commissioner, Chen Caineng, also focused on how to resolve the land seizure problem.

On April 22, 2011, netizen Wang Changming (2011a) put up a public post on *Matsu Online* with the title: "On August 23, we will take to the streets of Taiwan to demand the return of the rights and interests of the Matsu people." In the piece, he gives an impassioned description of the land problem in Matsu and recalls the 1987 protest for freedom by the Matsu people in Taiwan, calling for locals to once again rise up and demand their rights. The post not only sparked a chain of discussion on *Matsu Online*, but it also gave rise to the 823 March for land reform on Ketagalan Boulevard in Taipei (Fig. 5.6).

Wang Changming is the village head of Banli, Beigan. He had lived through the oppressive treatment of military officials during the WZA era. When martial law was lifted in Taiwan in 1987, but the government still maintained military control over Jinmen and Matsu, Wang, who lived in Taiwan at the time, participated in the first protest march there

Fig. 5.6 Matsu people at the 823 March with the building of KMT
Central Party Department in the background
(Photo by Wang Chun-Hui)

on August 23rd of that year. He moved back to Matsu in 1998 and was
elected village head in 2006. He was unstinting in his efforts to redress
the problems of land in Matsu. Because of their common interest in the
issue of land seizures, Wang Changming and Chen Caineng gradually
came into closer contact with each other. When ordinary people's land
appeals were ignored or dismissed by the government, they were increasingly attracted to political outsiders for assistance. On September 7,
2010, when Chen appeared before the county legislative assembly,
Wang also came to participate. On that day, the "Return Our Ancestral
Lands Association" was established, and Wang was put forward as the
head of the association. It agreed upon a deadline of March 1, 2011. If
the government did not produce legislation by that date, the association
would launch recall petitions against the county commissioner and the
entire legislative council.

Matsu Online thus became a platform through which Wang could
communicate with citizens and confront the land issue. He posted continuous updates about the situation and emphasized the importance of
the return of Matsu land. After 2010, he commenced even more active
efforts. He publicly posted a petition and forms online and frequently

announced new signatures and information, thereby turning *Matsu Online* into a center for news about the land issue. By October 4, the petition had garnered 687 signatures (C. Chen 2010).[7]

As a result of the online activity and the insistence of leaders, a protest march gradually took shape. A degree of planning and coordination were needed in order to concentrate forces effectively. Holding the protest on August 23 was a clever decision. The 823 bombardment of Jinmen had heightened tensions between the two sides of the Taiwan Strait, and the date had special historical significance. Aside from the date, the marchers also needed a new slogan and something eye-catching to emphasize the idea behind the protest and attract more participants. Wang (2011b) posted twenty-some slogans online and asked people to choose between them. Chen (2011a) recommended the idea of "the power of a single cloth!" This post was the most hotly discussed of the group, and it attracted a total of 6,641 readers by August 14, 2011. Chen recommended that every person with a specific land complaint should write down the lot number, location, and civil defense number on an 8 x 23 cm piece of cloth. These cloths would then be sewn together into a huge flag and carried in the procession. The purpose was to recall the 823 March and to symbolize the land they had lost. It also aimed to unite the people together to rally for justice. Although the idea of the flag was not ultimately implemented because of practical difficulties, it undoubtedly absorbed and concentrated the fury of the netizens.

This protest movement is an important case of an event being fomented and organized online, and then implemented in the real world. *Matsu Online* played an important role throughout: it allowed people from across the world to learn about what was happening, and it offered a conduit for the anger of those who were plagued by land problems. It also exposed the seizures by the state, the inflexibility of bureaucrats, and the impotence of politicians. When the online community's discontent reached a certain level, its force was redirected towards real-world action. On the day of the march, demonstrators often mentioned *Matsu Online*, and when participants met each other, they even introduced themselves by their online comments. The internet gathered people, produced ideas, and generated concrete action in the real world.

Discovering Matsu

The discussion above clearly demonstrates that Matsu today is neither the transient fishing island of yore, nor the military warzone frontline. The variety of mediating forms—words, photos, music, films—offered by *Matsu Online* also shows the different angles from which the people of Matsu write, imagine, and discover a new Matsu.

The bottom right of *Matsu Online*'s main page contains a listing of blogs by local writers and artists, exploring Matsu's language, culture, and natural landscape. They show us how "today's Matsu" has been newly understood. For example, there is a thread for schoolteachers' discussions of traditional Matsu religion and folk culture. There is also a "Blog of a Cool Principal" in which the "cool principal," Wang Jianhua, focuses on describing Matsu's natural world. Along the left-hand side of his blog are options such as "Flapping Feathers," "Summertime Feathers," and "Ecology Notes." By clicking on one of the links, one is directed towards his careful reflections on the island's ecology. "Flapping Feathers" provides his observations of birds; for example, in "Small Pool, Unbridled Life-force," he wrote:

> These past two days, the rainy season has covered the land, and the water has been pooling up
>
> From my car, I've made records of the birds in the little pools (I won't startle the birds if I photograph them from the car)
>
> There are egret, yellow-headed heron, yellow wagtail, brown-backed shrike, white-bellied water rail, pintail snipe, painted snipe, pheasant-tailed jaconda…

He continues by telling netizens how they can enjoy these Matsu birds:

> At 5:30pm I returned to school after hosting ballplayers from Xiju, and I went to observe again
>
> The painted snipe, which I thought had already moved on, reappeared when disturbed by a white-bellied water rail
>
> If you want to appreciate the birds, don't cross the pavement
>
> Just wait quietly, and you'll see some wonderful things! (J. Wang 2010a)

In "Ecology Notes," he posts about creatures other than birds. For example, the article "Let our children learn to do more—going clamming" talks about his experience taking his children to dig up clams. "If You Don't Do It Now, You'll Have to Wait Until Next Year!" (J. Wang 2011) offers a picture of Fuji cherries and tells people where they can find and enjoy them. One can also observe how he focuses on helping people to "discover Matsu" and to experience the unique aspects of the islands.

Matsu Online also has a blog, written by Cao Yifeng, that younger people enjoy called "Ascending Feng's Valley." Cao is part of a younger generation; and his way of expressing himself in his blog is to post mainly photographs, with text serving an auxiliary role. His photos all have to do with daily life, as witnessed by the post containing the comment "It's bass season and you can see it from every household" (Y. Cao 2011), followed by a long succession of photographs about hanging the dried fish. Photographs cannot transmit the same quantity and depth of information as words, but recording daily life and one's experiences in photos can often bring a sense of immediacy.

In short, both schoolteachers and cultural workers actively apply different kinds of media on *Matsu Online* in order to share what they know about the history, culture, and natural ecology of this place. In doing so, they hope to bring new perspectives of Matsu to the netizens.

Conclusion: A Place with its Own Value

This chapter has shown how *Matsu Online* has achieved a level of unprecedented influence in these islands. Its popularity can be explicated first from its geographic condition. Previous scholarship shows us that whether a community website can have a significant impact on a place or not is closely related to its situation in that given locality. Community websites often thrive in newly developed suburbs in which immigrants have just arrived and modern technologies are more readily accepted (Hampton and Wellman 2003; Postill 2011). The Matsu archipelago is located on the furthest northern border of the ROC, and its inherently dispersive mountainous island topology had traditionally made communication for people scattered across Matsu difficult, both between individual islands and between the islands and the outside world. The linkages provided by the World Wide Web appear to be all the more important in this context. Second, with its particular historical background as a military zone, Matsu's main news medium, *Matsu Daily*, has long been controlled by the government, though local dissidents had established self-founded journals such as *Matsu Light* and *Matsu Report* for several years and had gathered considerable energy. This is why the internet, when it came to the islands at the end of the twentieth century, successfully collected the readers of print media, and used its new technology, which can combine words, music, and images, in more powerful ways to attract a bigger readership. *Matsu Online* thus built extraordinary momentum and influence.

Overall, *Matsu Online* changed the way in which the islanders access information, providing an entirely new platform for the dissemination of news. In the age before smart phone-based communication software became popular, it was the most important media technology of the time, which changed how people communicated with each other and the social rhythm of the entire archipelago. In contemporary Matsu, people live in both the physical and the virtual worlds; local residents and netizens create the reality of Matsu together.

Nevertheless, for a small archipelago, the importance of *Matsu Online* perhaps has even more to do with the fact that it allows people to transcend the self and traditional social relationships. The rise of *Matsu Online* gave any individual on Matsu a new virtual life—that is, a blank page to write on. It allowed individuals to hide behind an account number and express their opinions freely. In this virtual world, netizens can be reborn as beginners and grow up into experts, gradually gathering influence and affecting the real world. Although these new selves do not entirely throw off traditional social roles, they have already superseded the geographical borders of the islands and have become interconnected to form a new Taiwan-Matsu-China existence. They stretch across the Taiwan Strait, and are able to generate social movements that demand greater rights for the Matsu people.

Taking one step further, *Matsu Online* has not only created a new kind of community, but also a different sense of place: in this instantaneously linked online world, Matsu is no longer the periphery, but the center. *Matsu Online*, therefore, offers us an excellent example to understand how new media have created a different imaginary, that is, "a new place"

(Boellstorff 2008; Miller and Horst 2012). If in *Imagined Communities*, Anderson (1991 [1983]) told us how print capitalism could change local communities into homogeneous and empty social units, then *Matsu Online* demonstrates the opposite: that the internet can turn a locality into a new homeland of the mind towards which the diasporic people feel a sense of belonging and to which they anchor their emotions. This is likely not only unique to Matsu, but is rather a phenomenon that can be seen in other online emigrant communities (Basu 2007; Mitra 1997). In other words, internet technology has become an important means of producing place. Matsu people around the world can depict and imagine "the new Matsu" online, creating intimate ties with it that did not previously exist. Via online media, Matsu today has already transformed itself from a peripheral archipelago and a Cold War "anticommunist frontline" into a place with its own value and worth.

6   Online War Memory

The previous chapter gives a comprehensive examination of *Matsu Online*, and demonstrates the influence that the internet has had on local society. This chapter focuses on individuals and the ways in which they have undergone transformations in the online world. Beginning on September 14, 2005, a husband-and-wife team began to publish a series of posts on *Matsu Online*. The images were drawn by Chen Tianshun, a Matsu islander who had emigrated to Taiwan, and the text was written by his Taiwanese wife Xia Shuhua, who had never been a resident of Matsu. Given the enthusiastic response of netizens, the duo continued their collaboration for three years, culminating in the book *The Wartime Childhood of Leimengdi* (Fig. 6.1, hereafter *Leimengdi*), published in 2009. "*Leimeng*" means "hooligan" in the Matsu dialect, and the expression "*leimengdi*" is often used as a general term for boys. The book, narrated in the first-person by Leimengdi, thus represents both Chen Tianshun's experiences as well as those of most Matsu children. It describes in great detail the ecology of the Matsu Islands and people's lives during the period of military rule. The unique products of the island, the eastern Fujian culture, and the difficulties of living while governed by the military state all come alive in Chen's vivid illustrations and Xia's nostalgic storytelling which together constitute his memories of Matsu under military rule. Much beloved, it was selected as a "Book of Matsu" (*Matsu zhi shu*) in 2010.

This chapter will first examine the writing of *Leimengdi*, analyzing how Chen Tianshun's experiences growing up in Matsu contain two kinds of self-consciousness, namely an island sociocultural self and a militarily oppressed self. Then I will discuss how online writing became for him a

Fig. 6.1 The cover of *The Wartime Childhood of Leimengdi*

process of subjectification (Moore 2011:80), allowing Chen to transcend
these two kinds of self and become a new imagining subject brimming
with morals, emotions, and hopes for the future. New media technology
played a vital role in this process (Dijck 2007), since its inherent connectivity and immediacy can evoke, respond, and animate intersubjec-
tively, linking netizens in different spatio-temporal locations. In this
process, the borderlines between the inner and the outer, the individual
and the social are transgressed; new subjects, social relations, and,
importantly, a collective wartime memory thus take shape.

Leimengdi in *Matsu Online*

On the old main page of *Matsu Online*, one could find a link to "Xia Shuhua-
Leimengdi Stories" on the right side under "Recommendations" (Fig. 6.2).
Clicking it gave access to posts beginning in 2005 and continuing up to the
present day. Each of the posts received a large number of hits when it first
appeared, and they continued to be frequently visited. When the web page
was redone in 2016, this section was merged with the "Star Writers"
(*dakuai*) section, under the name of Xia Shuhua. Nevertheless, it has
remained one of the most popular series on the website. What prompted
this couple to write the posts? How did they work together, and what did
they want to express?

Fig. 6.2 Xia Shuhua-Leimengdi stories on *Matsu Online*

The Denial of Matsu

Let me begin with the creation of *Leimengdi*. I first met Chen Tianshun at the invitation of a Matsu commissioner, Yang Suisheng. Chen was already quite famous in Matsu because of the success of *Leimengdi*. The commissioner was interested in promoting a recent archeological discovery on Liang Island, and hoped he would put out a series of books about the lives of the people on Liang Island in the style of *Leimengdi*.[1] Later, as I was writing about the online Matsu "land reclamation" movement (Lin and Wang 2012), I found him very keen on writing blog posts and drawing pictures criticizing the government's occupation of the Matsu people's land during the military period. When I contacted him to express my interest in researching *Leimengdi*, with the hope that I would be able to interview him and his wife, he invited me to his home.

In my interview with Chen, I asked why his family had come to Taiwan. He told me that the Matsu fishing economy had declined, and his father could no longer support their family by fishing in their village of Qiaozi, Beigan. His elder brother and sister were sent to Taiwan as child laborers, and were followed there by their father, who made a living selling Fuzhou noodles. When Chen graduated from middle school, he moved with his mother to Taiwan, and with that, the whole family had left Matsu behind. Chen then studied fine arts, and after graduation worked as a cartoonist for several animation companies. He lived in

Taiwan for twenty-seven years without returning once to Matsu. I asked him if he hadn't missed it, and he frowned and said:

CHEN : As far as I was concerned, it wasn't such a great place. Shuhua had been telling me for a long time that she wanted to go back with me to see it, but I just told her that it's a barren and dying place. I only went back in 2005 because of the land dispute with the government. Here in Taiwan, we've tried so hard to get our land back, and when we actually got a chance to reclaim it, would it have been right if we hadn't gone back?

AUTHOR : When you came here, did you contact other people from Matsu in Taiwan?

CHEN : I didn't get to know any others from Matsu, aside from occasional contact with some high school classmates.

This snippet of conversation shows that when he moved to Taiwan, Chen Tianshun's memories of Matsu under military rule were very negative. He did not return for nearly three decades and only rarely had contact with others from Matsu. He married a Taiwanese wife and lived with his family in Taipei, unwilling to face that part of Matsu's past.

Nevertheless, during this time, he would occasionally post a few cartoons on *Matsu Online*, criticizing the state for fooling the people, occupying their land, and coming up with all manner of excuses to justify not handing the land back to its rightful owners. The longstanding anger he holds against the government is still evident (Fig. 6.3) (T. Chen 2008).

I asked Chen why he started drawing the *Leimengdi* series. His wife Shuhua, sitting beside him, answered by saying that when she joined her husband as he went home to negotiate the land dispute with the government, she was very moved to see his hometown for the first time. She wrote about her feelings in an essay entitled "Total Lunar Eclipse" (*yue quan shi*) (Xia 2005a), and posted it in the "Life & Culture" section of *Matsu Online*. In the piece, she describes how after she visited Matsu, her husband's childhood memories turned into her own longing. The first couple of pieces were all text, with a few photos she had taken appended to the end. To her surprise, the click rate was extremely high. She then wrote three or four more essays, and each essay broke the Matsu Online record for number of views. Encouraged, she continued to write.

The enthusiastic response of netizens not only gave Xia Shuhua the impetus to continue the series, it also inspired her cartoonist husband to begin illustrating her work. On October 27, 2005, he published the first

Fig. 6.3 "Return our land" cartoon

Fig. 6.4 Qiaozi, Beigan (circa 1960)

drawing in the *Leimengdi* series called "Faraway Childhood" (*yuanfang de tongnian*) (Xia 2005d). When I asked him why he decided to do it, he told me:

> When I went back to Matsu for the lawsuit, I saw how desolate my hometown had become, and it made me very sad. I wanted to leave something behind, since this was the place where my mother and father once lived and struggled.

This husband-and-wife web creation continued for three years.

Since *Leimengdi* is built around Chen Tianshun's recollections of growing up in Matsu, I will begin with his descriptions of local customs and his warzone experiences to analyze the implicit dual self in the text.

The Island Sociocultural Self

Leimengdi offers a rich portrait of Matsu's sociocultural context during Chen Tianshu's childhood. Below, I discuss how the author imagines himself from the perspectives of land, family, social lives, and individual fantasy.

Land

Opening the book, what immediately leaps to the eye is the carefully drawn Qiaozi, where the main character Leimengdi grows up (Fig. 6.4). The village is on the Matsu island of Beigan, and many of the villagers there rely on fishing for their livelihood. Some of their catch is sold to

Fig. 6.5 Leimengdi's siblings

Tangqi, the largest hamlet in Beigan. Chen Tianshun meticulously depicts the two inlets of Qiaozi, and as Leimengdi's father says: "They were like two precious pockets given to us by God, from which an inexhaustible supply could be drawn" (Xia and Chen 2009: 96). In this drawing of Qiaozi, Chen recreates the houses of the 1960s with incredibly accuracy (today, more than half of them have disappeared or fallen into disrepair). This precision undoubtedly shows that his youth was the most important period in his life.

Family and Social Life

Below the drawing, Xia provides a wonderful description of how Leimengdi's family managed to support eight people, two pigs, twenty to thirty ducks, and a dozen chickens. The father left each morning at 5 am to fish in the ocean, while the mother was constantly on the move, farming the slopes of the mountain, collecting seafood at low tide, and hawking goods to soldiers. Every child in the household had a job to do: the older children did the heaviest work with Leimengdi as a helper,

Fig. 6.6 Processing shrimp required the participation of the whole family

while his younger sister watched the youngest girl. Every member of the household took part in its maintenance (Fig. 6.5).

During Leimengdi's childhood, the ocean around the Matsu Islands still teamed with small shrimp. Processing shrimp was a complex process that required the participation of the whole family. When the fishing boats returned, the shrimp was first sorted on the beach, then taken back to each family's fishing hut to be boiled, dried, and laid out on bamboo mats to continue to dry in the sun (Fig. 6.6), all before it could be sold.

Chen also made extremely detailed depictions of village ceremonies and events such as weddings. In the small communities on Matsu, when a wedding was to be held, the family would borrow tables and chairs from anyone they could. A few days before the wedding banquet, all the able-bodied men in the family would carry a long bamboo pole through the village, tying chairs onto it as they walked the lanes, which became a fascinating part of the backdrop of the village (Fig. 6.7). The islands carried on the customs of eastern Fujian, where the tradition was that wedding celebrations lasted three days and three nights, with a separate "men's party," "women's party," and "children's party." The "children's party" would be held three days before the wedding, and before the

Fig. 6.7 Chairs needed for a wedding banquet

Fig. 6.8 A children's party

banquet began children would beat a gong and shout as loudly as possible, "The gong's ringing, come and drink!" When they heard the sound of the gong, the other children would happily run over to join the fun (Fig. 6.8).

The annual Lantern Festival celebration (*pe mang*) was an even happier occasion for everyone, young and old (Fig. 6.9). Adults would carry sedan chairs and the children would beat gongs as they circled the village. Children liked to hear the adults tell the story of Deity Yang fighting demons on the high seas (Fig. 6.10).

Fig. 6.9 Lantern Festival night in Matsu

Fig. 6.10 Deity Yang taming demons on the sea

Personal Fantasy

As he grew up, Leimengdi often played by the seaside and enjoyed the beauty of the ocean (Fig. 6.11). The section of beach that led to his grandfather's house left a particularly indelible memory. As he walked along the sand, the village seemed to rise like a mirage of a castle, while

Fig. 6.11 Leimengdi's personal world

behind him was fine white sand and the ever-changing ocean. In his mind, the scene resembled a girl curled up on the beach, and that image has remained etched deeply in Chen Tianshun's memory.

The exquisite scenery of Matsu was imprinted on his mind through his childhood games, as was the food that the women of Matsu made: noodle soup with fresh seafood and fish balls, jellyfish strips, and golden crab. These flavors became an unforgettable part of Leimengdi's memories. However, all of these wonderful memories came to be overshadowed by the military rule.

The Militarily Oppressed Self

Leimengdi is the first book to describe the physical and psychological harm that military rule wreaked on the islanders. The narratives and illustrations portray violent scenes with great vividness. The terror, oppression, and trauma of the time are evoked through the visceral content, paralleling the sociocultural context of Matsu described earlier.

Fig. 6.12 Newly arrived soldiers

Terror

Given the haste with which Chiang Kai-shek's army came to Matsu, many soldiers were billeted in the homes of islanders. The second floor of Leimengdi's house was turned into the military "Gaodeng [Island] Bureau." When young soldiers sailed in from Taiwan, they would frequently stay in Leimengdi's house (Fig. 6.12). When the weather and tides permitted it, they would then sail across from Beigan to the facing island of Gaodeng. Despite his youth, Leimengdi observed the fear of these unseasoned soldiers:

> [They] shrank back from the piercing cold wind, feeling for the first time the vibrations from cannon-fire at the frontline. Leimengdi heard the young soldiers' low sobs, mixed with their helpless terror. At night, it seemed they were orphans forsaken by the world…Even young Leimengdi could sense their feeling of near-despair (Xia and Chen 2009: 22).

Like the soldiers, Matsu islanders also faced terror, that of losing a loved one at any moment. Once, Leimengdi's father and a few other men from the village disappeared for several days after accidentally crossing a boundary while fishing (Fig. 6.13). At that time, the whole village was anxious, and wives and children who feared losing their husbands and fathers would

Fig. 6.13 Dad has disappeared

burst into tears unexpectedly. Every so often, mainland fishermen who had drifted off course in the mist would appear in the village, and Leimengdi would watch them be blindfolded and dragged off by the soldiers.

Trauma

The trauma of military rule was most keenly felt when loved ones met with violent abuse. The women of Qiaozi often went to the seaside to gather shellfish and seaweed in order to supplement their families' incomes. To get there, they had to walk near a slope where the garrison barracks were located, and great care was necessary to avoid the notice of the soldiers (Fig. 6.14). One day, Leimengdi's mother and aunts went to gather wild vegetables. They were caught and held by soldiers from the garrison, and only when village leaders came to negotiate, were they released. That night his mother kept crying in pain, and as Leimengdi salved her back, he saw that she was bruised as though she'd been beaten. Although she never told him what she had experienced, he had a sense of what must have happened. From then on, when he knew she had gone to the seaside, he would wait until dusk and gaze anxiously at the mountain

Fig. 6.14 Hiding from soldiers while gathering wild vegetables by the seaside

ridge until he glimpsed her and could relax. When Chen mentioned this memory, he said half-jokingly, "When you read that passage, you probably thought I was being filial, right? But it wasn't filial piety, it was a child's fear of losing his mother."

Oppression

Living under military rule, the fear and psychological trauma of oppression were omnipresent for Matsu islanders. The story entitled "The Disappearing Yellow Croaker" in the book best demonstrates the sense of maltreatment that they experienced during this period (Fig. 6.15). A soldier living on the second floor of Leimengdi's house received orders to leave Matsu, and he asked Leimengdi's mother to buy some yellow croaker and dry them in the sun to make "croaker jerky," a local Matsu specialty, for him to take back to Taiwan. At that time, the yellow croaker catch was minimal, and it rarely appeared in the markets. When they heard that a fisherman had caught some croaker, Leimengdi's aunt who lived in Tangqi bought a few. She put them in a basket, covered it with a gunny-sack, and told Leimengdi to take it on the bus back to Qiaozi.

Unexpectedly, there were two military policemen and the owner of a seafood restaurant on the bus. Seeing Leimengdi carrying a fish basket,

Fig. 6.15 Where are these yellow croakers from?

they demanded that he uncover it, and they examined its contents. They saw the fish and asked, "Where are these croakers from? Why aren't they for sale in the market?" They concluded, "These are illegally hoarded goods," and confiscated the fish. Tears welled up in Leimengdi's helpless eyes. He didn't understand why the fish had been taken from him. When he got off the bus, he was crying and felt confused and helpless as he walked home. When he told his mother what had happened, she immediately hurried off to Tangqi. When she reached the seafood restaurant, she saw that the owner had already gutted and cleaned the confiscated fish.

With this simple story, Chen demonstrated how soldiers were able to join forces with influential locals to wield power, invent excuses for their behavior, and run roughshod over the islanders. Tianshun mentioned this story in my interview with him. The oppression he experienced as a child still lingers in his mind and his anger has not faded.

Indeed, children experienced a special kind of oppression and terror under military rule. Another story in the book, Nighttime Trilogy, describes a separate incident. One night, Leimengdi's mother told him to take some fish to his uncle in Tangqi. Between Qiaozi and Tangqi was a

Fig. 6.16 Going to Tangqi at night

forest, a forbidden military zone, and a military blockhouse. These areas were viewed with complacency during the day, but at night they became terrifying; it is difficult to measure just how much courage it took for a child to go through them. Chen describes the journey in detail. After Leimengdi left the village, he first had to walk through the deep, dark forest. Concealed among the trees were graves, and the ghosts of the dead flashed here and there; Leimengdi dashed madly and made it to Juguang Fortress where the sentry pointed his rifle at him and shouted: "Halt! What's the password?" "I'm…I'm just a villager," Leimengdi answered softly. It wasn't easy to keep going, but he made it to a lookout post, where a group of cadres were training. Their dogs were famous for their ferocity; one had viciously bitten Leimengdi's younger brother. Leimengdi started to run through the dark as he heard his own frantic heartbeat and ragged breath, not knowing when his ordeal would be over (Fig. 6.16).

Bodily Injury

Aside from terror and oppression, ordinary people were also physically injured in the military zone that Matsu had become. Maimed or crippled

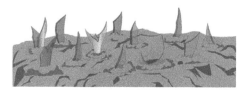

Fig. 6.17 Landmines everywhere

characters frequently appear in the *Leimengdi* series. One example is a man who often passed by Leimengdi's home. He had been hit with machine gun fire while fishing, and walked with a limp, perspiring heavily from the effort. His sadness makes a deep impression on Leimengdi, who also goes with his mother to visit a distant aunt who has lost an arm to a landmine. He sees her sitting in a dark room with sunken eyes, burdened by her struggle to support three young children with only one arm.

Children were not exempt from adult fates. Chen tells the story of a group of children playing by the seaside who discover a rusty metal case and decide to use it as a target. They take turns throwing rocks at it to see who can hit it, but just as they are getting excited, there is an enormous bang and the box explodes. Four of the children are blinded, including Leimengdi's older cousin.

Leimengdi's mother's story is perhaps the most tragic. As a young newlywed, her new husband was conscripted into a work gang and mortally wounded by a landmine (Fig. 6.17). Unfortunately, at that time marriage was a matter of agreement between two families, and the remote islands did not issue marriage licenses. These marriages were not recognized by the government, so not only was Leimengdi's mother ineligible for compensation, the young widow had to bear the burden of losing her husband all on her own.

Matsu Locked in Mist

These intractable problems seemed the inexorable fate of the islands. Leimengdi can only stand behind the barbed wire and stare out hopelessly at his own island of Beigan (Fig. 6.18). Xia writes:

Fig. 6.18 Leimengdi standing by barbed wire staring out hopelessly

The confinement of the islands coalesced into a song of the islanders' fate…In those years, the opposite bank surrounded us, as though we were surrounded by our own military. My mother couldn't go to seaside to gather shellfish, my father couldn't go out to fish, children couldn't swim in the ocean…What my mother lost couldn't be retrieved, what was taken couldn't be demanded back, and all of it just seemed to be a matter of course…Was this just part of the hopelessness of the larger situation, or was it a historical tragedy? (Xia and Chen 2009:53)

In *Leimengdi*, the word "mist" is frequently a metaphor for Matsu caught in a warzone atmosphere:

There had been mist for days. The whole village seemed glued to the ground—there was no sun and no breeze, only gray lumps congealed there…The earth and sky were moist and dark, and the tree trunks all looked darkened and wet with rain.

Waves of mist would come in on the breeze. The mist would cover everything and suddenly the sea would disappear, enshrouded. Then in an instant, the mist would lift and dissipate. It was like a demon, a blurry sea monster that came in with the wind and dreamily drifted there.

It was a special feeling to run through thick mist. It was as though you knew how long the road was but could never know how deep the mist was. (ibid.: 45)

The Matsu Islands frequently experienced fog, and all communication with the outside world would be cut off. Chen builds a metaphor of the warzone atmosphere as a mist that locks Matsu down so that the people are lost in a miasma, unable to orient themselves or tell which direction they're heading. For this reason, distant Taiwan became a "treasured island" (*baodao*) for them. Leimengdi was eager to grow up because his mother often said to him, "When you're older, you can go to the 'treasured island of Taiwan.'" When he was fifteen, his mother packed up household possessions, the family's ancestor tablet, a jar of sand from the coast near their home, and, with him and his younger siblings, left for Taiwan.

Healing through a Wife's Pen

These rich accounts of the warzone were written by a Taiwanese woman who has never lived in Matsu herself—Chen's wife Xia Shuhua. The duo's creative process generally involved Chen telling a story to Xia, who would then write it down. They would discuss it so that Tianshun's intended meaning would not be lost. Xia's writing was honed over many years of working in advertising and communications, and her posts have been admiringly received by Matsu islanders. Not only have all of her essays obtained a very high number of views, they have also been reprinted in *Matsu Daily*. Here is how Chen explains it:

> She manages to capture the experiences of the Matsu people. It would be hard for a local Matsu person to write that way. Her [relatively distant] relationship with Matsu allows her a certain objectivity.

There seems to be a special understanding between husband and wife that engenders a collaboration that is far from simple or one-dimensional. At times, Chen will simply draw a scene, and his wife will freely narrate, allowing her to express her own emotions and imagination. For example, in "New Years Performances," Chen told her a simple story about an unforgettable snowy New Years Day when he snuggled in his mother's arms to watch the snowfall (Fig. 6.19).

Xia meticulously wrote out the scene, describing Leimengdi's warm memories of his mother:

> As firecrackers and fireworks swirled through the sky, Leimengdi seemed to spot the first snow of the year. Just as on the first day of the lunar year, he and his mother joined the crowd in the big public square in Tangqi to watch the folk dances and performances. And that day, fine snow suddenly fell from the sky, the white snowflakes fluttering about like soft, delicate flakes of oatmeal, sparse and elegant. It fell gently and evenly, neither too fast nor too slow, coming to rest on his mother's black hair and the fur collar of her blue coat. It came down like

Fig. 6.19 Leimengdi's memory of his mother

eiderdown, silently floating through the air. Leimengdi lifted his young round face, and saw that his mother was spellbound, smiling happily. That day, that instant, was the calmest moment of his mother's life, just as it was the most tranquil moment during the hubbub of the midwinter scene. The beauty of the silent snow mingled with this lovely memory of his mother, and even when he was older, its beauty could still overwhelm him. (ibid.: 136)

Of course, Xia's texts do not merely transmit Chen's memories; she often adds a twist to Chen's mournful stories of military rule. For instance, in the example above, Leimengdi stares out hopelessly at the confined island of Beigan, not knowing where the islanders could turn. In the following narration, Xia turns this idea into a yearning for change:

Young Leimengdi stood on the rocks staring out at the ocean, the wind roaring past his ears and the sea roiling beneath his feet. Facing the freedom of the wind and the unfettered sea, when would the inhabitants of these isolated islands open their wings like seabirds and have a free and open spirit? (ibid.: 53)

Next, she provides some hope for the future of the islands:

The mist silently enshrouded the islands, and the sun diffused through the scattered clouds, shining on the wet treetops with dazzling sunbeams. Although that year layers of thick mist locked the islands down like the military rule, the sun that had disappeared behind the mountains would rise again the next morning, and the mist would finally be dispelled. (ibid.)

This hopeful future transfigured from past sorrows has helped Chen gradually face his painful childhood and reach a sense of self-transcendence and salvation through the creative process. As Chen told me in our interview, "Once it's written down, I can let it go." He hopes that his old painful memories will finally be exorcised by the writing.

Xia Shuhua plays an essential role throughout their creative process. For example, in the interview, Chen mentioned that the book was originally called *Leimengdi*, a transliteration of the name "Raymond" (雷蒙) which would have had fashionable foreign associations. But Xia changed one of the Chinese characters in the name to mean "alliance" (盟) implying that Chen and his homeland of Matsu were reconnected through his writing, and that he had taken an oath of allegiance to it. Undoubtedly, Xia recognized that the experiences of Leimengdi under military rule express Chen's deepest memories, even in spite of his immigration to Taiwan at a young age. This is also true for many other Matsu islanders who immigrated to Taiwan. As Leimengdi's senile old father drifts between waking and sleep, he still mumbles about getting on the boat in Keelung to go home.

Relay of Memories

The Leimengdi stories have received tremendous support and participation from Matsu islanders. Whenever a story is published online, netizens often enthusiastically share similar experiences of their own and exchange their intimate feelings publicly. For example, the day after "The Dark Night Trilogy" was published, a netizen responded:

> Many thanks to Shuhua and Leimengdi for helping us remember how we used to go to the seashore when we were young to dig for clams to make a little money. Foggy mornings were even scarier than nighttime—you couldn't see the village in front of you or the shops behind you, and it was terrifying. So it turns out I wasn't the only coward...Because of your wonderful posts, when I get off work, I often go on *Matsu Online* and look for more solitary pleasures. (Maimian Xishi 2005)

Similarly, when the webmaster of *Matsu Online* saw that Leimengdi's father had been captured by the Communist Party, he immediately shared the following post:

> Lots of similar things happened in Dongyin during the Cold War. Dongyin fishermen were captured by the mainland fishing authorities, but there were

also mainland fishermen who drifted off-course and were imprisoned by our side. At one point in the fifty-some years of the Republic of China, a mainland fisherman was captured, and was able to meet up with his son who had been forced into the military by the Kuomintang many years before. Afterward, the two were once again separate. The famous author Sang Pinzai wrote the story up in the moving tale "A Meeting of Father and Son," which is included in the official Dongyin Gazetteer. (J. Liu 2006a)

Xia's evocative writing seemed to bring the faded, blurry past back to vivid life for many Matsu emigrants. For example, Huang Jinhua, who had emigrated to Canada, also responded:

> Reading Shuhua's work is like looking at an old photograph...suddenly I see how I made it through, and I know all about how things used to be, things that at the time were muddled and confusing. Now I use those memories to finally see my own childhood clearly, to see my old life in my hometown. (J. Huang 2005)

Netizens not only use *Leimengdi* to understand their own histories, they also help Chen to draw more accurate pictures by supplementing gaps in his memory owing to his long absence from Matsu. Their support has provided crucial emotional ballast for the couple to persist with the project. For instance, Tianshun wrote on *Matsu Online*: "This afternoon I exhausted myself revising a drawing of a kitchen. But when I saw the response of my fellow villager Mu'er, I felt revived..." (Leimengdi 2006). For Xia, the internet expanded her world, and the responses of netizens were the strongest impetus behind her writing. She once wrote on *Matsu Online*:

> I'm so grateful for *Matsu Online*—it's opened another window for me onto Matsu! (Xia 2005b)

> I would like to thank the webmaster and netizens of *Matsu Online* for all their encouragement. Your enthusiasm has been a source of constant motivation for us, and this beautiful, welcoming site has become a paradisal castle in my mind. (Xia 2008)

Indeed, one could say that this work of more than three years could not have been completed without netizens: throughout the process there was a collaboration between the writing and illustrations, the creators and readers, and the locals and non-locals, all of which brought the series to life. As one netizen commented:

> Each time, I'm not [just] moved by your stories. There are also all of those readers who are moved by you, and their responses really touch me. (Leayang 2005)

The associate webmaster of *Matsu Online* even asked, "Without *Matsu Online*, would there even be a book about Leimengdi's childhood under military rule?" (vice admin 2010). Another netizen's response speaks to the spirit of online creation: "[One is] like a dazzling dancer, and [the other is] like a beautiful stage, and when they come together…they create a moving performance." (Qiahogou 2010).

Unsurprisingly, when the *Leimengdi* series was collected and published as a book in 2009, it was celebrated by netizens, who felt that Leimengdi's childhood echoed a wider experience:

> Leimengdi's childhood under military rule is also our childhood. (H. Wang 2009)

> It's a period we all went through, and these are memories we all have. (Yuan 2009)

In sum, it was not Xia Shuhua and Chen Tianshun alone, but also their online readers, who completed this memory of wartime Matsu.

New Subject, New Matsu

The narrative practices of life stories usually exert an important influence on self-formation (Peacock and Holland 1993: 374; Lambek and Antze 1996: xxi). The writing of *Leimengdi* certainly changed Chen and his wife. Online media not only provided new forms of sociality to Tianshun, who had been displaced and had long refused to confront his past and his homeland, but also brought a new understanding of this place. He told me:

> Only through the *Leimengdi* series could I build a new connection to Matsu. I needed to understand Matsu better in order to draw it. When the book was published, we had open meetings about it, and the readers who came offered different opinions, which gave me a deeper understanding of Matsu. It helped me see a different Matsu.

Clearly, composing *Leimengdi* not only offered Chen a new connection to Matsu, it also constituted a process of discovering different aspects of Matsu. "Over the past few years, I've spent a lot of time in Matsu, so it's like I've made up for the previous twenty-seven years of absence! (*Laughs*)." He explained:

These past few years as I've tried to get my land back from the government, I've returned to Matsu to do land surveys. Only now do I appreciate how my parents had to work in this terribly remote and difficult place. But now we have new technologies, and we can have a different kind of lifestyle on Matsu from the one we had before.

That is to say, Tianshun has not only discovered a new Matsu, but also fresh possibilities for the future. In a new era, equipped with new technology, he imagines that he could remake his hometown into a new world to re-inhabit, and to transcend his painful past. As he said:

> I'm not asking for all of the land back from the government, only for places that have "stories." Like the spot on the beach where my mother used to collect shellfish. The soldiers didn't just prevent her from collecting there, they chased her and beat her until she was black and blue. And then there's what used to be the Chen ancestral fields where my grandfather is buried. When the army wanted to expand their barracks, they made my father dig up my grandfather's casket. By the time my father was notified, he didn't even have enough time to buy an urn. All he could do was put my grandfather's bones in a cardboard box and place it in a nearby mountainside cavern. Matsu has a lot of big black ants, and they came and nested in the box.

As he recounted this story to me, I could sense his deep anger at the military's injustice towards his family. He wants his lands back because they hold bodily traces of injustice and trauma; he is now prepared to confront the past oppressions and abuses by winning back his lands. When I interviewed him in early 2016, Taiwan was in the middle of a presidential election, and the leader of the opposition party had a real chance of winning. He told me: "When the new president takes power, I'm going to write to her personally." Not only is he demanding the return of his land, he also seeks to redress the issue of his mother's first husband.

> My mother hadn't been married to her first husband for more than six months before he was forced to work for the army. When his arm was blown off by a bomb, he was taken to the hospital, where he died the next morning. You know how he died? The hospital facilities were so bad that he bled to death.
>
> At that time, if you married on the outer islands, you weren't issued a marriage certificate. And without a marriage certificate or children, the government wouldn't recognize the marriage and wouldn't pay out benefits. It was such a horrible, cruel death, but as far as the government was concerned, it was as though he'd never existed at all.

Chen Tianshun's narration shows that what he is fighting for is not compensation, but rather the right to attach a sense of purpose to his life, a meaning for his existence. Having been reawakened in the process of creating *Leimengdi*, the afflictions of military rule, which previously caused him so much suffering, have now filled him with new power. He has started to confront his traumatic past by fighting for the ethical value of the unmourned and unremembered many who died because of military rule (see also Kwon 2010: 412). By grappling directly with the humiliation and oppression his family suffered, he is attempting to redis-cover his morals, emotions, and affects, as well as to restore ethical value to the people who were abandoned by the state.

As for Xia, she said:

> I've been writing advertising copy my whole life, but it wasn't until I started working on *Leimengdi* that I truly found joy in writing. Every day I still write something and put it up on Facebook.

Indeed, in the online series, Xia Shuhua not only puts Chen Tianshu's memories into words, she also frequently writes about her own feelings as a mother and expresses her apprehensions and her gradual coming to terms with aging in posts such as "My Invincible Little Warrior" (2005c), "A 33-Year-Old Mother's Disneyland," (2005e), and "Anxieties of Middle Age" (2006a). She says that she "wrote these pieces for myself," and that she enjoys sharing her youthful dreams and travel stories with fellow netizens. In the piece "The Slow Life" (2006b), she also writes of her love for music, fiction, and soap operas, and describes how a grown woman in the midst of her busy life can still find space for small acts of self-indulgence and ways to enjoy her life (Fig. 6.20). Although the *Leimengdi* series has ended, Xia has not stopped writing, but continues to produce work and post it on Facebook. Tianshun says: "She's got a lot of fans on Facebook now." Of course, after these interviews, I became one of them.

Conclusion: Internet Writing as Subjectification

Leimengdi is based on Chen Tianshun's personal memories of living in Matsu under military rule. It includes his longing for the land there, his family's common struggles, the oppression and trauma inflicted by the

Fig. 6.20 The slow life

WZA, his anger, and his uncertainty about the fate of the islands. For years after moving with his family to Taiwan, Chen Tianshun chose not to face this painful part of his past. It was only with the advent of the internet that he began to reconstruct his memories and imagine new possibilities for Matsu. He and his wife were in constant dialogue throughout the process of creating their online work. His wife retold the history of the area from her position as a Taiwanese, describing her hopes for the island's future. With the enthusiastic support of the online community, Chen was gradually able to face his own wounds and past misfortune, and to begin to heal. Through his *Leimengdi* stories, he was able to reconnect to the land and the people of Matsu. He not only repositioned himself, but also developed a fresh understanding of Matsu. He imagined different possibilities for the islands and himself – it is an island of hope for him now. For Chen Tianshu, writing is a process of subjectification. By drawing, writing, and sharing his work, he was gradually healed, turning himself into a subject. Bringing morals, emotions and affects together, he was able to transcend his old selves, and rediscovered a capacity to act.

However, *Leimengdi* was more than just Chen's personal reminiscence; it gave the people of Matsu an account of a shared history. It was chosen as a "Book of Matsu" precisely because it offered a "collectivity-in-the-person" (White 2000, 2001: 504), or a "memory of memories" (Cappelletto 2005a: 23), representing the painful and violent experiences of a people under military rule in the form of a single child's story. That this web-based series of wartime memories could be woven so quickly reminds us of a key effect of internet technology in contemporary society. Over recent years, scholars have probed the interface between individual and collective memory.[2] Many works have pointed out how focusing on narrative practices (White 2000, 2004) or new mediational means (Miklavcic 2008, Lambek and Antze 1996) can transcend the dichotomy of the individual and the collective, the psychological and the socio-structural. The ability to read and write provided by Web 2.0 meant that netizens could immediately receive and respond, and this made online collective creation possible. These choral effects are particularly clear in the *Leimengdi* series: the individual is no longer a sole writer, but in a relay of emotion. Whether living in Matsu, Taiwan, or elsewhere in the world, Matsu people can come together and interact in the virtual world, composing their war memories communally. Through the course of this process, netizens participate in a "social curation" (Macek 2013), mingling the individual and the social, thereby producing a new collective identity.

These memories, furthermore, carrying as they do the load of shared traumatic experiences, are imbued with a power and agency that can erupt at any moment. *Leimengdi* thus is an important foundation for Part III in which I will discuss how this history of common struggle has become an internal motivating force for the people of Matsu to pursue better futures for the islands after the suspension of military rule. In the face of an uncertain future, the people of Matsu not only use internet technology, but also apply all kinds of ways to connect themselves with the broader world.

Part III

Fantasia of the Future

7   Women and Families in Transition

Part III explores a pivotal transitional period for Matsu. As the army left and the islands gradually opened up to the world, both individuals and the island society faced a new situation. Chapter 7 follows the women of Matsu and the struggles they faced—between marriage and self, family and work, Matsu and Taiwan— through the late military period into the present day.

In Chapter 3, I discussed the changes that women experienced from the fishing period into the era of military rule. When fishing was the main source of household income, men were valued more highly than women, who had very few opportunities to receive formal education. Although elementary schools, and later some middle schools, were built across the islands under the WZA, most women who finished primary school promptly began to conduct G. I. Joe business to earn money for their parents' families. After marriage, their earnings went towards supporting their husbands' families. Although women's ability to engage in petty commerce and to contribute economically raised their status both at home and in the larger society (as shown in Chapter 4), their lives continued to revolve closely around the family. As a Matsu saying goes: "When the mother is there, the family is complete; when the mother isn't there, the family falls apart" (F. *noeyng ne duoli, suo tshuo iengnongnong. noeyng ne namo, tshuo tsiu sang lo*). A woman was the protector of her family, supporting its very existence, and sacrificing herself for it.

During the late military period, however, some women began to take their lives in different directions. Although women of this period were not afforded the advantages that men had access to, such as receiving government-guaranteed education in Taiwan, many of them left for

Taiwan in search of jobs to support their families financially. Others went
to Taiwan to study, if their families allowed it. Their experiences in
Taiwan had a huge impact on their later lives. This chapter examines
the new struggles that women confronted. I take three women, born
between 1950 and 1980, who lived through the era of military rule and
beyond, to discuss the rise of a new female self and the changing meanings of contemporary family and marriage. Rather than representing
Matsu women in general, their unique experiences provide crucial
insight into the changes in women's conceptions of themselves and the
challenges that contemporary Matsu society faces today.

Rising from Floriculture

Xiaofen is one of the most elegant women in Matsu. Her clothing always
exhibits a unique style, and she has meticulously turned the first floor of her
home into a café. Still, my most lasting impression of her is from 2008, during
a pilgrimage to China. She planned it as a reunion for her siblings' families.
The line of several dozen people in a pilgrimage procession was quite an eye-
catching sight.

Cao Xiaofen was born in 1956 and is the eldest of seven children. In
order to help share the burden of supporting the family, soon after
graduating from elementary school she began to work at a bookstore in
Shanlong as an assistant. She says that she always loved to study, and
even used the money she earned from her first job to go back to middle
school for a semester, returning to work only when she ran out of money.
At the impressionable age of eighteen, a matchmaker arranged for her to
marry into the Chen family in Shanlong. At that time, her husband's
family had opened a restaurant catering to the military, doing both G. I.
Joe business and raising chickens at the same time. Xiaofen was expected
to help with all of it, and that kept her extremely busy.

As G. I. Joe business became more and more competitive, the family
had to find other ways of making ends meet. In 1976, Xiaofen's mother-
in-law arranged for her to leave Matsu for Taiwan, and so she arrived,
pregnant, in the Bade district of Taiwan to work in the Lianfu Clothing
Factory. At that time, means of communication and travel between
Matsu and Taiwan were quite limited, and she had few chances to see
her husband. He would occasionally come to visit her, and each time he

prepared to leave again, she felt heartbroken and hoped that the ships between the Keelung harbor and Matsu would not set sail. Tragically, not long after her child was born, her husband fell ill with uremia. Since Matsu is fairly remote, and a lack of medical knowledge delayed his care even further, her husband had to spend many years on dialysis in Taiwan. When her husband got sick, Xiaofen left her work at the clothing factory and moved to Taipei to take care of him. Burdened by medical expenses, and with very little education and no professional training, she could only engage in manual labor to make money. In the winter she sold cakes in a market, and iced drinks in the summer at the hospital gates in order to supplement the family income. She says that one day after work she was pulling her cart home and heard someone behind her calling, "Mister, Mister!" and she realized with surprise that her skin had darkened from being out in the sun year round, and her appearance was indistinguishable from that of a man (J. Liu 2004c).

When her husband passed away in 1991, she finally had a moment to catch her breath, and she decided to take classes in floriculture. She said:

> I had a chance to study flower arrangement, and it was like I was back in primary school and could remember how happy studying makes me!

After many years of toil, however, she was diagnosed with cancer in 2000. During her treatment, the illness and the suppression of her emotions over many years of caring for the family led to depression. She stopped working in the market for nearly half a year, and this period of rest gave her a chance to reconsider her own life. She realized that the tense relationship with her mother-in-law had caused her to become servile and obedient. Because she was forced to take care of her husband, mother-in-law, and child who were all frequently ill, she found herself suffering from low self-esteem and had gradually begun to cut ties with people. After her own illness, her siblings and elementary school class-mates wanted her to come back to her childhood village, Ox Horn, to recover, so she moved in with one of her younger sisters. An old class-mate, Cao Yixiong, was promoting "Village Conservation" (see Chapter 8) at that time. He often came to visit, providing emotional support by taking her on walks to show her how the village had been transformed and renewed. He encouraged her to develop her artistic talents and to move back to Matsu for good to open a flower shop and a café in a historic building in the village. With the support of friends, Xiaofen gradually returned to health, and she decided to go back to Taiwan to learn to become a barista before returning to Matsu to open a café. She did not imagine that her flower shop would eventually do brisk business, and that her classes in flower arranging would prove to be very popular. Today, she is often invited to other islands to give lessons at women's associations and community centers. She said: "Floriculture helped me find my 'self,' and it also made me realize that Matsu is the place I'll always come back to." With her new chance at life, she is not only a florist, but now also plays the role of the central figure of "eldest sister" in her family. She arranges family events at specific times over the year, which helps to solidify and maintain their familial relationships:

> The place where I'm living now is the "family home" (*niangjia*) for my brothers and sisters. Each year, I organize a family reunion and we all go traveling together. My sisters and I also have a separate get-together, and it helps us all stay close.

When her florist's business does well and she makes some extra money, she sends it to her son in Taiwan.

> Over the past little while, I've done a pretty good business, so I've sent NTD $500,000 to my son and his wife in Taiwan. They have several children, so their financial situation is tight.

Xiaofen's case is particularly dramatic. After arriving in Taiwan, she suffered greatly from her illness, yet over the course of her sickness and recovery, she also managed to gradually free herself, slowly recognizing how severely she had been constrained by the traditional mother-in-law/ daughter-in-law relationship. A succession of family misfortunes caused her to withdraw even further, until eventually she was diagnosed with cancer and was confined to her own tiny world. Then, allowed the opportunity to study floriculture and to develop her talents, she was able to achieve a new selfhood. With the emotional support and practical aid of her family and former classmates in Matsu, she was able to recover from her illness, and now she has also established herself as the center of two different families. She not only serves as a bridge between her brothers and sisters, but also helps support the younger generation of her own family in Taiwan.

Torn Between 0 and 9

Xiufang loves to chat with us, but she only appears in the late evenings. Each time, she says: "I'm running around all day, and I can finally relax when I'm chatting with you." But she can't stay for too long, or her husband will call and urge her to come home.

Li Xiufang has a very busy job as an accountant. At 8 am each morning, she starts her day rushing back and forth between two different government agencies. She gets off at 6 pm and must hurry to the hostel that her mother-in-law runs to help keep the accounts. After dinner, she frequently goes back to the office, finishing up at 10 pm. She has been working in Matsu for twenty-one years, and these long days happen at least once a week and more often three times a week. She is transferred to a new government agency every four years and has already held positions in twelve different agencies.

Although she is kept very busy, when Xiufang speaks of her work, she always has a smile and a look of pride on her face. With her circumspect manner and her natural aptitude for numbers, she is often able to help her colleagues deal with the most complicated write-offs. When she is able to handle some thorny numbers, she says she always feels "a great sense of accomplishment!" Still, her demanding work reduces the amount of time she can spend with her family, and she reveals a sense of regret about her children. I asked her why she had chosen to work as an accountant, and she told me:

Because my dad's family had no money, he didn't have the chance to continue his education. He felt like he'd really missed out, so he always placed a lot of importance on our education. When I graduated from middle school, my dad sent the whole family to Taiwan so we could study there. When I was small, my mother washed clothes, tailored uniforms for soldiers, sewed military insignias, sold seaweed, working herself to the bone to make money. When we went to Taiwan, she came along to look after us and sold dumplings to help support the family. When I got into a business college, my dad encouraged me to get a degree.

After graduation, Xiufang got a job as an accountant in a government office. She married a man from Matsu, returned there for work, and had two children. Her husband also works in a government organization, and they are typical of many families in Matsu in which both husband and wife work for the government and enjoy a very stable lifestyle. Her husband makes allowances for her busy job, which often prevents her from coming home on time. He is the one who makes dinner and looks after the children. Xiufang is responsible for all of the cleaning, and in this way, the two cooperate in the running of the household.

When Xiufang speaks of her family, she often emphasizes that she is able to give her children ample time and space in which they can focus on their studies. This relates to Xiufang's own difficult experiences going to school in Taiwan as a teenager. Moving from a remote island to a metropolis, Xiufang was packed into a small apartment with her five siblings as well as five cousins to study and sleep together. She says that at the time, she did not have her own desk or her own bed. When she got home from school, she would have to make dumplings until late at night, and because of this, she tried her best to stay at school to study until 9 pm before returning home. Now, she is proud that she can offer her children their own personal space in which to grow up and develop.

Because of her hectic schedule, however, Xiufang has no time to cook for her children, and that is a source of deep regret for her. In Matsu, one very important traditional role that mothers play is to cook for the family. The meal that a mother prepares represents a maternal role that many Matsu people recall with deep emotion. Li Jinmei, who served for twenty-five years on the county legislature in Matsu County, says that during the time she was engaged in politics, she would come home each day at 5 pm to cook for her family, and only after they had eaten together would she return to her meetings. Today, we find a vibrant scene of married working women returning to their mothers' houses to eat dinner. Xiufang's family also often goes over to her mother's house to eat dinner. From this we can also see that for women in Matsu today, although their sense of self is indissociable from their work, they still identify strongly with the traditional role of the mother as the center of the household. The emotional intimacy fostered by a mother cooking dinner for the family and bringing everyone together is still irreplaceable for Xiufang in terms of how she views herself as a woman. For this reason, although she considers her career and her professional capabilities to be significant accomplishments, she still feels guilty about not being able to come home to cook for her children every night. As a contemporary woman, she is torn between striving for professional success and fulfilling the traditional role of the mother.

In Search of a Common Vision

Every time Lihong goes out, she's always meticulously made up. Her hair smells sweet, because she always washes her hair before she meets with us. Her eyebrows are carefully plucked, and her face is rosy and full. She puts on eye-catching necklaces, bracelets, and other jewelry, and even when she's in a tracksuit, she always shows her own sense of style.

Chen Lihong was born in 1971, one of five siblings, the youngest of whom is a boy. She recounted:

I'm the second oldest in my family, and my older sister and I both got good grades. But we were not well-off, so she and I decided not to go on with our schooling after graduating from high school, and instead to help make some money for the family so our younger siblings would have an easier time of it.

I asked her what she and her sister did to help. She told me they did all kinds of jobs, but that she was especially good at "carrying water" (*taishui*), and that she would collect nearly all of the water that the family used. Back when Matsu did not have running water, the water used by a household would be collected from wells and carried back to the home. She said:

I could carry a lot of water! In elementary school, I used to go with my sister. Then in middle school I would do it alone, and I'd hurry back from school each day to help out. The first gift my dad ever gave me was a stainless-steel water pail specially ordered from Taiwan. It's still there in my parents' house.

We can readily sense Lihong's satisfaction about the help she was able to give her family. In fact, like Xiufang, Lihong could have gone to Taiwan to study after high school, but she decided to stay so that the money could go towards the education of her younger brother. Years later, on his wedding invitation, he specially thanked her and her older sister, "and when I saw that, all of it [the sacrifice] was worth it," she told me with tears in her eyes.

Although both Lihong and Xiaofen sacrificed themselves to help their families and in particular their younger siblings, the former is different from the latter in that she grew up during the late period of the WZA. Lihong's family engaged in many different kinds of G. I. Joe businesses, including selling breakfast foods and snacks, and running a karaoke bar. As a girl, she would keep watch over the karaoke bar as she studied, and so had contact with the military from a young age. She told me that early on the soldiers would fight over her affections, and not a few of them tried to ingratiate themselves with her. "Were you ever interested?" I asked her. "I can't say I never was," she responded. However, one of her aunts had married a soldier, and after she went with him when he was posted to Taiwan, their marriage suffered. Because of this, Lihong felt that it was safer to marry a man from Matsu, with whom she would have a greater chance of having a secure life and a harmonious marriage. Doing chores and helping out the family as a girl, she had already started to develop her own ideas about the future.

After she grew up, she chose a local Matsu man with a steady income from among her many admirers. Her husband worked for the government, and she was also employed by the government at the time on contract, so together the two of them had a healthy income. After they married, they soon bought a house and a car, and a year later had a baby. Just as their life together seemed to only be getting better, her husband took up gambling, and then began to have an affair. Lihong said:

> When I found out that he'd been having an affair and I argued with him about it, he told me that I shouldn't poke my nose into what he did outside the home. He wanted me to be a traditional wife and stay at home. As long as I took care of the family, everything was fine.

Lihong could not accept her husband's attitudes, and once he had been unfaithful she allowed herself to become emotionally detached from their marriage. She worked even harder to make money, so that she could prove to the court that she had the economic means to take care of her son, hoping to be granted custody of him. She became licensed as a nurse's aid in order to get a better job with a steady salary. Still, since her husband could provide a better home environment, she agreed to allow her son to continue to live with him. She arranged a set time to come visit him and to take him out to do something fun. After her divorce, Lihong did not move back to her parents' house, as was traditionally expected of women, but instead rented a room, wanting her own private space in which to live. Each time we met, she would always be carefully dressed and made up. She felt that after her divorce, she needed to keep up her appearance, to make herself feel better than she had before. She told me: "Many women realize only after they get divorced that they have a lot of capabilities. The struggle for survival brings out latent potential."

Like many traditional women in Matsu, Lihong has sacrificed for her family since she was a young child. In the process, however, she has also slowly been developing herself: she planned out the kind of marriage and family that she wanted, and made it happen. Despite all of her careful planning, her marriage unfortunately ended in divorce, but she described the outcome this way:

> My husband and I struggled for a long time to build the kind of family that we had. But as soon as we had everything we'd been working for so hard, we lost sight of a common goal for the future.

Lihong's reflections reveal that she did understand that her husband's leaving might also have been caused by his pursuit of "another kind of self [beyond the family]": it was precisely because husband and wife lost their common vision that their marriage failed and their home life collapsed. In any case, Lihong is no longer willing to submit to a man's demands, as women had done in the past. Her decisions demonstrate how different contemporary Matsu matrimony is from the traditional model. In the past, as long as men brought money home to support the family, they were free to gamble in their spare time; even affairs were tolerated by their wives. But Lihong and most of the other women in Matsu no longer want to be traditional wives. In other words, contemporary Matsu households can no longer successfully operate on the assumption of the self-sacrifice of one of the partners (most often women). Quite the opposite, creating a common vision that both partners, along with the entire family, can work toward together has become the foundation of contemporary marriages and families in Matsu.

Conclusion: Struggling Women, Families, and the Future of the Islands

The cases of Cao Xiaofen, Li Xiufang, and Chen Lihong clearly show that the women of Matsu did not have much chance to receive higher education during the military period. Most women ended their education after elementary or middle school, and immediately began engaging in small-scale commercial business to help support their families or to provide their siblings with more opportunities than they had been given themselves. After marriage, they were expected to take care of their husbands and their families, and also to raise children. Although, as Chapter 3 indicated, they did obtain a kind of free space and greater power than they had in the earlier fishing period, most of them still struggled to be loyal sisters and filial daughters-in-law (e.g. Lee 2004). Cao Xiaofen and Chen Lihong are clear examples: they both enjoyed school but were unable to continue their education because of family responsibilities. Despite her pregnancy, Cao Xiaofen had to obey her mother-in-law's dictates and move to Taiwan to work in a clothing factory, living separate from her husband. The family took precedence over the individual.

Nevertheless, the examples of Xiaofen, Xiufang, and Lihong also show how a new female self-consciousness, one that was distinct from the sociocultural self, developed between the military period and the contemporary era. For instance, Xiaofen is the eldest of the three and the most constrained by traditional culture, encountering shattering separation, deaths and illness throughout her life; however, these sufferings have prompted her to reflect on the ultimate causes. With the support and care of her siblings and friends in Matsu, she was able to regain a new life. She became a new subject, not only managing her successful flower business but also putting great effort into sustaining emotional ties between her siblings. She works hard to reach a balance between her business self and the sociocultural one (playing the kinship roles of mother and eldest sister).

Xiufang also had the opportunity to go to Taiwan when she was young. She was fortunate in that she received higher education there and so was able to get a stable job in the Matsu government when she returned. Becoming a successful accountant is clearly a point of great pride for her. She is also proud of the fact that she is able to provide a comfortable home environment for her children. Nonetheless, she is upset that she cannot play the role of a "proper" mother—who cooks and cares for the family, holding it all together. Whether in life or in work, she is torn

between two extremes—between 0 and 9, the traditional and the
contemporary.

Lihong is very different, and from her situation we can see an intermediate stage between the traditional and the contemporary. Compared
to Mahmood's (2005) depiction of the ethical formation of Egyptian
women, Lihong's example presents an even better case of the burgeoning
of a modern subjectivity. Lihong made the kinds of sacrifices that women
in the traditional culture have long made, and she even took the decision
not to study further so as to afford her younger siblings the opportunity to
finish school. In the process, however, she began to develop her subjective consciousness, and formed plans for her own future and imagined
what her life could be like. As a result, when her marriage began to
flounder, she rejected a role of further self-sacrifice and refused to
continue as the traditional wife. As she encountered myriad difficulties
in the divorce process, her subjective consciousness became all the more
engaged, and she pursued economic independence so as to gain custody
of her son. Of course, after the dismantling of military rule Matsu society
developed in myriad ways, and the new job options in Matsu have given
Lihong more varied opportunities to develop her subjectivity. She can
now make investments in her future, and actively seek out new employment so as to better herself and her situation.

Lihong's case underlines the fact that marriage and family in Matsu
today differ significantly from the past. That is to say, in contemporary
Matsu, women's self-awareness has come to the fore, and the continuation of a marriage and family depends on whether husband and wife are
willing to negotiate and create a common vision for the family. In fact,
this is true not only of marriages. In the Chapter 8, we will see that Matsu
as a whole—from villages to islands—faces a similar challenge: how to
find a common sense of the future in the midst of these multitudinous
new selves.

8   Community Materialized through
       Temple Building

When martial law was lifted in 1992, Matsu entered a new era brimming with freedom, openness, and hope. A civilian county government and county council were elected in 1994, and in that same year the first airport for civilians, albeit a small one, was completed, allowing people to visit Matsu freely. In 1997, a new ferry, "Tai-Ma lun" (Taiwan-Matsu ferry), replacing the old military personnel transport ships, began to sail between Matsu and Taiwan. The Taiwan government also initiated a route, called "three small links" (*xiao santong*), connecting Taiwan to Fuzhou, China via Matsu in 2001.[1] With the widespread availability of the internet since 2000, Matsu became open to the entire world.

However, these forward-looking prospects did not obviate the many challenges Matsu still faced. The fishing economy was in the doldrums and many people had emigrated from the islands. Having lost its strategic significance in cross-Strait relations, Matsu was no longer as important to the state as it had once been. In 1997, the Taiwan central government launched a program of troop reduction, severely threatening Matsu's economy which was heavily reliant on military supply. The situation worsened after Taiwan and China finally reached an agreement on mutual communication and implemented the "three great links" (*da santong*) in 2008. As a result of that policy, flights, voyages, and postal services could bypass Matsu (and another demilitarized island, Jinmen), and flow directly between China and Taiwan. In short, at the very moment that it gained its freedom, Matsu lost its significant role in cross-Strait relations. A strong sense of instability and uncertainty pervaded the islanders' minds.

180

In the face of these enormous changes, many Matsu people, in particular those who went to work in Taiwan or made their way there via the
guaranteed admission program during the WZA era and later returned to
take important government positions, began to offer their own visions of
the future by proposing new blueprints for Matsu. Over the next three
chapters, I explore the processes by which these new visions, or new
social imaginaries, have struggled to take form up to the present day.
Unlike the top-down analyses of Anderson (1991 [1983]), Appadurai
(1996), and Taylor (2004), I will begin with the imagining subjects
themselves in order to investigate how a social imaginary takes shape.
As Chapters 5 and 6 describe, the dismantlement of the WZA and the
advent of online technologies had already liberated individuals to a great
extent. Once individual imaginations have been engaged and developed,
the question a society faces is how a collective consensus can be reached.
Thus, in order to understand this era, it is crucial to examine the
individual imagination and the process by which it is potentially transformed into a larger social imaginary. This is important for understanding not only Matsu but contemporary society in general.

Chapters 8 to 10 look at the capabilities of specific individuals and the
tribulations they faced during the WZA era, synthesizing their life experiences to show how their daring and risk-taking spirits were fomented,
and how individual imaginations are formed. I then discuss the different
mediating forms through which they transform their individual imaginations into social imaginaries. In other words, I take these mediating
forms as "technologies of imagination," exploring how they create new
social relationships and cultural capacities. These forms could be material, such as community projects and the building of a temple, as will be
discussed in this chapter, or conceptual, such as new pilgrimages and a
proposed fantastical gaming industry on Matsu, as explored in
Chapters 9 and 10. My analysis in these chapters draws on Foucault's
thoughts on "ethical subject" (1985, 1998) and Moore's writings on
"ethical imagination" (2011); however, the imagining subjects I define
are not just individuals, but also cohorts of different generations,
genders, and social categories. Having undergone similar life experiences
and hardships, they are more likely to share common imaginaries. In

these chapters, I give special consideration to these cohorts and scrutinize the new ways they evolve to reach out to others.

Community Building Projects in Taiwan and Matsu

In many ways, Matsu is similar to Taiwan, in that it has been under authoritarian rule and is wedged uneasily between two big political forces (China and Taiwan for Matsu, and China and the USA in the case of Taiwan). Both faced many similar and pressing problems such as how to reintegrate and redefine themselves after the authoritarian regime had gone. On reflection, it is not surprising that the Taiwan government started a "Community Building Project" (*shequ yingzao jihua*) in 1994, attempting to create a new sense of community which was previously suppressed by the authoritarian government. The project was launched by the Council for Cultural Affairs (CCA). The main project coordinator at the time was the vice-chairman of the CCA, a cultural anthropologist, Chen Chi-Nan. He observed that after Taiwan had freed itself from the rule of the Nationalist Party in 1987 and experienced economic growth, what was needed most was the rebuilding of communities (1996a: 109). He claimed that Taiwanese society had always embraced a strong sense of "familism" (1992: 7), "traditional localism," and "feudal ethnic consciousness" (1996b: 26). Religion in Taiwan only functioned in the "private" and "mental" domains and was never directly involved in the public sphere (1990: 78). Therefore, it was necessary to build a new sense of community through community development projects. Only by doing so could Taiwan truly turn toward modernization and democratization (Chen 1996b: 26; Chen and Chen 1998: 31).

What actual steps needed to be taken to achieve this? Since the purpose was to create a new community consciousness, values, and identity, Chen suggested that culture was the most fitting starting point. By organizing various cultural activities and encouraging community members to participate, a sense of group identity could be fostered (1996a: 111). The activities promoted by the CCA were mostly related to art and culture, such as rebuilding the village landscape, organizing arts activities and architectural restoration, and researching local history and literature (Chen and Chen 1998: 22).[2]

It is important to note that Chen Chi-Nan's intriguing ideas and proposed project were not a rehabilitation of old values or culture, but rather a new national imaginary in the global terrain (Lu 2002: 10) and a response to the global economy and the multiculturalism of Taiwan (Hsia 1999). They thus received strong support from the president at the time, Lee Teng-hui (1995), who was steeped in Taiwanese consciousness and incorporated Chen's ideas into many of his speeches. These ideas were disseminated through different government institutions, and various subsidies and promotional activities quickly reached towns and villages everywhere in Taiwan. The surge of interest in community landscape building drew an avid response from professionals in architectural and civil planning fields (Hsia 1995, 1999). The idea of community development soon became closely linked to village preservation and had a huge impact on Taiwan.[3]

These ideas were brought from Taiwan to Matsu mainly by Cao Yixiong when he became a county councilor. Cao had not tested well enough to enter college after high school, so in the early 1970s he went to Taiwan at the age of eighteen to look for work. Drifting from a shoe factory to an electronics factory to a ceramics factory, he moved around quite a bit and was unable to settle into any vocation. He said that if given half a chance, he would just sit and read. It was a way for him to escape his feelings of discouragement and inferiority from not having gone to college. At that time, he encountered famous books of world literature rarely seen in Matsu, which were first translated and introduced to Taiwan under martial law by the Zhiwen Press's "New Wave Series."[4] He was impressed by Hermann Hesse's works: Beneath the Wheel (*Unterm Rad*), which severely criticizes education that focuses only on students' academic performance, seemed particularly appropriate to his own situation. Reading *Siddhartha* and *Der Steppenwolf* also offered him a way out of his own struggles with his soul. As he put it, "These novels set my own imagination free...I felt that my life had meaning and a sense of dignity." He also read a number of popular Western novels such as *Gone with the Wind*, *One Hundred Years of Solitude*, and *The Thorn Birds*. Remembering those years in Taiwan, he recalled, "That was my life: it was in the process of brewing." He found great stimulation in these humanistic books, and the ideas he encountered penetrated deep into his consciousness.

In 1982, Cao Yixiong's former classmate, Cao Eryuan, who worked for an agricultural improvement station, helped get him a job in the engineer corps of the Matsu Bureau of Public Works, and he returned to his hometown to work as a bulldozer operator at the agricultural improvement station. Later, Cao Eryuan joined the Matsu democracy movement, and Cao Yixiong also became active in politics, participating in the "823 Jinmen-Matsu March" and the "507 Anti-Martial Law" protest led by Liu Jiaguo (see Chapter 5), and was eventually elected a county councilor. When Liu Jiaguo then decided to leave politics and to throw his efforts into the media realm, it came as a major blow to Cao Yixiong, who began to ponder what his own path should be. At that time, the WZA had just been dismantled, and he had to consider how Matsu could position itself anew. He chanced upon a series of books titled *Changzhu Taiwan* (Taiwan for the Long Term) at a bookstore in Taipei, written by Hsia Chu-Joe and some civil planning scholars (Wu 1995). Cao was deeply inspired by the ideas about the value of local traditions presented in the series, and subsequently invited Professor Hsia to Matsu to give talks on "Local Development and Community Building." Hsia introduced the ideas of the civil planning scholars and those of Chen Chi-Nan to people in Matsu. Later Cao had the opportunity to visit Tsuma go yuku in Nagano, Japan, a place known for its successful preservation of historical streets and buildings. After the visit, he began to promote the community building project *Changzhu Matsu* (Matsu for the Long Term) in his hometown, Ox Horn.

This chapter uses examples of community projects carried out in Ox Horn to explore the question of whether religious practices are necessarily an obstacle to modern thoughts as claimed or implied by policy makers and intellectuals. In the Matsu Islands, we will see that earlier efforts at community building—which included literary and historical research, art and cultural events, and activities connected to village preservation—yielded little success in terms of creating a sense of community identity and consciousness. It was not until the community building activists became aware of the importance of religion and began to negotiate with villagers and to participate in building the temple that a sense of community began to emerge. In this case, religion and in particular the process of its materialization through temple building serve as a basis for the formation of a new community. They also function as important mediums for absorbing modern concepts of cultural preservation, environmental aesthetics, and imagining tourism development.

Village of Nostalgia

As I stated in the introduction, Ox Horn had once been the biggest fishing village on the island of Nangan. Because of the decline of the fishing economy, the population was greatly diminished during the military period. From 1970 to 1990, the population decreased from 1,300 to 750. Abandoned and dilapidated buildings were everywhere. With village preservation as its core objective, "*Changzhu Matsu*" began by reorganizing and restoring the eastern Fujian-style stone houses in Ox Horn. Responding to the county councilor's appeal, a group of Matsu educated elites participated in the project; they came not only from Ox Horn, but included teachers, cultural workers, and artists from different villages, and even many young architects who were doing their military service in Matsu. The group held a variety of cultural and artistic events, and invited renowned music, art, and dance groups to perform. In 1999, a "Civil Planning Workshop" (*chengxiang gongzuofang*) supported by the government was set up in Ox Horn to design a number of village preservation plans. The figure below shows the prospective appearance of Ox Horn, according to the plans of these community development activists (Fig. 8.1).

The figure demonstrates the initial concepts of the community development activists. They invented new names for places to convey a strong nostalgic flavor or to make reference to local history, such as the Fishing Hut Café, Ox Horn Teahouse, and Local Classroom. Although the actual implementation process did not always follow the original plan set out in this figure, it did not stray too far from it. After the successful execution of the project, Ox Horn attracted much attention in the media, thanks in part to its county councilor's networking ability. The results of the development project also garnered numerous national awards.

Nevertheless, the media reports and national awards were recognitions gained outside the village. For the development of a community, it is essential that community activities elicit the participation and interest of

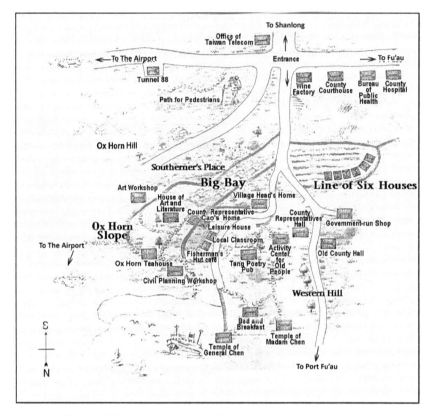

Fig. 8.1 The spatial design of Ox Horn community development
(Source: Report on the Community Development of Ox Horn,
Lianjiang County. Map based on Wang Huadi)

local residents. And the fact was that local villagers, especially the elderly residents (who were still highly influential in village affairs), played a
very passive role in most of the activities.[5] Perhaps it was their fishermen
background that made them feel awkward about being involved in these
elite-led cultural projects; in any case, they were uninterested in taking
part. In fact, they frankly told me that restoring the old houses was simply
"doing dead things" (F. *tso silai*), something that was for them utterly
pointless and meaningless. Therefore, the old houses were still demolished one after another and rebuilt in cement. The vast horizon of Ox
Horn became gradually blocked by tall, modern buildings.

The community development leaders, however, still moved ahead. Under the influence of new community concepts such as "sustainable management" and "cultural industrialization," they raised funds to open businesses in these restored historical buildings. It may come as no surprise that these stores ended up vying fiercely with one another for business owing to stiff market competition (see also Y. Huang 2006a). The community development implementation process created new groups working in parallel to the village's administrative system, as also happened in other places in Taiwan (Chuang 2005), resulting in friction and conflicts. In the end, many activists withdrew from the project and some formed other associations.

At about the same time that this community development was being carried out, a temple committee was formed by the local people on their own initiative, with the goal of building a temple in Ox Horn. The role of religion in Matsu therefore deserves consideration.

Religion in Matsu

The deities in Matsu have strong eastern Fujian characteristics that are distinct from the southern Fujian belief system in Taiwan (H. Wang 2000). Ox Horn presents a useful example of this difference. The deities of Ox Horn worship can be divided into four main categories. The first consists of deities of a higher status who were brought over from mainland China, such as Wuling Gong or Wuxian Gong, whose origins can be traced to the Five Emperors from Fuzhou (Szonyi 1997: 114). Second are the deities who possess special powers, such as the Lady of Linshui (Linshui Furen or Chen Jinggu) who is venerated for her powers relating to childbirth (Baptandier 2008). In Ox Horn, villagers set up a shrine for her after some local women experienced difficult labor. The third category comprises gods who came to be deified because their corpses or statues floated to the shores of the village and over time the villagers associated certain miraculous events with them. After having found the bodies or statues, the villagers buried them or built simple huts to shelter them from the rain, and as some wishes were answered, particularly for big harvests of fish, they started to be revered and worshipped. General Chen (Chen Jiangjun) and Madam Chen (Chen Furen) are two such examples. The last category is that of the territorial deities who ensure the wellbeing of the place, such as the Lord of the White Horse (Baima Zunwang) and the Earth God.

As mentioned, many of these deities mentioned above have strong eastern Fujian origins, such as Wuling Gong, the Lady of Linshui, and the Lord of the White Horse, but religion in Ox Horn is also inseparable from a particular physical characteristic of the islands: the sea, which continually brings things to their shores. The religion of Ox Horn, or of the Matsu Islands in general, is therefore a unique combination of eastern Fujian culture and elements of the oceanfront geography inherent to Matsu.

The deities are indispensable to the villagers' lives, as they journey through life's stages, experiencing birth, old age, illness and death. The Lady of Linshui is a goddess in charge of pregnancy and taking care of children. Before weddings, an elaborate day-long rite (F. *tso tshuh' iu*) is carried out to show gratitude to her. When villagers encounter illness or misfortune, they seek help from Wuling Gong, Wuxian Gong, or General Chen. They are also the deities who protect fishermen at sea. The Lord of the White Horse, as a territorial deity, is in charge of death: when anyone dies, his or her family has to "report the death" (F. *po uong*) to him.

The Ox Horn villagers initially did not build a temple for their deities, but only set up incense burners for them and kept the burners at villagers' houses, either because of their poverty or because they saw the Matsu Islands as just a temporary home. Nevertheless, if the house in which a deity's incense burner was kept became dilapidated, the villagers would raise funds to renovate or rebuild it. Sometimes, if a family built a bigger house, the incense burner would be moved there so that the deity could have a better dwelling place. If a deity had exerted special powers to help a family, such as curing their son of a serious illness, the family would set up an incense burner in their house dedicated to the deity to invite the god to stay with them permanently. Becoming "the adopted son of a deity" (F. *ngie kiang*) is a very common custom in the Matsu Islands. Thus, villagers' lives are intimately connected with their deities.

The relationship between the villagers and their deities was not limited to the domestic domain, however. Since Matsu residents came over in waves from mainland China, their homeland kinship ties influenced their

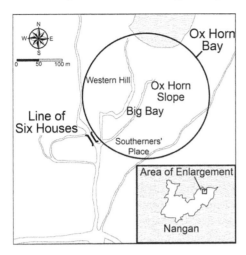

Fig. 8.2 The neighborhoods in Ox Horn

choices of residential location. The first arrivals congregated in areas populated by families from the same region in China. Over time, each area was then further subdivided according to the particular deities worshipped by its families; the settlement gradually became fragmented into several distinct neighborhoods.

Bordered by a bridge, Ox Horn is divided into "Ox Horn Bay" towards the north and the "Line of Six Houses" towards the southwest of the village (Fig. 8.2). Ox Horn Bay is mainly populated by families with the surname Cao, though families with other surnames are also interspersed throughout this region. In the past, the majority of the population made their living by fishing or running small businesses. The Line of Six Houses, on the other hand, was inhabited by a mixture of different surnames who moved into the neighborhood from various places in China. As revealed by the name of the neighborhood, the earliest settlers lived in a row of six houses and had the surnames of Li, You, Cao, and Zheng—thus, it was a rather heterogeneous composition. Surrounding the Line of Six Houses is a large stretch of farmland. The early residents made their living by farming and fishing.

The residents of Ox Horn Bay and Line of Six Houses further differentiated themselves by venerating different deities. The former worshiped Wuling Gong, who was brought from China by a Cao family,

General Chen, the Lady of Linshui, and the local deities the Lord of the White Horse and the Earth God. As I described earlier, most of these deities originally resided in the residents' houses but were then moved to a temple in Ox Horn Bay after it was built in the 1970s. The latter, the Line of Six Houses, also have their own deities, such as Wuxian Gong, brought by a Yu family, and Gaowu Ye (a minor deity). Although the inhabitants of the Line of Six Houses also worship Wuling Gong and the Lord of the White Horse, these deities had their own incense burners and statues and did not mix with their counterparts in Ox Horn Bay. Every year during the Lantern Festival (F. *pe mang*), the two neighborhoods held their own nighttime rituals, but on different dates. Each neighborhood had its own percussion band, and if the bands crossed paths, they usually ended up in heated competition with each other.

Looking more closely, Ox Horn Bay is further divided into different territorial units: for example, the Ox Horn Slope along the mountains, Southerners' Place (populated by residents from southern Fujian), Big Bay (which includes the old market street), and Western Hill. Each unit has its own deities and festivals. Every year during the period between Chinese New Year and the Lantern Festival, the whole village has to celebrate the same festival as many as eleven times! This high frequency of nighttime rituals became increasingly difficult for most people in Ox Horn, especially as many Matsu people had shifted from being dependent on a fishing economy that dictated the pace of life according to the tides and the fish, to having a lifestyle determined by the new county government that was set up after the military government was abolished in 1992. The new nine-to-five work routine created a need to integrate the various rituals. The construction of a new temple presented a possible solution to this problem.

Giving Way to Religion

Aided by the county government, the Ox Horn Community Development Association (*shequ fazhan xiehui*) was established in 2001, and a second phase of community development started. Since most of the non-local members of the first phase had left the group, the association was largely composed of village inhabitants. They elected Yang

Suisheng as the chair; the county councilor, Cao Yixiong, was also invited to join the association.

Yang is a typical Matsu educated elite who was sent to Taiwan by the government guaranteed admission program to study medicine thanks to his outstanding scores in high school, and who then came home to serve his community in 1981. As a doctor, he received modern medical training and was inculcated with a love of scientific ideas and values; he was the first person in Ox Horn to build a Western-style house, which he designed himself. At the same time, his attachment to his hometown is also strongly emotional. Motivated by the idea of preserving and reforming his hometown, he decided to lead the association. Most of the members in the association were similar to him: most were middle-aged and had gone to Taiwan or Europe to attend university and returned home to work, but there were also some members who were of the older generation.

Given the intellectual background of its members, the association began, unsurprisingly, by holding art and cultural events resembling those in the first phase. But Yang also designed many other activities for older people. For example, he invited migrant elders back home to tell stories of the past, and, understanding that they were mostly fishermen, he executed an environmentally conscious project to prevent sea waste from flowing into the bay. Although a greater variety of events were organized than in the past, the association soon faced the same problems that had plagued community development activists of the previous phase: their plan did not capture the interest of locals, and participation was low.

Though frustrated, Yang noticed that older members (along with other villagers in general) showed a strong enthusiasm for temple building. Whenever the subject was brought up, they discussed the issue fervently. He gradually realized that the association's ideas of community could be accepted and implemented effectively only if they changed their view of religion as mere superstition, participated in temple building, and engaged with the residents about their conceptions of Ox Horn. He thus reinterpreted local religion as "folklore" (*minsu*) without much religious implication, a view that was embraced by the intellectual activists on the committee, who began to actively engage with building the temple.

After that, the Community Development Association worked closely with the temple committee and often held joint meetings. In order to formalize their coming together, a member of the association proposed integrating the temple committee into the association. Although this proposal did not receive support from the older population, it helped the middle-aged members to realize that they had to change their ways of thinking in order to succeed in implementing their ideas of community development. Yang said:

> Originally, we thought of the community as a big circle, and the temple committee as a smaller circle within. But then we had to change our way of thinking... we had to hide ourselves [the association] within the temple committee and use their power to strengthen our own.

This statement shows that the community activists came to understand, after reflection, the importance of religion in local society and were willing to change themselves, and even to "merge the association with the temple committee." A shared imaginary of the village was finally taking shape.

Materializing Community through Temple Building

Aside from the religious reasons and the need to adapt to modern life rhythms, the enthusiasm for building a temple also stems from the highly competitive electoral politics in Matsu after its democratization. Elections depend on votes, and thus on the support of local communities. While other villages had successfully integrated different neighborhoods through joint construction of their temples, Ox Horn faced more thorny issues and remained fragmented, much as it was during the fishing period. Since Ox Horn had once been a major village, its residents were very anxious to build their own temple. It is for this reason that the villagers initially only elected proprietors of construction businesses as the directors of the temple committee. However, as Ox Horn is located between two mountains, with many houses built along the slopes, it was very difficult to find an ideal site for the new temple; even though discussions had been going on for almost a decade, the five previous directors had not been able to decide upon a suitable location. Faced with increasingly heated elections, and with the temple still unbuilt, the committee decided to organize a ritual to bring the whole community together. As I indicated above, different neighborhoods originally celebrated the most important ritual—the Lantern Festival—on different days. After negotiation, one day was chosen for all the households to get together on the same night. This unification was initially successful, and Ox Horn-born Cao Erzhong, who spearheaded the effort, was voted into the national legislature. Unfortunately, the success was largely superficial: he later lost his bid for re-election (as we know, one quick ritual may temporarily assuage an urgent predicament, but it cannot resolve the underlying issue), and only then did the plan for construction of a temple return to the fore. However, the process of temple construction was tortuous.

The Temple Location and Sanctuary

After failing to win re-election in 2001, Legislator Cao Erzhong decided to restart his political career by devoting himself to temple building. The first problem he encountered was finding an ideal location for the new temple, which was a challenging task because of the mountainous geography of Ox Horn. In the beginning, a suggestion was made to build the temple around Ox Horn Bay by filling up part of the sea with earth from the mountain, but the committee members held differing opinions on the matter and an agreement could not be reached. Later, someone suggested the old location of the County Hospital, but there were problems with the property rights and the idea had to be abandoned. Then the thought of using the site of a liquor warehouse was brought up, but the villagers were opposed to this location because it had been used earlier as an execution site and a military brothel by the army. The committee members looked everywhere for a suitable location, and after numerous thwarted efforts, the focus returned to Ox Horn Bay. After much discussion and re-examination of the location, the villagers managed to come to a final decision. This brought joy and excitement to the village, and Legislator Cao was widely recognized for his dedication to the matter. In the next election in 2004, he was able to garner 69.8 percent of the votes from Ox Horn, an increase from 61.5 percent in 2001. His opponent's votes decreased to 26.9 percent from 38.5 percent. In Ox

Fig. 8.3 The seven sanctuaries in the Ox Horn temple
(Photo by Liu Meiyu)

Horn alone, Legislator Cao won by nearly 300 votes over his opponent and was easily elected.

Besides politics, the new temple also effected a successful integration of the various deities from the two neighborhoods of Ox Horn: Ox Horn Bay and the Line of Six Houses. As described above, the two neighborhoods are peopled by residents of diverse surnames and deities, and the building of a new temple presented an opportunity for people from the two long-separated neighborhoods to sit down and discuss how to combine their respective deities and festivals. When they came to an agreement on the hierarchy of the deities and arranged them accordingly into the seven sanctuaries in the temple (Fig. 8.3), the people of these separate neighborhoods were also unified. As one important temple committee member put it: "Once the temple is built, it will unify not only the deities, but the people as well." Since that time, the villagers have worshipped each other's deities, and also combined the eleven separate times of worship into two.[6] Other rituals, hitherto practiced separately by the people of Ox Horn Bay and the Line of Six Houses, have since been united.

The Architectural Form

The process of deciding on the architectural form of the temple demonstrates the politics of negotiation between elder villagers and middle-aged community activists. The older members of the temple building committee favored a palace-style temple of the kind recently completed in a neighboring village. They were impressed by its ornate and opulent

Fig. 8.4 Temple in palace-style (left) and Eastern Fujian-style with "Fire-barrier Gable" (right)
(Photo by the author)

appearance, displaying the substantial wealth of the village (left panel of Fig 8.4). The middle-aged community activists, however, preferred the common island-wide architecture style, called "fire-barrier gables" (*fenghuo shanqiang*) (right panel of Fig. 8.4).[7] They believed it would better represent the eastern Fujian heritage of Matsu culture, and they made great efforts to convince the village elders of this idea.

Perhaps the idea of valuing distinct local characteristics as advocated in the first phase of the community project had influenced the older committee members over time, since it did not take long for them to accept the suggestion. A draft of the new temple was quickly drawn up by the same architect who had participated in the first phase of community development. Using the structure of the old temple as a basis, he expanded and modified it, and also added new elements. This version was later made more attractive by painting it colorfully, and it was unveiled at the banquet of the Lantern Festival celebration (Fig. 8.5). The temple committee successfully raised almost NT$10 million on that single night!

The next debate was over the material for the temple walls. The members of the older generation leaned towards green stone, which is not only resilient to climatic changes, but also serves as a symbol of wealth and high social status. In the early days, when the people of Matsu acquired wealth through their businesses, they would go to China to buy high-quality green stone to build new houses, and for this

Fig. 8.5 Coloring the draft of the temple
(Photo by Yang Suisheng)

reason village elders naturally preferred green stone for the walls of the temple. But the middle-aged activists had been nurtured by concepts of community building, which approaches architecture from environmental and aesthetic perspectives. They favored granite because its color complemented the traditional stone houses of Matsu and the surrounding greenery of the mountains. They thought the temple would look too subdued and dull if the walls were green. The two sides held strongly to their own opinions and consensus proved elusive for quite some time. In one of the rounds of negotiation, a middle-aged member used sharp rhetoric to express his stance, which seriously offended the elders and caused them to withdraw from the meeting. Although middle-aged members softened their attitude, efforts to establish communication between the two sides proved to be in vain. In the end the issue had to be resolved through an open but very tense vote by show of hands, in which granite won over green stone by a single vote.

Next in question was the color of the fire-barrier gable. This time it was the middle-aged activists themselves who held diverse opinions. Legislator Cao preferred red, which is traditionally seen as a festive and auspicious color, but a local artist who had studied in Spain proposed black. By doing so, he hoped to present a unique color aesthetic through the stark contrast between the red outer walls and the black gable. But painting the gable black was seen as too subversive and was not easily accepted by other members. In the end, the members suggested the idea of dropping divination blocks to ask the deity for guidance on the final decision. Knowing that he would not be able to win the older members over, the artist did not show up for the divination, and the proposal for red was accepted.

As for the interior of the temple, the middle-aged members had always thought the village lacked a large public space that could be used for gatherings by the entire village, so their design of the temple offered a substantial common area suitable for community activities and events. For instance, their plans included a courtyard for small-scale public events. This concept had not previously been applied to any temple in Matsu. The temple as a whole was designed as a two-story building in which the ground floor could be used to hold an important banquet for all the villagers after the Lantern Festival. Further, the middle-aged members of the temple board extended the staircase leading towards the entrance of the temple for future use when a stage will be constructed to present Fuzhou operas and other entertainment programs.

The Trails, the Little Bay, and the Old Temple

The trails next to the temple used to be part of the lives of the people in Ox Horn, but the area was closed off and became a "forbidden zone" during the military period. After the abolition of the military administration, the community development association applied for government funds to clean up and restore the trails. The new trails do not necessarily preserve the old look, but instead expand towards the coast, and are designed to connect with the new temple, as part of the greater aim of linking the important tourist sites in the village (Fig. 8.6).

The little bay behind the temple holds a similar meaning for the villagers. Although filling it with earth would have created a larger area for the temple, the little bay is also a cherished and protected memory from the childhoods of most of the villagers who recount vividly how they played in the water or were chased by the coast guard soldiers. Therefore,

Fig. 8.6 The old and new Ox Horn temples
(Photo by the author)

rather than filling in the bay to create more land, the temple committee decided to preserve the villagers' precious memories.

The most spectacular aspect of the temple area, however, is the manner in which the new and old temples exist side by side, aligned back to front. All the other villages demolished the old temples when building new ones. The construction team of Ox Horn temple initially also sought to do the same, and the elder villagers did not show any strong opposition to the idea. But the middle-aged activists, keen on preservation, were reluctant to do this, as they considered the old temple to be a part of their history. When the committee visited the root temple in China, they asked for the deities' opinion by dropping divination blocks. The deities indicated that the old temple should not be demolished, as it was there that the Ox Horn deities had attained their power (*dedao*). As mentioned above, the new temple was designed according to the old temple's form, with the addition of new elements. Now the new and old temples are juxtaposed: the old one is small but exquisite and the new one modern but culturally sensitive. They look similar in form but differ in detail, complementing each other and bringing out a unique aspect of Ox Horn.

Surrounding Landscape

The design of the new building also takes into consideration the issue of how to connect the temple with tourism. In the overall design, the middle-aged activists further contributed the idea of building a mezzanine between the first and second floors: a space in the shape of a half-moon. Its location is such that it allows people to see the contours of the northern island, as well as the beautiful scenery formed by the tiers of houses overlapping the slopes of Ox Horn. The design of the mezzanine was initially part of an effort to link the temple to future potential tourism, but interestingly, this space gradually developed a kind of religious meaning. In other villages, people say that it is the deities of Ox Horn who requested that the mezzanine be built so that the temple, situated between the mountain and the sea, would have a more solid foundation and in order that the "gods can sit firmly" (*shenming caineng zuode wen*). This example shows how the concepts of the community activists were translated into ideas with religious significance and subsequently became widely accepted by the Matsu people.

In order to attract more tourists to the village, the committee members also designed two separate entrance and exit paths. The committee applied for funds from the Matsu National Scenic Administration to build a pavilion (which was later changed to an observatory) above the temple that would allow tourists to admire the surrounding scenery from different angles. The eaves of the temple are engraved with a "legendary bird" that was recently found to be close to extinction—the Chinese crested tern (or Thalasseus bernsteini)—which all the more highlights the local characteristics of the Ox Horn temple.

Temple, Community, and the Matsu Islands

The description of the temple reveals how the temple building not only provides a space for the two distinct neighborhoods to develop a unified sense of community, but also a way for the local people to adapt to the pace, especially the nine-to-five workday routine, of modern society. It successfully merged the deities from different neighborhoods into one temple and reduced the frequency of rituals to help the people cope with the rhythm of work in modern society. Residents from different generations negotiated with each other throughout the construction process: the activists infused the new temple with their own ideas about architectural aesthetics, local characteristics, and concepts of organic living. Older members offered their knowledge of traditional beliefs, and local residents provided the necessary funding and labor. Together, they built the temple for both the past and the future.

This process has been enthusiastically recorded online. A person with the username "Intern" (Shixisheng) posted one picture each day on *Matsu Online*, throughout the two-year long period of construction. "Intern" finally made a GIF animation, dedicating it to:

> all the villagers who contributed to the construction of the Ox Horn temple and the villagers who moved out. Many thanks to the craftsmen from mainland China and to all the community members who worked together to support this project! (Shixisheng 2007)

Many new community activities were organized after the temple was completed. After its inauguration on January 1, 2008, the temple launched an unprecedented pilgrimage to China in July, in which more than 300 villagers participated (to be discussed in Chapter 9). When a disastrous fire destroyed the business area in Shanlong as I noted in Chapter 5, Ox Horn temple held a fire-repelling ritual for all inhabitants to ward off the fire spirit.

The momentum of the new Ox Horn was also demonstrated in the elections for county commissioner in 2009 and legislator of Matsu in 2004. The director and other leaders of the temple construction project obtained an unprecedented number of votes; two of them were duly elected to these two positions. Nowadays, the temple in Ox Horn plays an even more significant role in integrating traditional culture and modern society in Matsu. Since 2011, for example, the temple committee has cooperated with the Matsu Cultural Affairs Bureau to hold an annual coming-of-age activity. It combines the traditional Matsu ritual of *xienai*, in which teenagers turning sixteen offer thanks to the goddess Lady Linshui, with the values of a modern high school education.[8] This ritual gives high school students in Matsu a chance to celebrate their coming of age while sustaining their traditional customs.

The close connection between temple leaders and elections, however, has cast a shadow of factionalism. Criticisms have appeared on *Matsu Online*, with claims like "the temple has turned into an election tool" (Shenhua 2010). Others have said that the temple committee elections are "preliminary battles for legislator seats" and that "the village leader's faction is being oppressed by the temple board." Voices of dissatisfaction can also be heard in private settings. Indeed, the discord between the village leader and the community building committee that had developed in the previous phase of the community project persisted throughout the process of temple construction. It would obviously be a gross exaggeration to claim that the building of the new temple could resolve all of the longstanding disagreements about elections and disputes between political factions and disgruntled individuals. Nonetheless, we should not overlook the importance of the temple building in breaking many of the deadlocks that had formed during the community building project, nor should we underestimate the hard work contributed by the majority of the inhabitants. This ethnography, in a very important way, provides us with a lens through which to examine how a divided community can reach a consensus in contemporary Chinese society. Yang Suisheng, former chair of the community development association, later the head of the temple building committee, and subsequently elected Matsu county commissioner, gave a vivid description of this process:

> The temple of Ox Horn not only integrates traditional architecture, folk beliefs, and local culture together, but also provides a space for new community activities. There have been many ups and downs in the process of building the temple. Each step along the way has been full of compromises negotiated in locally democratized ways. The result is a collective achievement of grassroots democracy (S. Yang 2007).

Grassroots Democracy

It is worth examining the idea of "grassroots democracy" a bit more, particularly the process through which the middle-aged activists communicated and negotiated with their elders. As I mentioned earlier, during the negotiations the so-called "democratic" method of voting was often only used as a last resort, when a consensus could not be reached after substantial communication. Usually, the middle-aged members would talk to the older members in private, and if the two sides strongly insisted upon their own views, they would decide the matter through the use of divination blocks. What is worth noting is that this method does not always yield yes or no answers; the responses often fall into a grey area, necessitating further communication among the members.

The divination blocks consist of two crescent-shaped blocks with a flat side and a convex side. Dropping the two blocks can yield three different combinations: a positive answer (meaning the deity gives its consent: one block facing up, the other facing down, $+-/-+$), a negative answer (meaning the deity disagrees: the flat side of both blocks facing downwards, $--$) and an ambiguous answer (also called a "smile," meaning the god smiles but refuses to answer: both blocks facing upwards, $++$). In other words, by the laws of probability, there is a 25 percent chance that the deity will refuse to answer and will throw the question back to the worshippers. This allows them to modify their question before coming back to the deity for another answer, thus providing a chance for the various participants involved to renegotiate and reach a form of consensus. The worshippers can also set up certain rules depending on how significant the questions might be. If the issue is one of little controversy, then it needs only one positive answer from the god. If it is one of great importance or could lead to severe consequences, three (or more) positive answers in a row may be required to validate the result. By this method, the local people are given more opportunities to communicate. The whole process exemplifies another kind of democratic civility (Weller 1999), in which final decisions on contentious or significant matters are reached not just through group discussion, but with the support of the deities.

Conclusion: Community, Mediation, Materialization

This chapter probes how old conflicted and fragmented social units in a settlement came to be integrated after the reign of the military ended and formed a new community. Since the beginning of the twentieth century, popular religion has been seen as an obstacle to the modernization of

China, and thus suppressed by the state and discounted by intellectuals (Duara 1991; Goossaert and Palmer 2011; Nedostup 2009; C. K. Yang 1961; M. Yang 2008). This chapter shows that their counterparts in contemporary Taiwan, and even the educated people in Matsu, have similarly taken a dismissive view.

The role of religion was initially overlooked in cultural policymaking and in its local execution. The first phase of community building in Ox Horn focused on literary, historical, and cultural activities, like most community building efforts in Taiwan at the time. But such activities failed to elicit the participation of local villagers. It was not until the second phase of community building, when Yang Suisheng, the chair of the community development association, and the middle-aged activists understood the expectations of the local residents and the important role played by religion in their daily lives, that community building experienced a breakthrough. After their ideas changed, committee members began to participate actively in building the temple, which in their own words was an attempt to "build from the inside" (*neizao*) rather than "build from the outside" (*waizao*)—meaning to take part in the construction of a building that occupies a significant place in the heart of the villagers, instead of organizing activities that are only valued by the middle-aged generation. On one hand, they incorporated local religion into their ideas of historical preservation, environmental aesthetics, and tourism development. On the other hand, their concepts of community were translated into ideas with religious significance and subsequently became widely accepted by the Matsu people.

This chapter demonstrates how religion and, in particular, its process of materialization through temple building, could provide an important medium for creating a new community. Taking inspiration from important works in material culture (Miller 1987, 2005), we have seen how cultural concepts (of community) and social relations (of Ox Horn) have been reconstructed by the residents and by their deep engagement with the temple. The process of temple building, and how it materialized the negotiation of conflicting ideas, provides us an excellent example of contemporary community formation.

In fact, not only the temple, but also myths of deities and the practice of dropping divination blocks can create a civil space of negotiation and help to translate the ideals of community building into concepts that are accessible to the villagers. Different individuals or generations with varying values were able to find a way to resolve their disagreements, and the two neighborhoods that had long excluded each other were able to integrate into a unified community. The temple building process demonstrates how religion and religious artifacts can serve as the basis for the emergence of a new community and as a means of absorbing modern ideas. Without them, new and external concepts often only have a short-term influence and very rarely can take root in a local society.

I am not arguing, however, that the case of Ox Horn's temple construction is merely a revitalization of traditional culture or values. Instead, I aim to show how religion, community, and space in the contemporary Matsu Islands have more complicated articulations than in the past. Religion, by subsuming diverse elements, has become more collage- or montage-like in contemporary society. It has transcended its previous form and challenges us to reconsider what it is today.

9 Novel Religious Practices as Imaginative Works

After the inauguration of the new temple on New Year's Day of 2008, Ox Horn organized a five-day pilgrimage to China, from July 5–9. Because the completion of the new temple had realized a long-awaited dream of many Ox Horn villagers, this pilgrimage won strong support from local residents and village emigrants living in Taiwan. Including pilgrims from other islands, more than 300 people took part. In the procession, one could see the temple committee members holding statues of Wuling Gong and the Lady of Linshui, young people carrying sedan chairs and puppets, women playing drums and gongs, and pilgrims following behind.

That this pilgrimage was aimed at more than religious renewal is evident in its name: "Matsu-Ningde First Sail: Changle Pilgrimage." That is, they did not directly head for their ancestral temple in Changle, but instead undertook an elaborately planned journey across the Taiwan Strait, starting from Taiwan and arriving in northeast Fujian Province (Map 1). The five-day itinerary was as follows:

> 5 July—Keelung, Taiwan → Matsu → Ningde, China
> 6 July—Ningde → Pingnan (Baishuiyang Scenic Spot)
> 7 July—Pingnan → Gutian (Linshui Temple) → Fuzhou
> 8 July—Fuzhou → Changle (Longshan Temple) → Fuzhou
> 9 July—Fuzhou → Mawei → Matsu

The organizers rented the Hofu Ferry and departed from Keelung Port in Taiwan, where they invited officials from the Ministry of Transportation and the mayor of Keelung to a press conference. After stopping in Matsu to pick up local residents, the ferry proceeded north-west into Sandu'ao Port and reached Ningde City in Fujian, China, where the city government welcomed the pilgrims in celebratory style. The next day, the pilgrims boarded a bus and headed northwest to the Baishuiyang Scenic Spot, before traveling south to the Linshui Temple in Gutian County, the root temple of the Lady of Linshui. They then continued further southward to Fuzhou, where they finally arrived at the ancestral Wuling Temple in Changle.

We may wonder why a pilgrimage held by people from Matsu would choose Keelung as its starting point? Why was Ningde, a city not well known in Taiwan, chosen as the point of entry into China? Why did a pilgrimage to the ancestral temple have to take a detour towards the northeast and arrive at Changle only after visiting the Linshui Temple in Gutian?

This chapter begins with this pilgrimage and moves on to discuss the successive, newly invented religious practices initiated by the islanders in the first decade of the twenty-first century, including Matsu-China "direct-sail" pilgrimages, the myth that "Goddess Mazu was buried in the Matsu Islands," ascension rituals for the goddess, and the construction of her tomb and a giant statue. The "Goddess Unbound" (Weller 2019), material practices, and invented rituals will also be discussed. I will first explicate how these inventions were responses to the drastic changes in Taiwan and China during the period 2000–10 when, in particular, a series of "direct links" were promulgated to connect Taiwan and China. These transformations seriously challenged the status of the Matsu Islands, and left islanders with a great sense of confusion and uncertainty about their future. The Matsu people thus devised various rituals, myths, and material practices to break through the cross-strait political impasses. Second, I will show that these innovative religious practices are not only responses to the changing cross-strait political and economic situations, but also the processes of the islanders' subjectivity and subjectification. It is through these mechanisms that they attempt to recentralize themselves, create new social relations, and imagine novel possibilities for the islands.

Imagining the "Cross-Strait Economic Zone" in the Neoliberal Era

After the Warzone Administration was disbanded in 1992, the progressive retreat of the army had severe effects on the local economy. When

Map 9.1 The route of the Ox Horn pilgrimage

the "three great links" across the Taiwan Strait, by which flights, sea voyages, and the post could bypass Matsu and move directly between China and Taiwan, were mooted early in the twenty-first century and finally implemented in 2008, the islanders experienced a strong sense of doubt about their future and even felt abandoned by the Taiwan government. These worries were revealed in the Matsu people's own accounts: they used to consider themselves "the Fortress of the Taiwan Strait" (*taihai baolei*) and "a springboard for anticommunism" (*fangong tiaoban*). Nowadays, in sharp contrast, terms like "orphans" (*gu'er*) or "second-rate citizens" (*erdeng gongmin*) frequently appear in *Matsu Online*, expressing people's disaffection owing to what they see as neglect by the Taiwan government.

With this in mind, we can better understand why the Matsu-initiated pilgrimage to China was designed to start in Taiwan and pass through Matsu before reaching China: it is an expression of hope that Matsu can become a mediator between Taiwan and China. Looking again at

Map 9.1, we can see that the pilgrimage route's clear message is that Matsu is no longer an insignificant archipelago between Taiwan and China, but rather a "central point" connecting them. In other words, Matsu's people imagine the pilgrimage as transforming their marginal position and bringing them back as the focus of cross-strait relations.

It was the then head of the County Tourism Bureau and secretary of the temple committee, Cao Eryuan, who offered up this vision. Cao studied agriculture at Tunghai University in Taichung, Taiwan through the guaranteed admission program. Not long after arriving in Taichung, he appealed to other schoolmates from Matsu to follow him there to study, establishing the Taichung Matsu Association and inviting Matsu students from other nearby schools to participate. This was an early indication of Cao's gregarious nature and his desire for collaboration, as well as his ability to make connections far and wide. He has spoken about how he absorbed democratic ideas while studying in Taiwan, and how he participated in opposition activities to fight for independence upon returning to Matsu (E. Cao 1988). What had the deepest impact on him, however, was his experience working with military officials in an agricultural improvement station after returning home.

At that time, the station was still controlled by the military, and was in the midst of carrying out a "war against isolation and hardship" (fan gukun zuozhan jihua). This program was intended to improve Matsu's agricultural production, as well as to encourage young people to engage in "pioneering work" and "collaborate [with the army] to build factories" (hezuo zaochang). Most of the funding for the project was provided by the army. The remainder came in the form of loans from the military to young people. In order not to lose money, however, the military officials demanded interest rates even higher than those charged by banks. When Cao Eryuan told the officials that young people would only be able to participate in the program when interest rates were lowered, the military's response was to fret about potential financial losses. In a fiery argument, one officer even accused him of being a "turncoat." Cao said:

> I was really disappointed. These military officials weren't actually interested in developing Matsu, and they didn't really want young people to participate. The whole thing went on for a year without a resolution. ...[That is why] when I became the head of the Tourism Bureau, I launched direct flights between Matsu and Meizhou [in Fujian], and later one to Ningde to bring in more

people and to make more connections for Matsu. Only with more people will Matsu be able to prosper.

Bring in more people, make more connections to Matsu: after his experience with the army, Cao became increasingly fixated on this idea, which was consistent with his natural inclination to bring people together. Like many people of his generation, he returned to Matsu to serve in government after studying in Taiwan. He began at the agricultural improvement station, moved on to the County Government, and gradually climbed his way up. When he eventually became the head of the Tourism Bureau, he had a chance to put his convictions into action. At the time, there were radical changes in the relationship between the two sides of the Taiwan Strait; with the implementation of the "three great links," Matsu's marginalization came to a head. As Matsu was seeking a new position for itself, his goal developed into creating new links for the islands. In an interview in 2008, he proudly said:

> When I was invited to give a talk at the Ningde Tourism Exhibition last year, I told the audience, "Matsu is not just an archipelago along the coast of Fujian; neither should it be considered as Taiwan's outlying islands. Matsu belongs to the world! If I draw a circle around Matsu, it will encompass all of you. In the future Matsu will be able to connect you with Taiwan. ...Matsu is a connecting point in the Taiwan Strait, but it is also the central point.... We will soon launch a direct-sailing route to Ningde." "After the demise of the War Zone Administration," he went on to say, "Matsu should play the role of fulcrum in the balance of cross-strait relations."

In other words, the direct-sailing pilgrimage is an important medium, through which he hoped to be able to bring to fruition his long-term thoughts about how the islands could prosper in the period after military rule. More importantly, pilgrimage was also a means of connecting his own life experiences with the collective desire of recentralization, since the direct-sailing pilgrimage was seen as a way to draw out the hope and imagination that could reverse Matsu's marginalization and restore it as a focal point between China and Taiwan.

From this perspective, we can understand why the pilgrimage started from Keelung in Taiwan, and also why a pre-trip, formal press conference was held, to which government officials were invited. But why was the relatively obscure city of Ningde chosen as the point of entry into northeast Fujian? Cao Eryuan explained this as a way to explore a new route in addition to the existing "three small links" between Jinmen-Xiamen and Matsu-Fuzhou. Moreover, he pointed out that Ningde could connect to north Fujian, further north to Zhejiang Province, and even to Shanghai after the 2009 opening of the Wen-Fu (Wenzhou-Fuzhou) high speed railway. Convinced that Ningde had the potential to become an economic relay point between Taiwan and Shanghai, they thought that such a route could make Keelung-Matsu-Ningde-Shanghai into a new path for economic development, as well as a unique cultural route combining tourism (to east and north Fujian) and religion (through the Lady of Linshui) (see also Keelung-Matsu-Ningde 2008).

This idea encapsulates the Matsu people's imagination of the "Western Taiwan Strait Economic Zone" (*haixia xi'an jingjiqu*, hereafter "Cross-Strait Economic Zone"), a policy the Fujian government proposed at the beginning of this century. The Cross-Strait Economic Zone was first proposed in 2004 as both a political strategy and a regional economic development plan (Haixi: cong 2009). Its ambit stretches beyond the province itself, most importantly east to Taiwan, and its main goal is to increase development in Fujian, which, due to the longstanding tensions in cross-strait relations, had been neglected relative to the Yangtse and Pearl River deltas. This is to be accomplished by augmenting cross-strait exchanges, developing modern transportation and networks, and advancing manufacturing and tourism along the strait (Haixi tengfei 2009).

For example, one of its projects was the construction of the Wen-Fu Railroad, launched in 2005 and completed in 2009. This route reduced the travel time between Fuzhou and Shanghai from fourteen hours to a mere five, and Ningde is the first northbound stop from Fuzhou. In the past, the development of Ningde had been rather limited and relatively slow compared to other southern cities in Fujian owing to its proximity to Sandu'ao, an important military port. With its high-speed rail connection, the Matsu people now see Ningde as a place with high potential for development. Envisioning the future, Cao Eryuan said:

> Very soon, this place [Ningde] can attract people from the Yangtse river delta, Hangzhou, Wenzhou. [If the sea route is implemented] they can come to Matsu first before continuing on to Taiwan. That way, Matsu will become a center and a kind of hub. ...We will have our own niche.

This statement shows that this pilgrimage was rooted in an important imaginary and hope for the future: in short, Cao longed for Matsu to join in the development of the Cross-Strait Economic Zone, and by making the islands a link between the mainland and Taiwan, Matsu would become a key pivot in the region.

From a wider perspective, the Cross-Strait Economic Zone is an example of neoliberal design "with Chinese characteristics" (Harvey 2005; Ong 2006: 98–9). Since the 1980s, many such economic zones have appeared along China's southeastern coast, and the Chinese government is in the process of constructing highways and high-speed railways to link these zones with interior cities. However, one consequence of this policy is that the cities in these zones are perpetually in ferocious competition, each scrambling to outdo its neighbors in business and cultural affairs. An important question for their ruling elites has become how to produce cities or regions with distinctive qualities and attractions (Harvey 1990: 295; 2005: 132).

It is from this neoliberal perspective that we can better comprehend the enthusiasm of the people in Ningde to make this pilgrimage a success— for them, connecting to Taiwan through Matsu was a major breakthrough. The Ningde government's website trumpeted how the pilgrimage could accelerate development of tourism and religious culture in northern Fujian (Mou 2008). The city's top administrator came to the welcoming ceremony held in Ningde's city hall on July 5 and declared,

> The Hofu Ferry brought a full boat of Taiwanese fellow countrymen to Ningde, realizing the first direct-sailing between Ningde and Taiwan, and marking a historic breakthrough in the exchange and cooperation of Ningde and Taiwan" (Ningde xiying 2008).

Afterward, he talked about developing Ningde into an important city in the Cross-Strait Economic Zone:

> Ningde is a large port bursting with business opportunities … the entire city … [will in the future] put forward its best efforts to push [Ningde into becoming] a central city in the northeast wing of the Cross-Strait Economic Zone (ibid.).

Thus, this pilgrimage was significant for Ningde in many important ways: not only did it allow the city to transcend its previous status as a military port with little contact with the outside world, it also immediately gave it a higher profile and greater prominence in the Cross-Strait Economic Zone. By carrying off the pilgrimage successfully, Ningde recreated itself as a place with economic and cultural potential. Thus, the pilgrimage is without a doubt the result of a joint vision of a new politico-economic zone in the neoliberal age.

Virtual Recentralization through the Welcoming Ceremony

We can go one step further by exploring exactly how this pilgrimage brought about the imaginary recentralization of Matsu. To facilitate the arrival of the pilgrims, Ningde city officials were extraordinarily coopera-tive with regard to customs and transportation. The city government cleared the port to welcome the ferry, and in order to process the Matsu pilgrims quickly they erected a temporary customs office in a former cement factory next to the port. The pilgrims were treated with the utmost courtesy during the pilgrimage events over the following five days. For instance, the group was escorted everywhere by important officials, such as Ningde's deputy mayor and the deputy chairman of the city's People's Congress, and police were stationed at every intersec-tion along the route to assist with traffic control. The nine tour buses carrying the pilgrims seldom encountered a red light and roamed the streets with ease.

A carefully designed welcoming ceremony further reinforced the image of Matsu linking China and Taiwan across the Strait. Just after disembark-ing, the pilgrims were escorted to an auditorium where a long red carpet had been laid at the entrance to welcome them. On either side, arrays of people danced, played gongs and drums, and set off firecrackers in cordial welcome. Walking into the auditorium, they were confronted by a gigantic picture depicting a boat sailing westward toward the Lady of Linshui (Fig. 9.1). On either side hung a large golden medallion decorated with shining lights, with Taiwan, Matsu, and Ningde prominently marked, making explicit the significance of the direct pilgrimage in binding together the three places. The design and decorations of the event palpably conveyed the Matsu people's role as intermediary, for it was they who had managed to connect Ningde and Taiwan for the first time.

Fig. 9.1 The auditorium for the welcoming ceremony in Ningde
(Photo by the author)

Apart from the pilgrims, the auditorium was full of officials from all levels, and media from the Ningde area and even Fuzhou. Leaders from both sides—the top administrator of Ningde and the county commissioner of Matsu—delivered long speeches brimming with visions of future political and economic interaction. They formalized their alliance by exchanging gifts, including votive tablets (*bian'er*) and local products (*techan*). In fact, such political alliances were stressed throughout the pilgrimage; wherever the pilgrims went, local government officials held banquets in their honor, and accounts and photographs of the numerous ceremonies during the trip were published in newspapers and on websites in Matsu, Taiwan, and China. The imaginations here differed from those expressed in traditional pilgrimages through religious symbols, legends of saints, or sacred topography (Turner 1967; 1968; Turner and Turner 1978); here, what made possible Matsu's imaginary of a mediatory role, or more specifically, its virtual recentralization, was the careful organization of rituals, the administrative and transportation privileges extended to the pilgrims, and the accounts of the journey rapidly disseminated by the media.

Extending Sociocultural Space

We may wonder why this political and economic project should have been realized by means of a religious activity such as a pilgrimage. Sangren (2000: 100) has shown that the relationship between a branch temple and its ancestral temple is a special, cultural-spatial one. It operates by a mechanism that is not readily reducible to political orders, as has been further shown by Yang's research (2004: 228) on the ritual space of the Goddess Mazu stretching across China and Taiwan. In this pilgrimage, we see that the cultural-spatial relation between Ox Horn and its homeland, Changle, was expanded to connect Taiwan and northern Fujian. It imaginatively articulated the Matsu residents' changing political and economic circumstances (see Kapferer, Eriksen, and Telle 2009: 3) and helped them to envision new prospects for their future.

To understand this contemporary pilgrimage, we must further examine the different types of Taiwanese pilgrimage from which the Matsu people have borrowed. The first, pilgrimages to ancestral temples, occur regularly and the entire community usually participates in them. Most famous of these is the annual pilgrimage organized by the Zhenlan Temple in Dajia (Chang 2003; Sangren 1987). In a second type of pilgrimage, which scholars have studied less, owing to their irregularity, people or interest groups organize visits to popular temples that are combined with tourism. These are usually more impromptu and have no fixed route or destination.

The pilgrimage held by Ox Horn combined these two types. It had the first type's community-based and root-searching quality—the destination was their homeland, Changle, and the more than 300 participants were mainly Ox Horn residents and their relatives in Taiwan. They included couples, parents, and children, and sometimes relatives from three generations. One family seized on the pilgrimage as a chance for a "reunion" (*jiaju*) of twenty-six of its members. Many older people went along to seek the well-being of their families; having experienced warfare and poverty, many of them led austere lives and consented to travel far from home only for this reason. Younger participants saw the pilgrimage as a chance to show filial piety to their elders. I also observed many emigrants bring their families back from Taiwan to meet their relatives in Matsu.

And yet the pilgrimage also had its improvisational and flexible aspects. For the Chinese, the boundary between pilgrimage and tourism is sometimes difficult to draw clearly (Oakes and Sutton 2010). Many pilgrims, when asked why they participated, frequently answer: "We come for fun" (*women lai wan*), and in fact much of their time was spent visiting cities and scenic spots. For example, reaching Baishuiyang, a new tourist spot promoted by the Ningde government, involved traveling a long route that circled to the northeast of Fujian. Also, as the itinerary shows, three out of the five days were spent in the vicinity of Fuzhou, and once there the pilgrims immediately went their separate ways; those in politics and business did their share of networking, while those interested in buying houses went to see prospective properties. Still others went on shopping excursions, or for a massage. The actual worship at Changle Temple took up only one morning.

Given that the pilgrimage tried to juxtapose and satisfy so many disparate aims, it was inevitable that paradoxes and contradictions would arise. For instance, the organizers deliberately arranged to visit Gutian first, both to promote the Lady of Linshui in Matsu and to attract her followers in Taiwan to pass through Matsu when making pilgrimage to her root temple in Gutian. To do so, they opted not to journey directly to Changle, where the main deity of Ox Horn came from, but rather made the Lady of Linshui the focus of the pilgrimage. Although the Lady of Linshui is commonly worshipped in Matsu, she is considered a deity of lower status. In the new Ox Horn temple, she is ranked fifth among the eight deities. The route's itinerary therefore implied an inversion of the deities' hierarchy, and this sparked protests from elders who insisted the pilgrimage should first visit Changle, the ancestral temple, before proceeding to Linshui Temple or elsewhere. Although Cao Eryuan was able to persuade them that "what comes later is more important" (*houzhe weida*), this modern pilgrimage clearly gave greater prominence to political, economic, and entertainment aspects than to its traditional religious meanings.

This pilgrimage is only one of many new rituals which were designed to connect Matsu with China and Taiwan. Many other novel religious material practices—such as promoting the myth that "Goddess Mazu [was buried] in Matsu" and constructing the Goddess's sacred sites— were invented to attract people to visit Matsu.

Sacred Constructions, Material Echoes

The name "Matsu" was originally taken from the "Mazu" temple. This temple is also called the Tianhou Temple, and it has always occupied a special place on the islands.[1] Indeed, all of the powerful figures of Matsu want to leave their marks on this temple. As I stated in Chapter 1, when the pirate Zhang Yizhou defeated Lin Yihe in 1942, he reconstructed Tianhou Temple and set up a stele to commemorate his victory. During the WZA period, the military took pains to manage and maintain the temple. The projects to rebuild the temple were all funded by the military: the cement reconstruction in 1963 and the renovations in 1983 were both completed by soldiers. Upon completion, the military commander came in person to host each inauguration.[2] The temple management had to follow his instructions, and the annual ceremony to celebrate Mazu's birthday was arranged by him and hosted by the county commissioner. Military cadres of all ranks and officials from the central government in Taiwan also frequently visited and toured the temple.[3]

When the military rebuilt the Tianhou Temple using cement in 1963, the commander erected a stele:

Reconstruction of the Mazu (Tianhou) Temple

The Goddess Mazu was a girl surnamed Lin who lived in Meizhou in Fujian during the Song Dynasty. She showed remarkable filial piety. Her father and brother met with an accident when fishing at sea. She threw herself into the sea to save them but died afterwards. Her corpse floated to this island. Later, she performed many miracles to protect fishermen at sea. In gratitude for her grace, the people built a temple here and renamed this island as Matsu. During the reign of the Kangxi Emperor, Mazu was proclaimed to be "The Queen of Heaven." At a time when the Red menace was ascendant, and the people were dispirited, I was given an order to protect this island and pacify the bandits. As commander of an army, I understand that the mind is the most important. [I have to] protect the political boundaries, enrich people's lives, and correct society's trends as well as people's thoughts. I have the responsibility to protect this land, administer the territory, and reform society. We deeply understand that the heart is the root of everything, and filial piety is the most important of all virtues. The deeds of this pious girl can serve as an example of virtuosity. Her filial piety shines as brightly as the sun and moon. This temple has been rebuilt in honor of her virtue. This stele shall forever commemorate her virtues in stone.

Commander of the Matsu Garrison Area
Lieutenant-General Peng Qichao
Erected in Autumn of 1963

重修媽祖廟（天后宮）碑記

媽祖娘娘宋代閩省湄洲林氏女，事親至孝，父兄捕魚遇難，投海覓親，殉身抱屍漂流斯島，後常顯靈異，護佑漁航沿海。居民感受恩澤，立廟宇尊祀，易島名曰馬祖。康熙年間冊封天后。時際紅禍橫流，人心陷溺，超奉命戍守斯島，進剿寇逆，治軍之餘，身體治心為本，固疆圉裕民主，端風氣正人心守土有責，庶政並舉，正本清源。深維心為萬事主，孝居百行先，而孝女之事蹟足式懿範可風，孝義足昭日月，廟時宜享千秋。敬重修廟宇以張孝烈，用勒於石，永崇祀典。

馬祖守備區指揮官
陸 軍 中 將 彭啟超撰書
中華民國五十二年仲秋 吉立

The stele records that after Lin Moniang jumped into the sea to save her father and brother, her corpse floated to the edge of Mazu bay; her remains were buried where the Tianhou Temple is located now. From the inscription as a whole, one can be sure that the commander clearly understood that "the heart is at the root of everything" during cross-strait wartime, and "filial piety is the most important of all virtues." He erected the stele to praise Goddess Mazu for trying to save her father's and brother's lives and sacrificing herself; the implication, of course, was that the army and residents were similarly attempting to protect Taiwan. Although there is no actual evidence to confirm that the corpse of Goddess Mazu floated to the Matsu Islands, emphasizing her sacrifice could provide a boost to the morale of soldiers and residents in the battlefield and a means of acclaiming their own sacrifices for the country.

Locals have varying opinions about whether the goddess's corpse floated to Matsu. For example, the local gazetteer, *The Annals of Lianjiang County* (*Lianjiang xianzhi*), recorded this legend (Lianjiang xian 1980: 63); however, another gazetteer, *Records of the Matsu Islands* (*Matsu liedao zhi*) (J. Lin 1991: 236), questioned whether it was possible for the corpse of Lin Moniang to float all the way to the Matsu Islands, given that the distance between Putian and Matsu is over 100 nautical miles, which is approximately the distance between Matsu and Taiwan. I also asked many elderly Matsu residents their opinions about the myth. Most were unable to describe any details predating the arrival of the ROC army. They recount that Tianhou Temple was taken over by the navy command post which moved out after a fire. When I asked what the tomb was like at the time, a few elderly people who could vaguely remember said that it was "under an altar covered with a red tablecloth," so they could not see it. In short, none of them was able to recall what the tomb was like during the military reign, or indeed whether there even was a tomb. Some said that the military had once tried to build a cement floor to make the ground more level but that the cement above the tomb cracked the very next day. There are also rumors that when the temple was being reconstructed in 2000, the earth auger used to drill the cement cracked when trying to drill the area around the tomb; as a result, the tomb was not moved. Whether these legends are true or not, they have successfully created an atmosphere of mystery surrounding the tomb. The stele and these tales have become an important basis for the temple to promote the myth of "Goddess Mazu in the Matsu Islands."

From another perspective, the development of the floating corpse myth is congruent with the geographical and cultural context of the islands. In the past, it was common to find corpses floating to Matsu, owing to its island geography. According to Chinese custom, the remains had to be carried to land and buried; after some time, a little shrine or temple may have been erected because of spiritual apparitions. This kind of phenomenon was not uncommon in Matsu or other islands (H. Wang 2000; Szonyi 2008: 184). In fact, on the Matsu Islands, which encompass an area of less than 30 square kilometers, there are thirteen shrines or temples which can be traced to floating corpses (Lin and Chen 2008: 110). Thus, the myth of Goddess Mazu's corpse floating to Matsu and being buried there does not conflict with the geographical situation and cultural practice of the islands.

Tianhou Temple holds special significance for the Matsu people. It is located in the village of Matsu in Nangan, right on Matsu Bay and comprises several preexisting villages in the surrounding area, which were grouped together and established as an administrative village by the army. During the early war period, supply ships landed at Matsu Bay and transported people and goods back and forth between Matsu and Taiwan. People traveling to other islands, such as Beigan or Juguang, had to wait at Matsu Bay for the high tide before they could return to sea. Before the deepwater pier at Fu'ao was completed in 1984, Matsu Bay was the most important link between the archipelago and the outside world.

Tianhou Temple is located right in front of this very important bay. When residents left for or returned from Taiwan, the temple was right there to greet them. Gradually, the temple came to occupy a special place in the residents' life experiences. In fact, I often hear people say, "It is the place where we wait for the boat. The seas can be dangerous, so everyone burns incense at the temple to ensure safety." Today, in addition to their own village deities, many Nangan residents also go to the Tianhou Temple to worship Goddess Mazu during Chinese New Year. They say that their relatives living on other islands will even call to remind them to worship her. This collective experience of travel to Taiwan solidifies the importance of Tianhou Temple and Goddess Mazu in the hearts of most Matsu residents. This belief also served as the common basis for the later development of Goddess Mazu festivals.

Since 2000, a series of new religious and material practices surrounding the Goddess has appeared. When the Tianhou Temple was rebuilt in 2001, the temple committee added a burial vault in front of the sanctuary, emphasizing that it was the resting place of Goddess Mazu. As *yin* and *yang* must be separated, no temple in Taiwan would place a vault in front of a shrine, unless it is a ghost shrine (W. Lin 2018). But the Tianhou Temple daringly did it anyway to appeal to the adherents of Goddess Mazu. Immediately afterwards, the "Mazu in Matsu" slogan was proposed in 2004 (C. Chen 2011b), and then beginning in 2006, a "Mazu Ascension Ritual" was performed annually. In 2009, the temple built a giant statue of Goddess Mazu, modeled on a similar statue in Meizhou (Fig. 9.2). It reminds people that Meizhou is the birthplace of the Goddess, while Matsu is the place of her ascension, and encourages pilgrims to visit both places. It is through this "material echoing" that the residents of Matsu aspired towards a symbiosis with people across the strait so that both could prosper together.

Fig. 9.2 The giant statue of Goddess Mazu on a boat
(Photo by Yang Suisheng)

Exploratory Journeys of Increasing Scale

The Ox Horn pilgrimage can also be understood in the context of a series of pilgrimages that took place in the first decade of this century: that is, three other direct-sailing pilgrimages, and a pilgrimage-like exploration. Together, I show how the Matsu people deployed these rituals to confront the drastic changes in the cross-strait relationship during the period 2000–10.

Matsu people apply the term "direct-sailing" in a way that is slightly different from the general usage. "Direct-sailing" generally refers to traveling directly between two political entities that share no diplomatic relations, which usually requires going through a third country. However, Matsu residents apply the term to any significant travel by ship, even within the same country. Thus, a journey from Matsu to a city in Taiwan, both within the "Republic of China," is still referred to as a "direct-sailing" trip. This local interpretation shows again how much they value their role in directly connecting different places.

The first direct-sailing pilgrimage was from Matsu to Meizhou, China, via Mawei port. On New Year's Day 2001, the "three small links" were officially launched, allowing direct voyages from Jinmen to Xiamen, and from Matsu to Mawei.[4] Owing to disagreements with the Chinese government, the small three links were only implemented unilaterally by Taiwan. Skirting sensitive political issues, the Matsu government organized this first pilgrimage in January to mark the beginning of the three small links. The pilgrims arrived in Mawei by boat and took a bus to Meizhou, the birthplace of Goddess Mazu. The political significance of this pilgrimage was that of breaking the ice of cross-strait tensions.

By 2007, Taiwan and China had already maintained different kinds of contacts for several years, and a substantial number of Taiwanese tourists had visited the mainland. That year, the second direct-sailing pilgrimage was launched to promote Matsu's religious tourism. This trip, again from Matsu to Meizhou, and advertised as a journey from Goddess Mazu's burial site to her birthplace, was intriguingly named the "Sacred Sea Route" (*haishang shengdao*), in emulation of the ancient Silk Road. It was hoped that it would become a model route that Taiwanese pilgrims take through Matsu and on to Meizhou (Matsu xiangqin 2007). The "Goddess Mazu in Matsu" idea and a series of religious practices drew the attention of people on both sides of the strait, particularly in the homophonous "Lianjiang county" in China. Since 2007, Matsu's Tianhou Temple has been invited to participate in the "Mazu Cultural Tourism Festival of Lianjiang" and vice versa. This religious exchange has gone well beyond the previous interactions in scale.

The third journey, called "Direct-sailing to Taichung," was organized in September 2008, with a ferry going directly to Taichung Harbor in Taiwan, and pilgrims then going on to visit the Mazu Temple in Dajia. The group continued north and visited areas where Matsu emigrants had settled and other places with temples connected to those in Matsu. The purpose of this pilgrimage was to foster exchanges between the temples in Matsu and those in Taiwan (Mazu jinshen 2008).

A more unusual kind of pilgrimage occurred in 2009, when the temple and the county government sponsored Li Xiaoshi, a retired lieutenant colonel from Matsu, to lead an expedition to climb Mount Everest. After retiring from the military, Li devoted his leisure time to mountain climbing and painting. Upset by the fact that most Taiwanese consider

Fig 9.3 Li Xiaoshi carrying a figurine of Goddess Mazu
(Photo by Chen Jianing)

his homeland to be just an offshore military outpost, he decided to
undertake the most difficult challenge he could think of: climbing the
world's highest peak, Mount Everest, with the goal of generating publicity and so introducing Matsu to outsiders. He realized that to safely
climb Everest, he needed the protection of divine power. Thus, he
gradually formed the idea of carrying a statue of Goddess Mazu to
Mount Everest.

As he was casting about for funds for his expedition, the county
government heard about his plan. Seeing an opportunity to promote
tourism in Matsu, the government decided to give Li NT$2,000,000 in
sponsorship. Mazu Temple also contributed NT$300,000 and made a
16 cm high figurine of Goddess Mazu for him to carry to the peak
(Fig. 9.3). Since Mount Everest in Chinese is called "Mountain of the
Sacred Mother" (*Shengmu feng*), and because this female connotation
easily allows for an association with Goddess Mazu (whose official title is
"Heavenly Sacred Mother"), this journey bore all the markings of a

Fig. 9.4 Goddess Mazu heading for the peak of Mount Everest
(Photo by Li Xiaoshi)

pilgrimage. Indeed, the explorer was ceremonially sent off and heroically welcomed back with rituals, firecrackers, and drums.

On his way up the mountain, Li regularly sent pictures back to Matsu showing how he and Goddess Mazu were progressing towards the highest peak in the world (Fig. 9.4). The Tourism Bureau immediately forwarded these photos on to *The Matsu Daily* and posted them on their website as they received them. The photos were given labels such as "Goddess Mazu on the peak of Mt. Everest," "Goddess Mazu also climbs to the summit of Mt. Everest" and "Carrying Mazu to the peak of Mt. Everest," emphasizing the significance of Li's epic adventure (C. Cao 2009a; 2009b). Thanks to Xiaoshi's strenuous expedition, the two "sacred mothers" finally met. It was a moment that Matsu locals had been awaiting with bated breath; a moment when they imagined that they would at last be connected with the wider world! Li's adventure was of great significance because he brought the hopes of Matsu to humanity at large. The residents of Matsu not only longed to be linked to Taiwan and the mainland, but also desired to be seen by the world. Goddess Mazu

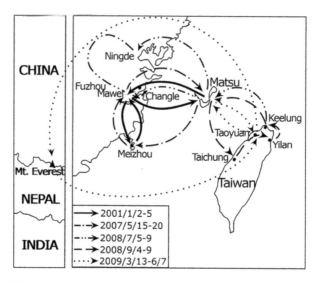

Map 9.2 Four direct-sailing pilgrimages and an exploratory journey to Mount Everest (not drawn to scale)

being carried up the mountain on the back of a Matsu local brought them one step closer to that goal.

Recentralization Imagined

Distinctive features of these Matsu pilgrimages can be seen more clearly from the routes pictured in Map 9.2, which, though somewhat complicated, shows how the Matsu-organized pilgrimages differ from Taiwanese pilgrimages in general. First, their timing betrays a lack of the regularity that is typical of Taiwan pilgrimages: they were improvised spontaneously to meet various needs. Second, the Matsu pilgrimages were deliberately designed to fulfill different purposes—depending on the particular needs of the local society, they could be organized to promote political communication, increase tourism, or expand networks. Finally, Map 9.2 most prominently shows that these routes were designed to create new connections, either with China, Taiwan, or the world. They represent the islanders' dreams of recentralization.

Note, too, that all of these pilgrimages occurred during a period when cross-strait relations were rapidly changing: tensions between Taiwan and China were improving, but a consensus had not yet been reached as to how their relations should develop. Those on Matsu, sensing the imminent danger of being forgotten in the new circumstances, were relentless in their attempts to attract the attention of both sides through pilgrimages. That is why these rituals appear to be contingent, instantaneous, and improvised, and inflected with fictive and novel tones (see Harvey 1990). To wit, they were performance-oriented, and intended to create more dramatic effects. Unlike traditional pilgrimages, they were eclectic in their combinations of different elements. Each was thus a peculiar religious reconfiguration in response to changing political and economic contexts. Together, they show the Matsu people's strong desire to engage with, and even to break, the constraints that came with being caught between the shifting tides of cross-strait relations.

A Mere Illusion?

Observing how the Matsu Islanders continue to change pilgrimage routes so as to forge more connections, several questions might be posed: Have Matsu residents succeeded in creating these economic, political, and religious links? What concrete results have the pilgrimages brought about? How much trade has flowed between Keelung, Matsu, and Ningde, and how many tourists? These questions do not seem to be important ones for the pilgrims or the temple committees themselves. The organizer of the Taiwan-Matsu-Ningde direct-sailing pilgrimage, Cao Eryuan, described their significance like this:

> In the future each island will be able to radiate out its own connections to the mainland, creating its own chances of survival.

In other words, Matsu residents recreate pilgrimages to generate possibilities for future development. Contemporary Matsu pilgrimages are thus like blueprints for the future, or to use Miyazaki's phrase, they are "methods of hope" (2004). They point to a future world that the Matsu people aspire to participate in.

The success of the pilgrimage to Ningde aroused the interest of Wenzhou in Zhejiang Province, the northernmost city in the Cross-Strait Economic Zone. City officials proactively contacted the Ox Horn temple committee and invited the people of Matsu for a visit. After visiting the Zhejiang administration in 2008, the committee soon planned a second trip that went through Fuzhou, moved north to Wenzhou, and finally arrived at Ningbo (July 6–11, 2010). This journey was not called a pilgrimage, but instead was referred to as an "incense exchange" (*huixiang*) between temples. However, in contrast with the traditional exchanges between temples in Taiwan, the people from Matsu conveyed no deity statues or incense burners, nor did they play gongs or drums.[5] The team's leaders carried only incense flags and used them just to indicate directions their team should move in, much as tour guides do. Though the group visited a Buddhist sacred site, Mt. Putuo, it did not meet the heads of the temple there. Generally speaking, the religious significance of this exchange was peculiarly downplayed. Its main purpose was revealed by the group's official title—the Pioneer Group to Zhejiang from Matsu, Taiwan—which was meant to emphasize that this group from Matsu was the largest entourage from Taiwan to have visited Zhejiang. The temple committee had the participants wear uniforms to show their unity, and indeed 450 people appearing in bright orange uniforms was a magnificent sight.

However, the connections that the Matsu people longed to forge through their pilgrimages and religious exchanges suffered setbacks during this 2010 trip, owing to changed external circumstances. The Wen-Fu High Speed Rail, commissioned in 2009, greatly shortened the journey between Wenzhou and Fuzhou, allowing people from Taiwan to fly directly to Fuzhou (following the official opening of the "three great links") and conveniently proceed to Wenzhou. Officials from the latter city therefore no longer had a strong incentive to encourage visits through the sea route from Matsu. Without reaching any consensus with these officials regarding the trip's itinerary, the Ox Horn temple committee decided to travel by railway and had only a short layover at Wenzhou. Though the original purpose of the trip had been to facilitate connections between Matsu and Wenzhou, the leaders of the two sides did not interact at all.

Equally telling was the way they were received in Ningbo City, the trip's final destination, to which direct flights from Taiwan are now available. A local newspaper referred to them as a "tourist group" (Peng 2011) and only travel agents were sent to accompany the people from Matsu as they toured Ningbo. The highest-ranking official they met was the relatively junior deputy director of market development, a department of the city's Tourism Bureau. This was in stark contrast to what the Matsu people had experienced in Ningde two years before. On the Ningbo trip I frequently heard them reminiscing about the high-profile reception they had enjoyed in Ningde and wondering why they were not being escorted by police cars. One woman told me, "I miss the gongs, drums, firecrackers, and boisterous atmosphere (re'nao) of the Ningde trip."

Indeed, the Zhejiang exchange could not compare on any level with the journey to Ningde—in neither Wenzhou nor Ningbo was it considered an important political, economic, or even religious event. Undoubtedly, the status of Matsu in the cross-strait relationship had quickly diminished due to macro politico-economic developments, including new direct flights and sea travel between China and Taiwan, China's regional policies, and its greatly improved transportation infrastructure. In the midst of these fast-changing neoliberal dynamics, this trip nearly dashed the islanders' dream of recentralizing Matsu between China and Taiwan by means of pilgrimages and religious exchanges.

It is undeniable that, lacking political, economic, or religious significance, the pilgrimage was little more than a sightseeing tour. For the temple committee, however, the trip still had importance: "We have already gone beyond Fujian, and moved northward to Zhejiang." In other words, the imagination entailed in pilgrimages and religious exchanges continues to generate opportunities and hopes. On the way home, I heard discussions about their next destination: Tianjin in northern China.

Conclusion: Explorations of Potentialities

While on the 2008 pilgrimage to China, I was surprised to learn that, like me, the Matsu people were unfamiliar with Ningde. But I was reminded of something once said by a ninety-year-old Matsu immigrant living in Taiwan, who had once been a fisherman: "Before Chiang Kai-shek's troops came over, people from Ningde or even further north would come by boat to Matsu to buy fish. At that time, Matsu people could travel anywhere. Matsu was a free place then!" The war separated the two sides of the Taiwan Strait and isolated the Matsu Islands. Today, the people of Matsu are trying to use religion to reestablish links between the two sides. The new temple in Ox Horn has created a new sense of identity for the residents, and the process of building a temple and traveling across the Taiwan Strait has strengthened relations on both sides. After the completion of their new temple, the Ox Horn residents took their deities on a pilgrimage to the ancestral temple in mainland China, witnessing and commemorating the bitter history of separation over the previous fifty years (see Jing 1996).

However, there is more to the Matsu pilgrimages than cross-strait reunion or religious renewal. In earlier times, Matsu merely served as a temporary stopover for fishermen, and most of the cultural activities were performed on the mainland. Since pilgrimages and other important rituals were never a part of Matsu's historical tradition, the islanders can be relatively spontaneous and improvisational in planning them now. In other words, although the Matsu pilgrimages may be inspired by those in Taiwan (M. Yang 2004; Hatfield 2010; Stewart and Strathern 2009), they are in fact quite different.

In this chapter, I have shown that these novel religious practices are imaginative works designed to attract attention from both sides of the Strait. I collectively refer to these imaginative qualities as "virtual recentralization." "Recentralization" connotes the Matsu islanders' longing to regain their important Cold War status as the focal point between China and Taiwan, even though this longing is "virtual" rather than real, as cross-strait tensions continue to be mitigated. These practices won the support of most of the Matsu locals, because they generate hope, potential, and point to future possibilities at the turn of the twenty-first century, when the Matsu Islands faced a strong sense of uncertainly.

Following along these lines, I posit that each of these rituals, myths, and material practices was not only a response to, but also a specific reconfiguration of, the dizzying political and economic changes in the relationship between China and Taiwan during this period. This is why the forms of all these religious practices appear to be improvised, contingent, and suffused with elements of fiction and fantasy. They differ from traditional religion in important ways: they are oriented toward performance and novelty, rather than transmitting permanent and solid religious values. Each attempt seeks a new kind of connection between the two lands, one that is more eclectic in purpose and less sovereign.

As these newly invented religious practices are the imaginary reconstitutions of cross-strait realities, they are inevitably susceptible to oscillations in the macro China-Taiwan relationship, as a result of which recentralization is sometimes on the verge of vanishing. However, I consider that the significance of these new rituals, myths, and material practices rests not on whether they succeed, but on the subjectivity they convey when people are faced with predicaments; they mediate social relations, rescale regional interactions, and forge possible developments for the islands in the future.

10 A Dream of an "Asian Mediterranean"

As I followed the Matsu people's pilgrimages to Ningde, Fujian (2007) and Ningbo, Zhejiang (2010), observing the ups and downs, and the build-up of expectations and the concomitant disappointments of Matsu's relations with China, I was constantly thinking that another project that sought to transcend the persistent cross-Strait adversities was perhaps not far off. As I expected, a plan to turn Matsu into an "Asian Mediterranean" arrived in 2012, and it quickly exploded and convulsed the islands. In this final chapter, I discuss this most controversial project, which will guide us deep into the Matsu society of today.

On December 25, 2008, the "three great links" between China and Taiwan were launched. These links allowed more frequent and direct travel between the two sides, but they also spelled the end of Matsu's role as a waypoint. The old "three small links" between Matsu and Fuzhou, which the government had been promoting since 2000, saw a steep decline in usage. Traffic between Matsu and Fuzhou numbered some 90,000 people in 2009. By 2011, it had been reduced to less than 40,000 people; in October 2011, there was only one voyage each day (down from two), and the ferry was usually nearly empty.

On the other side of the Strait, travel from Matsu to Taiwan has been a perennial problem. Although Matsu has two airports, in Nangan and in Beigan, they offer limited facilities, and owing to the unpredictable island climate, there are frequent flight cancellations. For instance, in 2011, the rate of flight cancellations for the two airports reached 19.4 percent (P. Zhang 2012). Some months are much worse than the average, such as May 2007, when a total of 135 flights were cancelled

230

(H. Yu 2007). Indeed, anyone traveling to or from Matsu even today will likely experience the frustration of cancelled flights and closed airports. Matsu locals often use a bit of doggerel to express their helplessness. The tourism bureau's motto inviting people to Matsu was reinterpreted by the local people as: "Come 'check out' Matsu— once you come, you'll never check out!" They also made up a joke offer, "Come to Matsu and get three free days in Guam!" (*Lai Matsu song guandao sanri you*) which was a pun for "Come to Matsu and you're not 'guam' to leave for three days!" Behind these jokes lies a reality of the difficulty of travel to and from Matsu, and a corresponding feeling of helplessness among the locals.

As for maritime transport, the Taiwan-Matsu Ferry (hereafter Taima Ferry), the main ship connecting Matsu to the outside world, frequently breaks down. Operating since 1997, the ferry is now over thirty years old.[1] Difficult sea conditions in the Taiwan Strait each winter often led to cancelled trips.[2] On February 20, 2010, an accident occurred during a voyage. The Taima Ferry had just had its annual maintenance check and was transporting passengers for the Chinese New Year. Near the end of the holiday period, the ship was passing through the Taiwan Strait when it unexpectedly lost power, leaving eighty-five passengers adrift at sea for four hours.[3] A new ferry, "Taiwan-Matsu Star" (*Taima zhi xing*) was built in 2015, only to become known as "the breakdown ship." After entering the water, the ship broke down at least once a month (J. Liu 2015), and in 2016 and 2017, the breakdown rate exceeded ten incidents per year. Although that has improved recently, travelers still find themselves on tenterhooks.

Transportation problems and the anxiety they cause appear constantly in *Matsu Daily* and in discussions on *Matsu Online*.[4] This chapter analyzes how a Matsu county commissioner attempted to face these transportation difficulties and to forge a wider regional network by bringing in a gaming plan proposed by an American venture capitalist— "Asian Mediterranean, Casino Resort" (*Matsu dizhonghai, boyi dujiacun*). This plan for a casino was hotly debated in Matsu before finally being put to a referendum. Even more importantly, a group of youngsters, the "post-WZA generation," mobilized and participated in this event and began to exert their influence in Matsu politics afterwards. In this final chapter,

I examine three important generations—the older fishermen from the fishing period, the middle-aged generation under the WZA, and the youngsters born in the post-WZA era, and explore their strikingly different imaginaries of Matsu's future.

A Different Vision

Elected county commissioner in 2009, Yang Suisheng was a major advocate for bringing the gaming industry to Matsu, though the idea had already been brewing for a long time. In 2000, Cao Yuanzhang, the leader of the democracy movement who was then a member of the Legislative Yuan (discussed in Chapter 5), proposed building a casino resort, but the commissioner at the time opposed the idea. On March 8, 2003, *Matsu Report* conducted a phone survey, showing that 62 percent of participants were against the idea, while only 26 percent supported it (Matsu minzhong 2003). Given the county commissioner's opposition, the proposal failed, but the issue continued to be actively debated on *Matsu Online*. After Commissioner Yang took office, the situation began to change.

Yang Suisheng was the first Matsu local to be sent to medical school in Taiwan under the guaranteed admission program. He began to participate in politics soon after returning to Matsu. In Chapter 8, I discussed Yang's role in building a temple in Ox Horn and followed his journey to the head of the county commission. Through it all, his leading concern was the problem of transportation. He personally oversaw the purchase of the Taima Ferry from Japan during his leadership of the Bureau of Public Works. When I asked him why he focused so much on transportation, he confided in me:

> In 1974, I began medical school in Taiwan, and each winter vacation I took a military supply ship back to Matsu. In the middle of a journey, an official military order came down saying that because important military goods were being carried on board, all non-military passengers would not be allowed in the ship's hold, but instead had to stay on deck. It rained all that day, and combined with the waves, everything got so wet that there was no place to lie down. After a journey of more than ten hours, we were all totally exhausted. I saw that there was a row of military trucks parked on deck, and so I suspended my body across the wheels of two adjacent trucks. After a

while, everything started to hurt, so I turned around and saw a cage of pigs on deck. I started to weep, thinking: "The Matsu people are even lower than the pigs."

Later, I got married and had my first child. When my son was eight months old, my wife and I took him to Taiwan to see his grandmother. Not long after the ship left harbor, my son got seasick and wouldn't stop crying. The ship officers were bothered by the noise and told us to go down to the anchor storage room. The waves were huge and the rolling ship sent the enormous anchor slamming into the walls, making an earsplitting noise all the way to Taiwan. I thought: I've had to suffer through a lifetime of excruciating sea voyages; will the next generation still have to be tortured in the same way?

In fact, because of ship or airline cancellations due to weather, both Yang and his son missed their respective university commencements in Taiwan (S. Li 2014: 7, 21). These wartime and personal experiences convinced him that only by improving the transportation to Matsu could the future of the islands be changed. When he was voted in as county commissioner, he began to implement a series of projects.

One of the projects involved replacing the Taima Ferry. After many complaints by Matsu officials to the Taiwan central authorities about the pervasive problems with the ferry, the Executive Yuan in Taipei finally approved the "New Taiwan-Matsu Ferry Purchase/Construction Plan" in 2009. The newly elected Commissioner Yang felt that if the new ferry were to be modeled on the old one, it would not prove competitive in the future. So in 2009, he put forth a proposal to purchase a trimaran instead (Fig. 10.1).

Fig. 10.1 shows a high-speed craft built by the Australian company Austal. It could make a one-way trip between Taiwan and Matsu in a mere three or four hours (compared to ten hours or more before); its hull was also resistant to high waves, making the journey much more pleasant (Qiuyue Liu 2010). The planned passage would take the ship from Taiwan's Keelung Harbor to Matsu, and then to Mawei in Fuzhou, before going back to Matsu and finally returning to Keelung. The commissioner felt that this route would be like a "high-speed rail for the sea" (*haishang gaotie*) since not only would the speed of travel increase convenience for the people of Matsu, but it would also encourage the movement of people between the three locations. The greater number of travelers would provide a boost to the local service industry and

Fig. 10.1 The old Taiwan-Matsu Ferry (left) vs. the fashionable new Trimaran (right)
(Photos by the author and Yang Suisheng)

businesses (Yong santi 2010). In his desire to purchase a trimaran, the new commissioner was clearly thinking not only about solving the transportation problem, but also was hoping to use new maritime transportation technology to develop Matsu more generally.

The only flaw in the plan was that building the trimaran would require an outlay of 2.8 billion New Taiwanese dollars, more than twice the anticipated cost of a new ferry. The commissioner began a tireless campaign to lobby the central government (Qiuyue Liu 2010). However, given that most Taiwanese were unfamiliar with trimarans and the high cost necessary to buy one, President Ma Ying-jeou finally declared in July 2010 that "the new Taima Ferry question should proceed in accordance with the original plan," thereby rejecting the proposal to buy a new technologically advanced high-speed craft. As the commissioner described these events to me in 2014, his face revealed no frustration or disappointment. He said mildly:

> Why am I telling you all this? Because even the president can't fix Matsu's problems. And that only made me more determined to bring the gaming industry to Matsu.

After that decision about the ferry, Commissioner Yang resolved to turn to outside capital.

Inspiration from a Poet

On January 12, 2009, the Legislative Yuan passed an amended Offshore Islands Development Act, with amendment 10–2 stating that the different islands could decide by legal referendum whether or not to allow gambling. In September 2009, the Pescadores Islands were the first to hold a referendum, and it was rejected. In Jinmen, a vote to allow the gaming industry was proposed in August 2009, but the proposal was withdrawn in October 2011.[5] Thanks to Commissioner Yang's persistence, on August 8, 2011, a gaming industry proposal was introduced in Matsu and produced a string of passionate debates and heated arguments. But how did the commissioner come up with the idea of bringing the gaming industry to Matsu in the first place?

Surprisingly, the idea originated with the celebrated Taiwanese poet Zheng Chouyu. After meeting the poet on three separate occasions, the commissioner decided to push the idea of bringing a casino to Matsu. The first meeting took place when the commissioner was involved in the development of Ox Horn (described in Chapter 8). At the time, he was the chair of the Ox Horn Community Development Association. He recounted:

> One of my Taiwanese friends pulled some strings and we were able to invite Zheng Chouyu to Matsu to give a talk. While we were having dinner together, he suggested that Matsu bring in casinos. He said that casinos aren't what most people think, and that they're places that offer many different kinds of entertainment. That was the first time I'd even heard of the idea of a casino, and I didn't really take it seriously.

The second occasion was at a banquet in Taipei, and this time Zheng Chouyu described in great detail the casinos on Native American reservations in Connecticut, which had proven to be very lucrative. The stories he told changed the commissioner's image of gambling. He wrote about it on *Matsu Online*:

> Three years ago, I had the chance to speak with Zheng Chouyu twice, and both times he mentioned the Native American reservations in the US. Owing to a lack of job opportunities, people had been leaving the reservations in great numbers. But in 1988, the US federal government issued the "Indian Gaming Regulatory Act," and tourists began to stream in, improving the economy, creating all kinds of jobs, and bringing people

back to the reservations. It completely changed the fate of the Native American reservations. (S. Yang 2008)

He also discussed the effects on Matsu of the recently developed religious tourism initiatives.

For the past few years, we've been trying to use the connection between "Goddess Mazu and the Matsu Islands" to develop "religious tourism" aiming at believers in Goddess Mazu. Although the effort has been ongoing for several years, we have yet to see any obvious results. (ibid.)

In 2009, the commissioner arranged to meet with Zheng Chouyu specifically to get him to expand on his ideas about the gaming industry.

The poet...talked about Macau and the Yunding Casino in Malaysia, and then mentioned how Singapore had recently built a casino, and then finally told me the story of how, when he was studying in Connecticut, he had worked as a dealer in a reservation casino. He had firsthand knowledge of and experience with the people who frequent casinos. As the poet said, a casino resort is like a goose that lays golden eggs, since people of all ages come together there and enjoy themselves. (S. Yang 2009)

He concluded:

Will Matsu vote to bring in the gaming industry? It might take a lot of discussion and public debate before we can have a vote. It could be an economic project, and good transportation will be a necessary part of that. It could also be a way of making a breakthrough on the transportation issue. No matter how you look at it, it's something really worth exploring. (ibid.)

From then on, the commissioner not only actively advocated for the gaming industry in Matsu, he also welcomed casino capitalists to the area and helped them hold informational meetings across the islands.

The Arrival of the Casino Capitalists

Over the past few years, there has been a surge of interest in the gaming industry, along with the construction of many casinos, especially in Asia. Quite a number of new luxurious, large-scale casinos have been built in Macao and Singapore, and they have attracted huge volumes of international tourists. In 2007, the total income from Macao casinos surpassed that of Las Vegas, making Macao the world's most popular destination for gamblers (Liang and Lu 2010). The gaming industry's success there has not only improved Macao's economy by leaps and bounds, but also made it an example for the rest of the world. Many experts conjecture that Taiwan may very likely follow in Singapore's footsteps and become the next country in Asia to allow casinos.

When Matsu spread the word that it might develop its gaming tourism industry, the American Las Vegas Sands Corporation, Australia's Crown Melbourne, Malaysia's Resorts World Genting, Macao's City of Dreams, and other international gambling enterprises all sent representatives to Matsu to inquire about the possibilities that might open up there. The most enthusiastic among them was Weidner United Development Corporation. The head of Weidner United, William Weidner, had begun as the general manager of the Sands Corporation in 1995. His team, selected from his days in Las Vegas, had taken part in the development and management of the Venetian Casino Resort and the Palazzo Resort in Las Vegas, as well as the Sands Casino, the Venetian, and the Four Seasons Hotel in Macao. He also participated in developing the Marina Bay Sands in Singapore. In 2008, he left the Sands Corporation after a dispute with the founder Sheldon Adelson. He now runs Weidner Resort Development, Inc., and has a joint venture partnership with Discovery Land Company. He has also formed a collaborative entity called Global Gaming Asset Management with the global financial firm Cantor Fitzgerald, which seeks out casino resort development opportunities across the globe.[6]

As a global venture capitalist, William Weidner follows gaming trends in Asia closely. In 2008, when the Pescadores Islands were enmeshed in disputes over the issue, he was there to gauge the possibility of setting up a gaming industry. When the referendum failed in 2009, he moved on to Jinmen, even staying there from June to September 2011. But the then commissioner Li Woshi was not interested in bringing casinos to Jinmen. Weidner said:

> Before I came to Matsu, I spent six months figuring out the situation in Jinmen. I could understand why the people of Jinmen didn't want to open a casino. They have a lucrative brewery which is topnotch. Their lives are really nice. Even I'd want to retire there! (Z. Yang 2013)

Weidner made his first trip to Matsu on March 4, 2011, when he met with the head of the county legislature. Having been thwarted in Jinmen, he turned his attention to Matsu. In October 2011, his staff began to come to Matsu to meet with local officials, and in January 2012, Weidner registered the "Taiwan Weidner United Development Corporation, Ltd." with the Taiwan Business Bureau and rented space in an office building in the Xinyi District in Taipei. That same month, he gave a brief report to the Lianjiang County Government and prepared to launch his campaign in Matsu.

Matsu in the Eyes of Global Venture Capitalists

With a public proposal to bring the gaming industry to Matsu, many people in Taiwan began to pay attention to where a casino might be built. Even the billionaire businessman Terry Gou (the chairman of Foxconn) had something to say about the matter:

> If you're going to build a casino in Taiwan…it would be better to do it in Danshui. Not only would it bring jobs to the island, but it would also make Danshui an important site for tourism, technology, exhibitions, and so on, all in one spot. (Cai et al. 2013)

Weidner was of a different opinion:

> If you look at Google maps, you'll see that the key cities of Fuzhou, Quanzhou, Xiamen, and Guangzhou are just an hour and a half away. So the way i see it, Matsu isn't an "outer island"—it's right in the middle of everything. (Z. Yang 2013)

A reporter asked some follow-up questions about Terry Gou's thoughts:

> Question: Foxconn chairman Terry Gou has stated that building a casino in Danshui would be more profitable. What do you think about that? Is there somewhere on the main island of Taiwan that is more suited to a casino?

> Answer: If you want to make money off of the people of Taiwan, then Danshui is a fine location. If you want to make money off of people from China and around the world, you should build it in Matsu. You'll be making money from people who can afford to buy a plane ticket, instead of from people who are driving to the casino. (ibid.)

Weidner was clearly not thinking about Matsu in terms of Taiwanese consumers. China (or at least southeastern China) was his main object- ive. He had carefully analyzed how mainland China's high speed rail system connected the major cities along the southeastern coast and had concluded that as far as land transportation from the west was con- cerned, Beijing, Shanghai, Wenzhou, Fuzhou, and other major cities were all linked by high-speed rail. In a single day, Chinese travelers could take advantage of the convenient transportation system to get to Fuzhou, the closest city to Matsu, and from there take a ship to the island. Once Matsu's new airport was finished, tourists would also be able to fly there directly. Similarly, from the east, travelers from Taiwan could fly in from airports along the high-speed railway that connect all of the major cities from Taipei to Kaohsiung. Accordingly, he calculated that once the casino resort was operational, it could handle 12,000 visitors a day, or a total of around 4.5 million people a year, 70 to 80 percent of whom would come from mainland China. For a global venture capitalist, south- eastern China was likely only a starting point: in the future, he would aim to bring in all of East and Southeast Asia (Weidner 2013: 89). Moreover, Weidner could take care of the finances and technologies without having to ask for government subsidies. He said confidently:

> Some people say that the basic infrastructure of Matsu is lacking, such as water and electricity. I'm always surprised when I hear that. Haven't these people ever heard of Dubai and Abu Dhabi? We built a city in a god-forsaken desert and accomplished so many impossible things.
>
> At this point, there are all sorts of technologies like seawater filtration systems and biofuels to help us solve any problems we encounter. (Reporter: Are you saying that you plan to build a water filtration plant in Matsu?) I plan to build whatever will help me succeed. I can do it all myself, but I also would welcome help from the government if they wish. I've long since learned to deal with any limitations nature might throw my way. (Z. Yang 2013)

Weidner boldly declared that he could do what the government could not; water and electricity for him were just the starting point. What other incentives did he offer?

Encroaching Neoliberalism

What Weidner wanted to build was not a simple casino, but rather a large-scale, integrated resort like Singapore's Sands or Sentosa resorts.

Weidner said: "To me, Matsu is like a charming little village in southern Italy" (C. Cao 2012a). Thus, he named his planned resort village "Asian Mediterranean," choosing Mt. Da'ao in Beigan and Huangguan Island in Nangan as his development sites. Beigan would house the Matsu Asian Mediterranean Resort Village with gaming facilities, while Nangan would be home mainly to five-star hotels and individual rental villas.

In order to attract tourists to these resort areas, Weidner would have to make major improvements to the basic infrastructure of Matsu, and this was a major part of the appeal the plan had for locals. These plans later developed into his so-called "four big pledges" (*si da baozheng*). First, he promised to build a Code 4 airport in Matsu (Codes 1–4 are designations used to indicate the length of a runway).[7] He planned to upgrade the airport in Nangan from a Code 2 to a world class Code 4 airport, complete with a high-tech instrument landing system. With that in place, Boeing 737 and Airbus A320 aircraft would be able to land, and the people of Matsu would no longer suffer from delays due to heavy fog and bad weather. It would also connect Matsu to cities across mainland China, East Asia, and Southeast Asia. In addition, Weidner also planned improvements to the wharfs on Matsu. In his envisioned future, it would only take forty minutes to get from Langqi Island in Fujian's Mawei district to Matsu, with each ship bringing up to 300–400 people.

To have a Code 3 or Code 4 airport has been a long-standing desire for the Matsu people. The county government carried out its own surveys and concluded that the airport in Beigan did have the potential to become a better-equipped Code 3 airport. However, it would require the removal of Mt. Duanpo, Mt. Feng, Mt. Da'ao, and Shi Island, among other areas, in order to allow for the safe approach of aircraft. A preliminary investigation of ocean depth also showed that if the runway were to be extended to a Code 4 standard, it would involve immense financial outlays. Meeting the Code 3 requirements was comparatively inexpensive and was therefore more feasible (P. Chen 2011). Even so, a Code 3 runway would require an investment of more than NT$8 billion.

Second, Weidner promised to build a cross-sea bridge connecting Nangan and Beigan. Since he planned to build the casino resort on Beigan and hotels and villas on Nangan, a convenient link between the two islands would be needed. This bridge was what Matsu locals had been longing for. It had been repeatedly discussed in *Matsu Daily*, but the nearly NT$4 billion price tag was prohibitive.

Third, Matsu locals had long been dissatisfied with the state of their educational system, with only one high school across all the islands. Weidner agreed to set up a university in Matsu to help train people in various aspects of the tourism industry.

Fourth was the issue of the public good. Weidner pledged 7 percent of revenues to the local government as a special gambling tax. He estimated that if the local government gave half of that amount back to the local people, in the first year each person on Matsu could receive NT$18,000, and that number would go up to NT$ 80,000 by the fifth year.

Weidner's "four big pledges" were undoubtedly an aggressive form of neoliberal infiltration, encompassing island-wide infrastructure (airport, bridge construction), higher education (university), economy (hiring workers), and public goods (dividends paid to Matsu locals). Were they to be realized, Matsu would doubtless become a "special economic zone" and the gaming businessmen would soon supplant the governance of the state.

Fantasy of an "Asian Mediterranean"

Weidner's "Asian Mediterranean" plan involved much more than the provision of basic livelihood or economic development for the people; it proposed a grand reformation of the landscape of Matsu, engendering a vision of a place utterly different from the Matsu of the military period. He widely advertised his plans on all kinds of media.

Isolated Islands vs. Interconnected Archipelago

Let us start with the cross-sea bridge connecting Nangan and Beigan. During the WZA era, each island was engaged individually in the war effort, with an emphasis on "one island, one life," and no one could ever imagine an inter-island bridge. Even after the dismantling of the WZA, each island's transportation system was developed separately. There was no way to share resources between the islands because of their dispersion. The fact that many vital constructions had to be duplicated on different islands was an enormous problem for the Matsu government (for example, Nangan and Beigan both needed to have an airport, which meant the facilities of each were simple and limited). If the islands were to be connected, resources could be shared; each island could then develop its own characteristics and functionally complement each other. Weidner's "four big pledges" thus struck a chord in the hearts of the people.

Marginality vs. Internationality

When I asked Liu Dequan, former head of the Matsu Tourism Bureau, about his thoughts on Weidner, with whom he often interacted, he said:

> Weidner and his team had a vision and painted a picture for us, while the other brokers just asked how much land Matsu has. They'd done a lot of research into the advantages of the area where Matsu is located—centered on Fujian, including Zhejiang to the north, and northern Guangdong in the south.

> They also had an understanding of Matsu itself. The places they proposed, Nangan's Huangguan Island and Beigan's Mt. Da'ao, are both chosen from the perspectives of the airports. They are also separate from the main islands, and the soil is poor there. Since no one lives there, it would be easy to develop.

He imagined a step further:

> After the plan succeeds, Matsu will be totally transformed from Taiwan's outlying islands into an international archipelago. Taiwan might one day even become an outlying island of Matsu!

Clearly, Weidner's imaginary of the future—namely of Matsu as an international archipelago—was deeply attractive to the Matsu people, who are facing an imminent crisis of marginalization.

Cold War Island vs. Luxurious Seaside Resort

The lure of a modern C4 airport was even more enticing. Not only would it solve the ongoing issue of transportation for Matsu locals, it would also bring in waves of tourists who would completely alter the bleak condition on the islands (Fig. 10.2). The global venture capitalists' "Asian

Fig. 10.2 Targeted land for building a casino resort in Beigan
(Photo by Yang Suisheng)

Mediterranean Project" promised to transform Matsu from a peripheral warzone island into a charming vacation island like the exotic resorts in the Mediterranean Sea. Matsu would be another Dubai, a fantastic vision erected in the middle of the ocean.

Let us look more closely at the theme of "Asian Mediterranean." The Matsu casino resort was quite different from the one designed for the Philippines, which we will discuss in the following section. Since the traditional dwellings in Matsu bear some resemblance to the style of villages in the Mediterranean, Weidner imitated the flavor of Italy—areas around the Mediterranean sea and in Southern Tuscany in particular—as well as villas in Monaco, to create a sense of the exotic for the resort (Fig. 10.3) (Hong 2013).

In the animated 3D images that Weidner designed, Matsu's bitterly cold winter that keeps people huddled indoors is completely absent. It is replaced by constant sunshine, villas, wharfs, speedboats, and a sparkling blue sea. The Matsu archipelago is filled with the bustling tourist atmosphere of the islands in the Mediterranean. This imaginary of Matsu was

Fig. 10.3 An exotic Asian Mediterranean planned by Weidner's firm
(Photo by the author)

endlessly circulated through publicity materials, in online venues, and across new media.

Reality or Dream?

We must ask, however, whether the image of Matsu propagated by these global venture capitalists was real or fake. Would it be possible to achieve in reality? For Matsu locals, it was impossible to judge. This new imaginary existed somewhere between truth and fiction. At the same time, Weidner packaged this imaginary with a series of neoliberal ideas: that is, his putative global, capitalist, non-local network (see Comaroff and Comaroff 1999, 2000, 2002). The mixture of his ceremony-like presentations with these neoliberal ideas only served to make the entire concept of an "Asian Mediterranean" even more indistinct and mysterious.

As described above, the plan that Weidner put forward was built with an understanding of the Matsu Islands' condition. When promoting his casinos, Weidner and his working team sought out contact with locals. They set up an office in Nangan and held large informational meetings on the two major islands. The members of his team also went out to each village to hold smaller local meetings. The day before the vote, they used the familiar Taiwanese tactic of "carpet campaigning," fanning out across areas likely to vote against the measure to try to sway voters. Below is a description by Xu Ruoyun, one of Weidner's team members, from July 6, 2012, the night before the vote:

XU RUOYUN: Starting at 4pm, we went door to door across Ox Horn and Shanlong. We knocked on every single door, talking to a lot of people who were against the casino and weren't happy to see us. We didn't even stop to eat. The worst of it was going to Shanlong [an area with a relatively high proportion of civil servants and school employees]. ...It was raining, and we were miserable [Matsu villages are built into the mountainsides, with pathways of uneven steps. They can be difficult to navigate in the rain]. In the end, the heavens were on our side, and we won in each balloting location! Only in Shanlong did we come in tied, 329 to 329. That means we didn't lose in a single district.

AUTHOR : And Weidner himself?

XU RUOYUN: He arrived three or four days before and canvassed with us. The night before the vote, he came out with us, going door to door to ask for people's votes.

However, in terms of "the reality on the ground," it truly was a "border-less fantasy." Weidner liked to display his wide network of contacts in well-laid-out advertisements and on official occasions. But these contacts were all from the outside world, and for Matsu locals, they were just a series of unknown faces. Weidner's publicity materials were full of international partners who were "big entrepreneurs" with no ties at all to the area. These contacts frequently appeared only for ceremonial occasions such as big informational meetings or press conferences (Fang 2012). No one knew who these men in fancy Western suits and women in perfume and heels were, nor what part they were supposed to play in Weidner's plan.

Moreover, Weidner held press conferences to keep a steady stream of publicity going, announcing that he had brought in more investments from international banks for the casino resort. Each monetary figure mentioned was higher than the last. The media was giddy with excitement:

> ...An American entertainment company held a high-profile press conference in Taiwan on the 9th to announce that it will head a team to develop Matsu's tourism industry, as well as to publicize its success in raising NT$60 billion from Wall Street financial institutions. (L. Li 2012)

> In America, he discussed raising capital with eight large financial institutions, including Goldman Sachs, Deutsche Bank, UBS, J.P. Morgan Chase Securities, Merrill Lynch, CLSA Capital Markets Limited, Credit Suisse, and the Macquarie Group. NT$60 billion is only for the first stage, and the plans have been extended to the third stage, with total possible investments reaching somewhere around $NT180 billion. (C. Cao 2012b)

> [Although] Taiwan's Weidner United holds NT$1 million in funds, Weidner's holding company does US$16 trillion worth of securities trading with companies on Wall Street. They pledge NT$70 to 80 billion for the first stage of development, and over the course of three or four stages in 15 years, the total investment will be more than NT$240 billion. The company has already raised US$3 million. (Fang 2012)

The proclaimed amounts of total investment kept on increasing, from NT$60 billion to NT$180 billion and all the way up to NT$900 billion, but for the Matsu people, there was no hard confirmation of these sums. For them, it was difficult to tell truth from fiction. Weidner also never directly addressed people's suspicions; for example, at an informational meeting in the town hall in Nangan:

> Weidner personally introduced the management for the project, including the Director General for Asia, his international gambling analysts and several other members of the development team who were present at the informational meeting. A video was shown by Weidner United describing their plans for Matsu. ...As for some concerns expressed online about the amount of capital raised, Weidner smiled and said that a Wall Street investment bank affirmed that Weidner United had received a single investment in the amount of NT$60 billion. (Q. Liu 2012)

Instead of responding directly, Weidner just smiled and dangled the number of 60 billion before the audience.

In order to further demonstrate his economic power and ability to raise funds, Weidner took advantage of the opening ceremony for the Solaire Manila Resort—in which he was one of the investors—to invite twenty-two reporters from Taiwan to the Philippines (Song 2013). He held a

Fig. 10.4 Weidner in the Philippines introducing plans for a casino
in Matsu
(Photo by Song Jiansheng)

press conference there so he could elucidate his plans for Matsu to them,
emphasizing how he would apply his experiences in Malaysia to the
planned casino resort in Matsu (Fig. 10.4). Solaire Manila Resort is set
on one hundred hectares of land overlooking the Manila Bay
Entertainment City. Plans for the Entertainment City included four
casino resorts, among which Solaire was the first to open, with the other
three still under construction. Weidner was collaborating with Solaire's

parent company, Bloomberry Resorts Corporation, and had provided around 10 percent of the total investment.

In this series of actions, Weidner, acting as a global capitalist investor, used borderless capital as a kind of underpinning for his plans (see Miyazaki 2006: 151). Aided by the extravagant ceremony-like meetings, he gave the marginalized people hope, even if it was for a fantasy-filled and as-yet undecided future.

Casino or Home?

The issue of whether or not to develop the gaming industry as a key part of Matsu's future was a pivotal one that affected everyone on the islands, and so it attracted wide attention. When an occasion arose to ask older fishermen about their attitudes towards opening a casino on Matsu, many expressed support for the idea. Aside from the "NT$80,000" payout to locals that would help support their retirement, they also felt that there was nothing wrong with gambling:

> We all used to gamble!
> Everyone on Matsu likes to "take a little gamble"—it's in our nature!

As Chapter 4 discussed, gambling was a part of the fishermen's life-style. Now that the fishing economy has declined, and the military is gone, the fishermen's attitude is "there's nothing left, so why not gamble and see whether we can get something (F. *huang lung tou mo lou, puh y tu luoh tu*)," according to a popular saying. The idea that something had to be done proactively in order for there to be any hope is not that different from the old belief of fishermen that every opportunity must be seized as soon as it arises, and it fed the feeling that any change for the better necessarily comes with a certain degree of risk.

There was another group that supported the gaming proposition, namely, educated people who had moved from Matsu to Taiwan. They not only conducted a forum on gambling in Taiwan, but also returned home to actively argue for the casino. Chapter 3 discussed how the guaranteed admission program led to the emergence of a new social category of civil servants and teachers in Matsu. Having fulfilled their obligation to return home and serve Matsu, they were then confronted with the difficulty of transportation to Taiwan and limited prospects for promotion, and many decided to return to better conditions in Taiwan. Their economic situation in general is better than the manual workers who had migrated to work in factories in an earlier era; many were able to buy homes in the greater Taipei area which were comparatively expensive. They even set up their own Matsu "Teachers and Civil Servants Association" (*wenjiao xiehui*) in 1997.

It quickly becomes apparent when speaking to these emigrants that many of them grew up in the WZA era and remember that period as one of constant hardship. They view the decline of the fishing industry and the limited job opportunities as part of life in Matsu, and see it as the reason they had to leave and make their mark elsewhere (L. Zhang 2012). They felt that if Matsu did not grow its own industry, it would continue to be reliant upon the central Taiwanese government, and the future would be bleak (J. Lin 2012). Others believed that large financial consortiums would have enough capital to develop the region (S. Cao 2012), thereby bringing hope to Matsu. Their memories of "hardship" and "being unable to stand on our own two feet," along with their support for "development," are primarily responses to their own histories as immigrants. These experiences are quite different from those of the younger generation who grew up in Matsu, and so their standpoints on the casino question also diverge.

One example from the middle of the age spectrum succinctly expresses the transition in the imaginaries of Matsu. Cao Xiangguan was born in 1970, and so was only forty-two years old during the push by the gaming industry. He is typical of many middle-aged locals in that he was sent to study in Taiwan as part of the guaranteed admissions program and came back to Matsu to serve in the government. He studied maritime engineering, which was badly needed in Matsu. When he returned home, the military government was just in the process of being dismantled; at the time, many of Matsu's harbors were very crudely equipped. He immediately began to work on wharf construction and improvement, spending a decade in the industry. Over the course of engaging in these projects, however, he came to realize that there was no long-term plan or overarching vision for Matsu's development, but instead only constant destruction: the thoughtless installation of docks, dykes, and anti-wave concrete blocks was destroying Matsu's shoreline and coral reefs. Obviously, Weidner's plans for a casino resort would involve a tremendous amount of land reclamation, at great cost to the natural environment and ecology of the area. When I talked to him in 2018, he used an image of a family to describe the support for the casino shown by the many educated Matsu people living in Taiwan:

> Take a poverty-stricken family, in which the father decides to leave the village to go out and earn money. He leaves behind his wife, who has the children to take care of and who works hard herself. After many years of struggling to make it, their situation improves. One day, the father returns home from his job outside the village. He doesn't understand how hard his family members have been working while he's been gone. He thinks of them as backward and behind the times, and he wants his wife and children to sell or rent out the family property to make money.

This story of "family" not only serves as a metaphor for the relationship between emigrants, locals, and venture capitalists promoting gaming; it also relates to the imaginary of Matsu that many of the younger generation hold.

Debate over the gaming industry had been going on in *Matsu Online* forums for quite some time, but the clearly demarcated camps for and against had little effect on the average people in Matsu. Taiwan's anti-gambling legalization association also came to Matsu and formed the frontlines of the battle early on, setting up a fan page on Facebook called "Long live Matsu, don't turn our home into a casino." But the page never caught on with Matsu locals, who saw it as outside interference. In contrast, the side favoring development was dominant under the influence of the Matsu government and the support of migrants. The opposition did not really get off the ground until a group of young anti-gambling activists joined in, and the numbers for and against the proposal began to fluctuate.

The Counterattack from the Post-martial-law Generation

Cao Yaping, the organizer of this group of youngsters, was at the time a 23-year-old student at a research institute for social development in

Taiwan. Born in 1989, she was different from other members of the opposition in that she had grown up in post-WZA Matsu and had no real experience with military rule. Cao said that when she studied the negative repercussions of development, the cases were all about indigenous peoples and disadvantaged groups. She had never considered that these issues might apply to her homeland until one day she returned home and was shocked to hear her father, the owner of a shop selling local products, expressing delight at the prospect of a casino being built in Matsu. "People of my generation first understand the outside world, and only then do we come to understand Matsu," she said. She went back to Taiwan and began to appeal to other Matsu youngsters by organizing an anti-gaming online community and setting up a Facebook page called "Matsu youth against gambling: We don't want a casino future."

This group slowly gathered steam and not a few young people expressed their feelings on the page. More importantly, the users took advantage of the different "share" functions, posting information from the anti-gambling page to other websites and thereby extending their reach. The most famous post was an essay titled: "A thirteen-year-old girl sent me a message to tell me that I have to keep up my anti-gambling efforts." It came from a message written to Cao Yaping by a girl who had gone to elementary school in Matsu, and it recounted the unspoiled beauty of the Matsu scenery as well as her dread of the islands becoming a gambling den. Cao first posted the essay on her personal blog, and then made public posts on Facebook and *Matsu Online*. It eventually went viral and received substantial coverage from all of the major media outlets in Taiwan. The Matsu casino suddenly became national news and attracted wide attention. In Matsu, educators began to see their students stand up, and they too started to support the movement. The energy and wholesomeness of the students moved many of the middle-aged generation, and brought more people to the cause. One of them wrote on Facebook: "Because [of them] we can see Matsu's future!" Public opinion, which had originally leaned toward the anticipated passage of the proposal, gradually became less and less certain (Pan 2012). In the end, even though the students lost the vote, the appearance of these young people opened up a different future for the islands. They constitute a growing force in contemporary Matsu politics.

The active political participation of the youngsters indicates that their image of Matsu, Taiwan, and even Fuzhou is very distinct from that held by the older generation of fishermen or the WZA generation. Importantly, this post-martial-law generation did not experience the hardships of military rule. The Matsu they know is developing tourism, and whether in terms of transportation, lifestyle, or accessibility of information, their Matsu is closely linked to Taiwan. For example, Cao Yaping mentions an experience from her childhood:

> I've been going to Taiwan since I was a kid. Over the summers, I'd meet friends in Taipei, and we'd walk around Ximending [the most popular shopping area for Taiwanese youth]. It just felt natural to visit Taipei from Matsu.

She even reverses the older generation's idea of the relationship between Matsu and its neighbors, Taiwan and Fuzhou:

> Taiwan and even Fuzhou are like Matsu's "backyard." We go there to hang out, to take extra prep classes, or to go shopping.

Thus, for the post-martial-law generation, Matsu is no longer an isolated place—it is neither a temporary stopover nor a military frontline. Thanks to the connectivity brought about by improved transportation and digital communications, Matsu has gradually become their "home," where they can live and work with a measure of stability. In contrast, Taiwan and Fuzhou are now their "backyards," which they visit for entertainment in their leisure time or whenever they want. This is a totally different image of their lived world. Their rejection of the casino project in Matsu reflects their longing for the sustainable development of their home that is no longer controlled by the army or damaged by outsiders.

Conclusion: Fissured Future

In the end, the proposal for the casino won 1,795 votes (57 percent) to the opposition's 1,341 votes (43 percent). Supporters propagated the idea that the proposal would provide a marginalized Matsu in crisis "another source of hope" (*duo yige xiwang*), or allow it to "seize an opportunity" (*zhangwo yige jihui*) , or even let its people "bet on the future"(*du yige weilai*), actively reaching out to a population mired in transportation and economic difficulties.[8] If we say that the Matsu people in the fishing period gambled with the ocean, and in the military period with the state, now in the twenty-first century they voted to gamble with their future. The fisherman's mindset continues to be a way for the islanders to struggle with uncertainty in the twenty-first century.

Matsu still does not have a casino resort. Although the measure passed a public vote, the central government must formulate a set of new laws, such as the "Regulations for the Supervision of Tourism and Casinos." Only when the local government sees the laws can it begin to attract subsidiary businesses and investment. The necessary bills, however, have been blocked in various ways in the national legislature. A February 2013 decision by mainland Chinese officials, indicating that they would ban travel to the Matsu casino, has made the plan seem even more unrealizable. Finally, in June 2015, Weidner announced that he would pull out of Matsu, as the Taiwan government had not shown any intention to cooperate for three years.

The fact that the idea of a casino resort could begin in an individual's imagination and go on to capture the imagination of a whole society is an expression of the constant vicissitudes that the Matsu people have faced. From 1992, the end of military rule, and all the way to the "three great links" between China and Taiwan, the people of Matsu have faced unprecedented challenges. It is undeniable that the imaginary of an "Asian Mediterranean" offered by the casino capitalists spoke to deep desires that the people of Matsu already harbored; or one could say that it fit their dreams. Through the image of an "Asian Mediterranean," Matsu locals were not only able to reimagine themselves as repositioned between the two sides in the Taiwan Strait, and to reframe the islands as able to reach the whole of Asia, they were also able to make an incipient entry onto the world stage. For most Matsu locals, this was indeed a "new opportunity"—irrespective of its complex mix of hope and despair, promises and disappointments, present and future.

This kind of new opportunity also reveals an important characteristic of the contemporary imaginary: the imaginary offered by the venture capitalist, William Weidner, did not come from traditional myths or stories (Taylor 2004: 23), nor was it based on local sociocultural forms. Given this circumstance, its resemblance to a fantasy is even more pronounced; it was mediated by global capital, non-local networks, and glittering "showbiz" performances. Reality and fantasy not only became difficult to distinguish, but also mixed with illusions to stimulate people's thoughts and fervor. Clearly, imagination is a crucial characteristic of local societies today. This kind of fantasy may appear absurd at first glance, but it is a genuine way for people on the periphery to respond to marginality and to explore their own possible futures.

The case of Matsu offers an excellent example of the process of imagination, which started with an individual and went on to become social and shared more generally by the greater society. As pointed out, in 2003, two-thirds of the population of Matsu opposed building casinos, while by 2012, the proposed casino resort won more than half of the vote. The important mediators were the grandiose dream offered by a global capitalist, and an imaginative figure, Yang Suisheng, who was able to connect the local and the global. As discussed earlier, Yang had received a modern medical education but was born and raised in Matsu. He was perennially caught between science and tradition. Early on in his career, he served as the chair of the Ox Horn Community Association and hoped to reinvigorate his home while also protecting the environment. With little success to show for his hard work, he threw himself into building a temple and gained the support of locals, eventually becoming county commissioner. While serving as commissioner, he realized that pilgrimages and other religious attractions would not usher in the benefits that locals were hoping for, and he decided to forge an alliance with the casino capitalists in order to bring new opportunities to Matsu. These sorts of figures, mediating between local places and the greater society, along with the kinds of imaginaries they offer, always prompt new thoughts and actions in local society, even if in the end they may not be able to solve the underlying problems.

The conflict, debate, and tension surrounding the casino proposal reveal the divisions between different generations in Matsu—the fishermen during the fishing period, the civil servants and teachers arising from the WZA era, and the younger generation born after the war period—and their different imaginaries of the future. Today's social imaginings are in no way unitary, nor can they be understood with a top-down model. How these different imagining subjects understand their lived world and their expectations for the future are important questions to consider when we study contemporary society.

Conclusion: Becoming Ourselves

For a very long time, Matsu sat on the edge of an empire, an outlying archipelago beyond the reach of state power. During a period of limited resources, people came and went, using the islands as a temporary shelter. In 1949, however, the happenstance of history transformed these isolated mountainous islands into a frontline: the occupation of the Nationalist army marked the start of more than forty years of strict military rule. The army carried out large-scale construction projects and provided new opportunities for education, but it also created many conflicts and traumas. As the US–Soviet Cold War came to an end, tensions across the Taiwan Strait loosened, and martial law was eventually lifted in 1992. After Matsu lost its military and tactical usefulness, its people were confronted with the existential question of who they were, and how to redefine themselves and their place in the world. Above all, how could the islands move forward so as to surmount their previous fate as either an ignored outpost on the periphery of the state, or a subjugated area under the strictures of military control? This book has discussed how the islands' middle-aged generation, who were sent to Taiwan to study during the wartime period, have devised a series of new imaginaries, or blueprints, for Matsu's future development. They grew up suffering the adversities of military rule, and after living and studying in Taiwan or in the world at large, they resynthesized their own experiences and knowledge and returned home with new ideas and inspiration. With diverse abilities, values, and beliefs, they built their individual imaginations of the islands and developed them through varied mediating mechanisms—including new media technologies, novel religious practices, and neoliberal economic concepts—in order to rescale and reposition Matsu in the world. We have seen how different imaginations were given an unprecedented chance to develop during this critical moment of uncertainty. The rich ethnography of these consecutive imaginaries of Matsu provide an unusual case for studying how the individual imagination can transform into a social imaginary.

As Anderson (1991[1983]) and Appadurai (1996) have shown with great foresight, print-capitalism and mass media have historically enabled national and global imaginings. This book goes one step further to analyze how imagining subjects can deploy new mediating technologies to explore their imaginations and extend them into the wider community; in other words, how individual imaginations can turn into social imaginaries. As an isolated archipelago in its early days, and as a military frontline for a significant stretch of the twentieth century, the imaginations of the Matsu individuals were less visible or simply hidden. It was only when the barriers were lifted, and the islands were no longer cut off from the world, that their imaginations had more opportunities to flourish and began to disseminate quickly.

Having experienced the longstanding oppression of military rule, how could individuals become imagining subjects? How could subjectification occur? And in what ways could the individual imagination reach the collective? Military rule undeniably left scars of varying severity on everyone living in Matsu at the time, but the military's withdrawal left the former frontline islands alone in the enormous ocean, facing a precarious future on their own. This book illustrates how the people of Matsu applied new imaginative technologies, invented rituals and myths, and even drew on the gaming industry in concerted attempts to relocate Matsu within different regional and global frameworks in order to find new possibilities for themselves. It importantly highlights that the serial island imaginaries that they evolved are also processes of subjectification. That is, social imaginary usually starts with individuals' reflections and combines their particular visions of the future. It then extends and spreads via different kinds of mediums and gradually coalesces a common understanding that motivates people to take concrete action. The imagining subject in previous literature has received less attention (Crapazano 2004: 1); in this book it is given primacy so as to better understand the key role it plays in contemporary society. Not all individual imaginations can develop into social imaginaries, owing to various social, cultural, and political factors. However, imagining subjects do not easily fade away; they remain latent and may take on renewed power at unexpected moments. This is important for understanding, in particular, the trajectory of the demilitarized islands after the Cold War.

★★★

The stories recounted in Part III of this book are still ongoing. On July 15, 2011, to commemorate the sixtieth anniversary of the first landing on Liang Island, the Matsu station troops sponsored a ceremonial trip called "Glorious Return of Heroes to the Island." During the event, the county commissioner Yang Suisheng happened to discover traces of a shell midden on the island. He invited archeologists to carry out an excavation, and they unearthed the skeletons of two people. Using carbon dating (AmsC14), they determined that the remains dated to sometime between 8,200 and 7,500 BCE, and named the bodies the "Liang Islanders" (liangdao ren). The Liang Islanders are not only the oldest Neolithic Age human skeletons ever to be found in the Min River basin area, they are also the oldest skeletons found in the Austronesian area of Taiwan. DNA analysis from 2013 further showed that the Liang Islanders' matrilineal line was most closely connected to the Austronesian lineage in Taiwan and the Philippines (C. Chen 2013).

The discovery of the Liang Islanders rekindled commissioner Yang's aspirations to connect Matsu with China across the Strait, after his plans for a gaming industry stalled. He visited the shell mound in Pingtan, Fujian in order to seek out opportunities to cooperate in archeological missions (Q. Liu 2013), and he held meetings at the Fujian Cultural Center and museum in an attempt to initiate communication and collaboration. He has also fervently participated in the One Belt, One Road initiative in China. For example, at the "21st Century Maritime Silk Road" high-level forum Yang boldly connected the archeological discovery in Matsu and its relationship to the mainland by placing Matsu along the maritime Silk Road:

> Matsu is just beyond the estuary of the Min river. ...It is a pearl along the maritime Silk Road. ...I hope that we can join with Fuzhou to head down the maritime Silk Road together, toward the world and the ocean. (D. Xie 2014)

The close linkage between the DNA of the Liang Islanders and the Austronesians gave Yang another new imaginary with which to attempt to push Matsu out "into the world." He wrote in *Matsu Daily*: "The Liang Islanders do not belong only to Matsu; they belong to the rest of the world even more."[1] He co-organized an international conference with Academia Sinica in Taipei, called "From Matsu to the Southeast Coast of Asia," in 2014 and invited well-known archeologists from around the world. After the conference, he invited academics and reporters, along with ambassadors from Kiribati, Tuvalu, and other Austronesian countries, to travel to Liang Island to advocate for its importance. In his county commissioner office bulletin, he said:

> The discovery of the Liang Islanders will turn Matsu into a new point of origin for the Austronesian people, uniting the two sides of the Strait as we head out toward the greater world, turning "the pearl of Eastern Fujian" into "the world's Liang Island."

Obviously, Yang's thoughts have become increasingly "rhizomorphic," ramifying connections in all directions. Despite all his efforts, however, the Liang Islanders inspired little enthusiasm among Matsu people. Even on *Matsu Online*, netizens have barely followed the findings. They doubted whether the putative connection between Matsu and Austronesia could bring any economic benefits; but the largest barrier to an enthusiastic response from the islanders was that the proposal that Matsu is the origin of the Austronesian people had little resonance among the residents (Xiong 2012). Since people saw no resemblance between Austronesian history and what they understood about themselves, the potential for the development of an imagination was rather restricted.

However, given that the individual imagination frequently comes from subjective experience and an individuated interpretative process (Rapport 2015: 8), it will not simply dissolve even when it does not develop into a social imaginary. For example, after Yang failed in his reelection bid as county commissioner and left public office, he quickly pulled himself together to start building his own "trimaran," his quixotic solution to the difficulties of traversing the Taiwan Strait (Fig. C.1).

This boat is without a doubt his bid to reset himself and strike out towards a new future. Its hull was fabricated from fiber-reinforced plastic

Fig. C.1 Yang Suisheng's handcrafted "Trimaran"
(Photo by Yang Suisheng)

and the outriggers made from used chlorine containers (such containers are discarded by waterworks after use in the disinfecting process), a demonstration of his long-term commitment to environmental protection. Vests designed during his reelection campaign were sewn together to make the sail, the message on which reads: "Pearl of Eastern Fujian, the World's Liang Island" (*mindong zhizhu, shijie liangdao*). Another motivation behind the sail, as he explained, was to commemorate his great-grandmother, whom he never met. As a sailmaker, it is said that her craftsmanship was exquisite; she had even made sails for the well-known "pirate" of early twentieth-century Matsu, Lin Yihe (Chapter 1). The completion of the boat demonstrates Yang's knowledge and competence developed from many years of research on sea vessels and the ocean itself. He intends to sail the ship from Nangan to the Liang Islands, and has even designed plans to turn it into an airborne sea-craft, dreaming that his boat will one day be able to fly. When that happens, the people of Matsu will no longer have to endure arduous travel to Taiwan.

A similar case is that of Cao Yixiong, who first proposed the Community Building Project in Matsu (Chapter 8); his dream of turning Matsu into an "Eastern Fujian Culture Village" was put into practice, but it proved to be largely unworkable. He then reconciled himself to the temple building project, even though it was not part of his original plan or interest. Along the way, he also went from being a member of the legislature to the chairmanship of the Cultural Bureau (he was appointed by Yang Suisheng). Following Commissioner Yang's failed bid for reelection, however, Cao reluctantly left office and asked himself what he should do with the rest of his life. Opportunely, the army on Matsu had recently disengaged from more than one hundred military fortresses and installations and had turned them over to the county government. Cao thought that he might apply for permission to "reutilize unused space" at Military Base No. 12 near Ox Horn, and thereby persist in his goal of preserving and revitalizing old dwellings. It was a very ambitious plan, however; now that he had no access to government resources, how would he manage to convert a military base? In the midst of his indecision, he remembered his itinerant days as a young man in Taiwan, and the novels with which he had whiled away his time. He recalled in particular one of the moving stories told in *The Thorn Birds*:

> There is a legend about a bird which sings just once in its life, more sweetly than any other creature on the face of the earth. From the moment it leaves the nest it searches for a thorn tree, and does not rest until it has found one. Then, singing among the savage branches, it impales itself upon the longest, sharpest spine. And, dying, it rises above its own agony to out-carol the lark and the nightingale. One superlative song, existence the price. But the whole world stills to listen, and God in His heaven smiles. For the best is only bought at the cost of great pain...Or so says the legend. (Colleen McCullough 1977)

He told himself that in the latter stage of his life, he should find a tree and sing out his last beautiful song, just like the thorn birds in the book. In that way, he would be able to demonstrate his own worth. He named the abandoned military site "The Thorn Bird" (*ciniao*) and has since expended great effort to renovate it singlehandedly, declining every offer of help and finally even moving there himself to live (Fig. C.2).

Today he runs a bed-and-breakfast at the site. Under his careful management, it has not only become a popular scenic spot in Matsu,

Fig. C.2 Cao Yixong at the renovated military base
(Photo by Chen Junwei)

but also the site of many art events. Now, he cuts a figure quite unlike a typical government functionary: darkly tanned, lean, and dressed, sometimes eccentrically, for his own pleasure. When he was first elected to the legislature, he always put on formal Western suits, but as he started to promote community building, he began to wear more culturally significant traditional Chinese dress, and now often wears a comfortable sarong. We may say that what he is doing now "...is an obstinate search for a style of existence, a way of being" (Moore 2011: 2). He has steadfastly continued to pursue and reveal his unique self; his self-stylization extends to every tree and bush in his own seaside corner.

Finally, what happened to Cao Yaping, who came to prominence during the public debates over the gaming referendum? Although her side in the referendum failed, Cao Yaping seems more disturbed by the fact that at the time she did not have a good grasp of the military history of Matsu and so was unable to understand the views of the older generation. When she returned to school in Taiwan to finish her Master's degree, she chose to research the fishing economy of Matsu during the wartime era in an attempt to come to terms with the island's history. After graduating, she came back to Matsu to work. In her webzine, she writes about her experiences in Matsu—she records her daily life, or interviews with people. For example, in an article called "The history of my family business," she records how her parents ran a shop catering to soldiers during military rule. She is looking for ways to understand Matsu and to reconnect with it.

Many other post-martial-law youngsters have similar confusion about themselves and their place in the world. With Cao, they formed the "Development Association of Matsu Youth" (*Matsu qingnian fazhan xiehui*) after the referendum. They gather together regularly to read and discuss, and they have started to participate actively in public affairs. In 2017, several people at the fisherman's association meeting suggested relaxing certain restrictions on fishing boats that hire Chinese workers, allowing them to spread nets beyond 300 meters from the islands' coasts (down from an earlier limit of 1,000 meters). Realizing that most of these boats were actually financed by Chinese investors rather than by locals, Cao Yaping and the Youth Association launched a vigorous "Defend Matsu's Ocean" movement. Thanks to their efficiency and finesse in internet advocacy, more than 2,000 online and paper signatures (out of 6,000 long-term residents) were collected within three days, thus preventing the motion from going forward and conserving the coastal resources.

Over the past few years, the group has continuously sought a place that could serve as a "base" (*jidi*) from which to develop their Association. Recently, they found a long-abandoned building which used to be an elementary school during the WZA. It occupies a mere 18 *ping* (640 square feet) and was originally a branch of the main school intended for first through third graders in Zhuluo. Yet the school does offer something special: the basement is an air raid shelter, where Zhuluo villagers hid from bombs during the military period. The Youth Association members felt that the space holds a special significance, and that it could connect them directly to the era of martial law. After persistent efforts, they finally got permission from the government and local villagers to use

Fig. C.3 Youth Association members together cleaning up the
abandoned Zhuluo Elementary School
(Photo by Cai Jiaru)

the abandoned school. They themselves rehabilitated the building, which
had been in disuse for fifty-three years (Figure C.3). It has become a base
for them to relearn the lost way of living on the island with its marine
ecology. For example, they regularly invite elders to share with them how
to collect seasonal shellfish and sea weeds, and make Matsu dishes out of
them; many of these practices were neglected or suppressed during the
military rule.

At the end of a long conversation, I once asked Yaping what they
intended to achieve now that they had found a base to work from. She
responded resolutely with a clear set of goals:

> We intend to learn about oceanic culture, and to understand the wartime
> history of Matsu. We want to redefine Matsu with respect to Taiwan and the
> rest of the world, rather than just returning to our ancient Fuzhou roots. We
> hope to open up this space, to make it a place where people across the
> generations can gather and learn together.

Eventually, however, she shook her head and admitted:

> To tell you the truth, I don't know what we really intend to become. All we can do is to keep exploring together with our members and the residents here. We hope someday that we can "become ourselves" (*chengwei women ziji*)!

I was thrilled to learn that the goal that she and the young members have set for themselves, out of this deserted school with a military history, is no longer self-stylization, as is the aim of Cao, or genealogical reconnection with ancestors, as Yang yearns for. Rather, by extending connections laterally and by cooperating with each other, they are pursuing a new ethic of belonging and living—in this new mode of being they could finally "become themselves."

In the present day, people diverge not only in their past experiences, but also in their increasingly varied individual imaginations whose scopes have been greatly enlarged. The question of how people in the twenty-first century can come together to face the future is a very thorny issue, and one which resists a tidy summing-up. Starting from the imagining subjects and the mediating mechanisms they deploy to reach out to others is important, and indeed imperative, for us to understand the contemporary world.

Glossary

a'bing'ge shengyi	阿兵哥生意
a'bing mei	阿兵妹
Bade	八德
Baima Zunwang	白馬尊王
Baiquan	白犬
Banli	坂里
banzhang	班長
baodao	寶島
baojia	保甲
baosong zhidu	保送制度
baozhang	保長
Beigan	北竿
bian'e	匾額
Caozhu	曹朱
Changle	長樂
Changzhu Matsu	長住馬祖
Changzhu Taiwan	長住台灣
Chen Furen	陳夫人
Chen Jiangjun	陳將軍
Chen Jinggu	陳靖姑
chengwei women ziji	成為我們自己
chengxiang gongzuofang	城鄉工作坊
da santong	大三通
dakuai	大塊
daliao guawang	搭寮掛網
danda shuang buda	單打雙不打
Danan	大湳
Daoguan	道光
Dawang	大王
dedao	得道

Di'er juntuan diyi lujun siling	第二軍團第一路軍司令
Donghai budui	東海部隊
Dongju	東莒
Dongyin	東引
Dongyin shendu zhilyu	東引深度之旅
dongyuan kanluan shiqi	動員戡亂時期
du yige weilai	賭一個未來
duo yige xiwang	多一個希望
E'tsai iong pei'ngiang, metsai iong ngoung'ngiang (F.)	寧願生敗家子，不願生傻子
erdeng gongmin	二等公民
erjie	二姐
fangong tiaoban	反共跳板
fan gukun zuozhan	反孤困作戰
feng zhou	封舟
fenghuo shanqiang	烽火山牆
Fujian jiuguo jun	福建救國軍
Fujian xianqian jun	福建先遣軍
Fuxing	復興
Fuzheng	福正
gangnguong si nuongma, me a si nuongne (F.)	甘願死爸爸，不願死媽媽
Gantang	竿塘
gaoshan gao, liushui chang	高山高, 流水長
Gaowuye	高武爺
gongfei baoxing	共匪暴行
gongchuan	貢船
guan	貫
guan, jiao, wei, yang	管, 教, 衛, 養
gu'er	孤兒
guangfu dalu	光復大陸
Hahahou	哈哈猴
hai huna (F.)	海皇帝
haishang gaotie	海上高鐵
haishang shengdao	海上聖道
Haixi jingji qu	海西經濟區
Haixia xi'an jingjiqu	海峽西岸經濟區
hezuo zaochang	合作造廠
hei shuigou	黑水溝
Hongwu	洪武
houzhe weida	後者為大

Huangguanyu	黃官嶼
huawai zhi di	化外之地
huanglung tou mo lou, puh'y tu *luoh tu* (F.)	反正都沒有了，不如賭一賭
huang ngiang nah (F.)	番仔搭
huixiang	會香
ia hyo ia tshiang (F.)	很騷很嗆
ia puongnëü (F.)	有本事
jiaju	家聚
Jiangtian	江田
jiazhang	甲長
jidi	基地
Jieshou	介壽
Jinma binguan	金馬賓館
jinma jiang	金馬獎
jinma linshi jieyan ling	金馬臨時戒嚴令
jinqu	禁區
Jinsha	津沙
Juntongju	軍統局
junmin yijia	軍民一家
kau seeming, ou tsieng theing (F.)	猴子洗臉，有錢賺
kho ngie lang (F.)	去外山
khui sydoung (F.)	開祠堂
kuo lang (F.)	過山
Lai Matsu, song guandao sanri you	來馬祖，送關島三日遊
lang a liang (F.)	兩個聲
laoban niang	老闆娘
Laobanniang, wo genni jiang	老闆娘，我跟你講
Lauma / nuongne sei thoeyngkhu (F.)	妻子/奶娘是桶箍
leimeng	雷蒙
leimengdi	雷盟弟
Lemah Toyuong (F.)	犁麥大王
liangdao ren	亮島人
Lianjiang	連江
Lianjiang Xianzhi	連江縣志
Lingnan	嶺南
Linshui Furen	臨水夫人
loeyh kang be (F.)	六間排
Luoyuan	羅源
mapi bao	馬屁報

maogan	茅干
Matsu dizhonghai, boyi dujiacun	馬祖地中海, 博弈度假村
Matsu Liedao Zhi	馬祖列島志
Matsu qingnian fazhan xiehui	馬祖青年發展協會
Matsu shi womende jia	馬祖是我們的家
Matsu shoubeiqu zhihuibu	馬祖守備區指揮部
Matsu xingzheng gongshu	馬祖行政公署
Matsu yun tai wang	馬祖雲台網
Matsu zhi sheng	馬祖之聲
Mephiu, metu, talouh kungtsu (F.)	不賭不嫖，打落公祖
meng	盟
Matsu	馬祖
Matsu zhishu	馬祖之書
Mazu	媽祖
Meishi	梅石
Meizhou	湄洲
Mindong wenhua cun	閩東文化村
mindong zhizhu, shijie liangdao	閩東之珠，世界亮島
minhai wangchao	閩海王朝
minsu	民俗
mo leing'uah, mo hiuong (F.)	沒生活 沒希望
nang nguang (F.)	南館
Nangan	南竿
Nanri	南日
neizao	內造
ngie kiang (F.)	義子
nguoyh (F.)	牛角
nguoyh biah (F.)	牛角陂
niangjia	娘家
Ningde	寧德
Noeyng ne duoli, suo tshuo iengnongnong.	有媽媽在，一家團圓；沒有
noeyng ne namo, tshuo tsiu sang lo (F.)	媽媽，家就散了
Ox Horn	牛角
pa ing (F.)	白犬
pe mang (F.)	擺暝
phiuphiu tutu, tsy'a thotsu (F.)	嫖嫖賭賭，自己作主
pi pe'ou (F.)	比牌九
piang tshoung (F.)	拼村
po uong (F.)	報亡
pohuai shanliang fengsu	破壞善良風俗

Putian	莆田
Qianlong	乾隆
Qiaozi	橋仔
Qinbi	芹壁
qingding shiliu, Matsu haozan	情定十六, 馬祖好讚
quanding kaoshi	詮定考試
Ren'ai	仁愛
re'nao	熱鬧
Sandu'ao	三都澳
sanmin zhuyi mofan xian	三民主義模範縣
se bieng nang (F.)	西邊山
Shanlong	山隴
shequ fazhan xiehui	社區發展協會
shequ zongti yingzao	社區總體營造
shenming caineng zuode wen	神明才坐得穩
shengmu feng	聖母峰
Siwei	四維
shi	市
shi'er jiemei	十二姊妹
shisan jinchai	十三金釵
shisi xiongmei	十四兄妹
shiye	事業
si da baozheng	四大保證
Sunlong	孫隴
suoh ba piengtang tang suoh kaui kho teiuang (F.)	一把扁擔挑所有家當到台灣
suoh ba tsheing yong lo suoh tshuo noeyng (F.)	一把秤養一家人
suongmuong (F.)	上門
taihai baolei	台海堡壘
Taima lun	台馬輪
Taima zhi xing	台馬之星
tanjing	探警
techan	特產
thoai ia siuai (F.)	討海很苦
Tian'ao	田澳
Tianhou	天后
Tieban	鐵板
Tie nëüng kungnaumo tuai, tie noeyng to sieh (F.)	誰的拳頭大，誰就拿去吃

ting noey o (F.)	陳大哥
ting nuo (F.)	停厝
toey o (F.)	大澳
toeyng' ing uonghua khoeyh tshui hai (F.)	東引黃花乞嘴害
tsau thauleing (F.)	跑前面
tshialiang (F.)	柴埕
tshui ia ie (F.)	嘴很饞
tso silai (F.)	做死事
tso tshuh' iu (F.)	做出幼
tsynoeyng niu na pienglau iu,	女人尿即使變油, 還是要男
toungmuonoeyng tang kho ma (F.)	人擔去賣
tuai luoh lieh tshuo, sa suoh tai (F.)	大石砌厝, 細石塞
tuoyou ping	拖油瓶
tuong tshuoli (F.)	回厝裏
uong' ua huah ya thie, mo huah ya	有黃花也哭，沒黃花也哭
thie (F.)	
waizao	外造
wenjiao xiehui	文教協會
Wenshi	文石
wode jia zai dalu shang	我的家在大陸上
wode xin zai zhuangqiuchang	我的心在撞球場
women lai wan	我們來玩
Wuling Gong	五靈公
Wuxian Gong	五顯公
wuyu	五育
Xifang gongsi	西方公司
xiang	鄉
xiaomie zhu mao hanjian	消滅朱毛漢奸
Xiju	西莒
Xiyang	西洋
Xiyin	西引
xiao san tong	小三通
Yazhou dizhonghai	亞洲地中海
yi cun yi xuexiao	一村一學校
yinian siji buyiyang	一年四季不一樣
yitian bu jiandao ni, wo jiu xin	一天不見到你, 我就心癢癢
yangyang	
yuanfang de tongnian	遠方的童年
yue quan shi	月全蝕
Zao'an Jinmen	早安金門

zhangwo yige jihui	掌握一個機會
zhen	鎮
Zhongtong	中統
zhuade yuejin, dude yuexiong	抓得越緊，賭得越凶

Endnotes

Introduction

1 Gammeltoft 2014; Gaonkar 2002; Kelty 2005; Marcus 1995.
2 Anderson investigates how print capitalism made the nationally imagined community possible by pointing out that although printing was invented in China perhaps 500 years earlier than in Europe, its impact there was not revolutionary precisely because of the absence of capitalism. Nationalism, he forcefully argues, was mechanically created by reproduced print-language capable of dissemination through the market (1991 [1983]: 44).

While Anderson makes the case that print capitalism laid the base for national consciousness, it was Harvey who thoroughly delved into the development of late capitalism and linked it to the appearance of postmodern imaginations. He elucidated how the flexible accumulation of capital compressed spatial and temporal experiences, which further mediated postmodern ways of thinking and doing (1990: 201). The cultural forms of postmodernism are the consequence of this mode of capitalism, or to follow Harvey's later usage, neoliberalism (2005).
3 This perspective is especially clear in recent work on southern and eastern Africa. Deploying a sharp sense of the economic changes in South Africa, Comaroff and Comaroff illustrated how the people's mounting preoccupation with zombie workers cannot be separated from neoliberal capitalism, which has created new classes, translocalized the division of labor, and rendered the financial order autonomous from production (1999; 2000; 2002). Zombies are thus an imaginative play, and a criticism of the world gone awry through grotesque figures imbued with despair, destruction, and terror (Comaroff and Comaroff 2000: 316). Similarly, Weiss has shown that the fantasies of urban youths in Tanzania, concretized in newly appearing barbershops (*kinyozi*), must be understood from the vantage of neoliberal reform in that country. Importantly, he points out that barbershops are forms of aspiration (2009: 36) that create possibilities and hope for young men. In these shops, where tradition and modernity are conflated, Tanzanians

273

imaginatively articulate the actual and the possible, and act on a world they remake for themselves.

4 I also conducted fieldwork on the island of Dongju; for more information, see Tsao and Lin (2013).

Chapter 1

1 Liang Kejia, *Sanshan zhi*, in vol. 2 of *Siku quanshu zhenben* liuji (Taipei: Shangwu, 1976), 7a.

2 Du Zhen, (1684) *Yuemin xunshi jilue*, in vol. 5 of *Siku quanshu zhenben* siji (Taipei: Shangwu, 1973), 53b.

3 *Fujian tongzhi* in the Qianlong years mentions that "in Hongwu 20, people were moved to the county seat, and the two mountains were deserted." See Hao Yulin et al. eds., *Fujian tongzhi* in vol. 3 of *Wenyuan ge siku quanshu* (Beijing: Shangwu, 2006 [a reprint based on the copy in the National Library of China]), 23a.

4 Huang Zhongzhao ed., *Bamin tongzhi*, in vol. 4 of *Beijing tushuguan guji zhenben congkan* shibu (Beijing: Shumu wenxian, 1988), 24a.

5 *Li* is a Chinese measure of distance. Its definition has varied in history. In general, it can be said that one *li* is roughly 1/3 of a mile (1/2 km) (Wilkinson 2013).

6 Xu Jingxi, *Fuzhou fuzhi*, eds. Lu Zengyu et al., in vol. 13 of *Zhongguo fangzhi congshu* (Taipei: Chengwen, 1967 [reprint based on the copy in Qing Qianlong 19]), 20a–b.

7 Yu Yonghe, *Bihai jiyou*, in *Taiwan wenxian congkan* no. 44 (Taipei: Taiwan yinhang, 1959), 41.

8 Taiwan yinhang jingji yanjiushi ed., *Fujian shengli*, in *Taiwan wenxian congkan* no. 199 (Taipei: Taiwan yinhang, 1964), 707.

9 *Qing shilu, Gaozong chunhuangdi shilu* juan 1363 (Beijing: Zhonghua shuju, 1986–7), Entry Jiachen on the 27th day of the 9th month of Qianlong 55, 292.

10 *Qing shilu, Gaozong chunhuangdi shilu* juan 1363, Entry Jiachen on the 27th day of the 9th month of Qianlong 55, 292.

11 Xu Shiying, "Minhai xunji" (Patrolling records around the sea of Min), in *Xu shiying* ed. by Anhuisheng zhengxie wenshi ziliao weiyuanhui and Dongzixian zhengxie wenshi ziliao weiyuanhui (Beijing: Zhongguo wenshi chubanshe, 1989), 77.

12 The nautical charts generally known as "Zheng He's Nautical Charts" were originally entitled "Zi baochuanchang kaichuan cong Longjiangguan chushui zhidi waiguo zhufan tu" (Charts for leaving Baochuan shipyard, sailing to the sea through Longjiang Pass and directly heading for foreign countries) in *Wubei zhi* ed. by Mao Yuanyi in *Xuxiu siku quanshu* juan 240 (Shanghai: Shanghai guji, 1995), 2b–24a. For relevant studies, see Xu Yuhu, "Zheng he xia xiyang hanghaitu kao" (A study on the nautical charts for the Great Voyages of Zheng He), *Dalu zazhi* 25 (12) (Taipei, 1962).

13 Du Zhen, *Yuemin xunshi jilue* juan 5, 53b–54a.

14 Viceroy of Minzhe Yude et al., "Wei nahuo zai yanghang jieshou huo daofei ji jiezang fuyi gefan shenming fenbie banli gongzhe juzoushi" (A deferential

memorandum reporting in detail how the main culprits, accessories and helpers that robbed the foreign firm were caught and sentenced), in *Gongzhongdang Jiaqingchao zouzhe* 12 (Taipei: Guoli gugong bowuyuan, 1993), entry in the 2nd month of Jiaqing 7 (vol. 2), 714.

15 "In Jiaqing 10, Cai Qian ordered this criminal to build shelters in Qinjiao Mountain in outlying Gantang …and to exact prescribed taxes from each fishing household." "The criminal Wu Xingdi, having his domicile of origin in Changle, procured rice for pirates four times and transported the rice to Qinjiao, where the pirates lived." "The five criminals Zheng Lian, Ke Zhe, Zhu Ding, Zeng Xun and Chen Dong testified that they were all hanging nets in Qinjiao and were forced by Cai Qian and his followers to fetch freshwater for them once." See Taiwan yinhang jingji yanjiushi ed. *Tai'an huilu xinji*, in *Taiwan wenxian congkan* 205th ser. (Taipei: Taiwan yinhang, 1964), 199, 123, 124.

16 The National Bureau of Investigation and Statistics, commonly known as Juntongju, was the military intelligence agency of the Republic of China before 1946.

17 By marked contrast, in my fieldwork in the agricultural communities in southern Taiwan (W. Lin 2015), people referred to the father as the "bucket hoop" of the family.

18 The cited passage has been edited for fluency.

19 This is not always the case now; some families have already bought altars for their ancestors. However, this is obviously influenced by Taiwan, and the altars are all purchased from there.

20 C. Cao (2011).

Chapter 2

1 Around 2014 a Matsu solider discovered a big wall painting of the United States map while stripping old paint off the walls at the site in Nangang. The map presents a lively panorama of the characteristic of each state. It was probably painted out of nostalgia by the American soldiers from the USA Military Assistance and Advisory Group who were stationed in Matsu sometime between the 1950–70s. Outside this former base stands a faded stele erected by an American colonel in 1958.

2 Over time this was reduced to ten days of training once a year.

3 Szonyi's book on Jinmen has shown in great detail how the military's policies and construction of infrastructure deeply influenced the islanders' social life. I won't repeat those demonstrations here.

4 The precise layout of the houses has been modified to protect the identity of the residents.

Chapter 3

1 Junguan hongpishu (2002), *Matsu Online,* July 28.
2 Yumingzheng (1961), *Matsu Daily,* June 9.
3 Y. Cao 2017: 52.

4 Y. Cao 2017: 52.
5 Y. Cao 2017: 52.
6 Nanbeigan yumin (1974), *Matsu Daily*, March 28.
7 Y. Cao 2017: 55.
8 Y. Cao 2017: 57.
9 Cao qije (1964), *Matsu Daily*, October 29.
10 Yuye xietiaohui (1965), *Matsu Daily*, April 14.
11 Yuye fuzeren (1965), *Matsu Daily*, May 21.
12 C. Liu (1965), *Matsu Daily*, May 30.
13 Sun (1966), *Matsu Daily*, October 17.
14 Xiapi jue (1974), *Matsu Daily*, June 30.
15 Zhihuiguan guanhuai (1962), *Matsu Daily*, August 15.
16 (Zhihuiguan) jian (1964), *Matsu Daily*, February 3.
17 Silingguan deyi (1966), *Matsu Daily*, January 18. *Jin* is the local unit of weight; in Matsu, 1 *jin* is equivalent to 500 grams.
18 Silingguan gwanxin (1967), *Matsu Daily*, November 18.
19 Chenzhi (1968), *Matsu Daily*, July 1.
20 Dafang (1969), *Matsu Daily*, January 13.
21 H. Liu 2017: 42.
22 H. Liu 2017: 44.
23 H. Liu 2017: 44.
24 H. Liu 2017: 83. NT$ (New Taiwan dollar) is Taiwan's currency. US$1 is equivalent to around NT$30.
25 Matsu Zhongxue (1960), *Matsu Daily*, June 25.
26 I conducted this interview in 2012. They swore their sisterhood in the 1970s.

Chapter 4

1 Lianjiang xianzheng (1959), *Matsu Daily*, February 1.
2 Chedi genjue (1965), *Matsu Daily*, August 13. Genjue dubo (1972), *Matsu Daily*, October 9.
3 Jinju chahuo (1972), *Matsu Daily*, October 7.
4 The WZA chair came to supervise the burning, see Du nai (1970). *Matsu Daily*, July 4. Other reports recording the public burning of gambling paraphernalia appeared in *Matsu Daily* in the following years: 1966, 1970, 1972, 1973, 1975, 1976, 1978, 1979.
5 Chedi genjue (1965), *Matsu Daily*, August 13. Du nai (1970), *Matsu Daily*, July 4.
6 Yan (1979), *Matsu Daily*, April 19.
7 Dujue xiansan (1970), *Matsu Daily*, August 2.
8 Zhengweihui chongshen (1982), *Matsu Daily*, January 20.
9 Minzhong tigong (1983), *Matsu Daily*, October 18.
10 Y. Li (1965), *Matsu Daily*, August 3.
11 A mahjong table, which is square in shape, can easily be kept folded to save space when not playing.
12 Dongyin diqu (1976), *Matsu Daily*. April 9.

13 The fish are able to float on the surface of the water by inflating their air bladders. I thank Professor Jen-Chieh Shiao, Institute of Oceanography, National Taiwan University, for supplying information about the yellow croaker.
14 Z. Chen 2013: 104.
15 Indeed, after the WZA was abolished and the government stopped making arrests, many said "it wasn't exciting anymore, so a lot of people just quit."

Chapter 5

1 For the process of democratization in Taiwan, see *Politics in Taiwan: Voting for Democracy* (Rigger 1999).
2 Banli guoxiao (2010a; 2010b).
3 For discussions of the physical and online virtual world, see Boellstorff (2008, 2012); Castells (1996); Miller and Slater (2000); Miller and Horst (2012).
4 According to current officials, this was due to the scarcity of arable land on the Matsu Islands.
5 See H. Liu's (2016: 22) article "Air-Raid Shelter," which describes an associate village head who commandeers a local yam field in order to build an air-raid shelter.
6 For example, see J. Liu's (1994) report on the Juguang villager, Yang Jiaojin.
7 The petition eventually garnered 1,402 names, a significant portion of the permanent resident population of 5,000 to 6,000.

Chapter 6

1 Liang Island is located in the north of Beigan. During an island exploration trip initiated by a Matsu comissioner in 2011, archeological remains were discovered there. They will be discussed in the conclusion of this book.
2 For example, Armstrong 2000; Kenny 1999; Winter and Sivan 1999.

Chapter 8

1 In 2000, the Taiwan government implemented the "three small links" as temporary channels connecting Taiwan and China through Matsu and Jinmen at a time when an official agreement on cross-strait communication still had not been reached. However, it was a unilateral policy not accepted by China.
2 After several years in community development, Chen Chi-Nan took over the position of chairman of the CCA, and his attitudes have slightly changed. For example, he no longer argues that religion had not existed in the public domain. He said: "During the Qing dynasty, Taiwan saw a lot of ethnic conflicts. Religion at that time played an important role. Temple grounds became places for people to discuss public affairs" (Chen Chi-Nan 2004). Nevertheless, he still maintained that "'Arts and culture' should be the main

public platform, in which a 'contemporary identity' should replace a 'traditional [religious] identity', so a new 'community of arts and culture' can be formed" (ibid.). In other words, his main thesis is still that contemporary arts and cultural activities should replace traditional religious practices in creating new communities.

3 The literature of research on community building projects is huge. For a recent and comprehensive analysis, see A. Lee (2017).

4 Under martial law in the 1970s, few presses in Taiwan published foreign works of literature or scholarship. Zhiwen Press established its pioneering "New Wave Series" in 1967 and began to systematically translate and publish essential Western books, including works of literature, philosophy, psychology, music, film, fine arts, history, and so on. The "New Wave Series" opened a window onto the rest of the world; it is difficult to overstate its influence in shaping the thought of a whole generation of Taiwanese.

5 Yang's research on southern Taiwan describes a very similar phenomenon (H. Yang 2007: 268).

6 The two days include the one earlier chosen for political unification, and the one selected in this second negotiation process.

7 A "fire-barrier gable" refers to a roof that is ridged, like fire moving along the outer walls of the Matsu temple, which can prevent fire from spreading.

8 The values are "five qualities of life" (*wuyu*), which include ethical, intellectual, physical, social, and aesthetic training (Timing 2011).

Chapter 9

1 Tianhou, literally "The Queen of the Heaven," is another term for Goddess Mazu.

2 Tianhougong zuori (1964). *Matsu Daily*, May 5.

3 Jiabin huilin (1970) *Matsu Daily*, January 24; Lu zhuwei (1971), *Matsu Daily*, September 17; Wu Jinzan (1978). *Matsu Daily*, January 8.

4 China initiated small-scale trade exchanges between its southeast provinces and Taiwan in 1994, but these were regarded as unofficial.

5 On the importance of carrying deity statues in temple exchanges, see Lin 2015.

Chapter 10

1 The forerunner of the Taima Ferry was a ferry across the Seto Inland Sea of Japan. It began service in 1985 and was bought by the Lianjiang county government from Japan in 1997, becoming Taiwan's longest serving ship (Pan 2010).

2 Each year, from October to the following March, northeast monsoons produce a very high rate of waves at level 9 or above, and the Taima Ferry attempts fewer voyages.

3 On April 29, 2017, as the ferry was returning to Matsu from Keelung, it was stuck at sea for seven hours. See X. Wang (2017).

4 For example, see S. Yang (2010) and Qiuhua Liu (2010).

5 In 2017, Jinmen voted on whether to allow the gaming industry, but the proposal failed.

6 Their website can be found at www.worldcasinodirectory.com/owners/ global-gaming-asset-management (Accessed December 25, 2017).

7 Code 1: less than 800 meters; Code 2: 800–1200 meters; Code 3: 1200–1800 meters; Code 4: more than 1800 meters.

8 For "another source of hope," see pinkheart (2012), for "seize an opportunity," see Feimaotui (2012), and for "bet on the future," see Hongbeiwang (2012).

Conclusion

1 Huigu 101 (2012).

Bibliography

admin. 2005. "Benzhan huiyuan zhuce, dengru, shengji, wangji mima ji qita shiyong wenti Q&A" (Member's Registration, Login, Upgrade, Forgetting PIN, etc. Q&A) *Matsu Online*, May 26. http://webarchive.ncl .edu.tw/archive/disk36/94/59/81/05/67/201606163005/20160617/web/matsu .idv.tw/topicdetailbc88.html?f=6&t=17773&p=1. (Accessed May 1, 2011).
———. 2008. "Nangan fasheng dahuo, zaiqing canzhong, xianzhang, fu xianzhang dou buzai Matsu." (Fire in Nangan Causes Heavy Losses—Neither County Magistrate nor Vice-Magistrate in Matsu). *Matsu Online*, January 20. www .matsu.idv.tw/topicdetail.php?f=176&t=51092. (Accessed May 1, 2011).
———. 2011a. "Qiuri guo Matsu nangan niujiao xiangdao oujian." (Autumn Scenes from Nangan-Ox Horn Tunnel in Matsu). *Matsu Online*, January 16. www .matsu.idv.tw/topicdetail.php?f=4&t=86689. (Accessed May 1, 2011).
———. 2011b. "LAG henjiu de Sun Xiaohao yu Wang Jingyi hunli zhaopian." (Long Awaited Photos of Wedding of Sun Xiaohao and Wang Jingyi). *Matsu Online*, January 23. www.matsu.idv.tw/topicdetail.php?f=143&t=86888. (Accessed May 1, 2011).
———. 2011c. "Taiwan bendao 40 nian lai diyici faxian de honghou qianniao, Dongyin xianzong." (A Red-throated Loon in 40 years, which hasn't been seen here or in Taiwan for Forty Years, has been Spotted in Dongyin). *Matsu Online*, January 24. www.matsu.idv.tw/topicdetail.php?f=4&t= 86904. (Accessed May 1, 2011).
Aide. 2008. "Shanlong dahuo jishi, tigong gejie cankao!" (Record of the Shanlong Fire, as Observed by Many!). *Matsu Online*, February 15. www .matsu.idv.tw/topicdetail.php?f=2&t=52086. (Accessed March 1, 2010).
Anderson, Benedict. 1991[1983]. *Imagined Communities: Reflections on the Origin and Spread of Nationalism*. London: Verso.
Anhuisheng zhengxie wenshi ziliao weiyuanhui and Dongzixian zhengxie wenshi ziliao weiyuanhui. 1989. *Xu Shiying*. Beijing: Zhongguo wenshi chubanshe.
Antony, Robert. 2003. *Like Froth Floating on the Sea: The World of Pirates and Seafarers in Late Imperial South China*. Berkeley: Institute of East Asian Studies.
Appadurai, Arjun. 1996. *Modernity at Large: Cultural Dimensions of Globalization*. Minneapolis: University of Minnesota Press.

2004. "The Capacity to Aspire: Culture and the Terms of Recognition." In *Culture and Public Action: A Cross-Disciplinary Dialogue on Development Policy*, eds. Vijayendra Rao and Michael Walton, pp. 59–84. Stanford, CA: Stanford University Press.

Armstrong, Karen. 2000. "Ambiguity and Remembrance: Individual and Collective Memory in Finland." *American Ethnologist* 27(3): 591–608.

Axel, Brian. 2003. "Poverty of the Imagination." *Anthropological Quarterly* 76(1): 111–33.

Banli guoxiao. 2010a. ""Heng "sao banli–banli guoxiao suimo" saojie huodong." (Clean Up Banli: Banli Elementary year-end street sweeping event) *Matsu Online*, December 22. www.matsu.idv.tw/topicdetail.php?f=143&t=85969. (Accessed July 28, 2011).

2010b. "Banli guoxiao huanle qing yedan: handong songnuan yimai yuanyouhui." (Banli Elementary Says Merry Christmas: Winter warmth charity bazaar traveling event) *Matsu Online*, December 24. www.matsu.idv.tw/topicdetail.php?f=143&t=86033. (Accessed July 28, 2011).

Baptandier, Brigitte. 2008. *The Lady of Linshui: A Chinese Female Cult*. Stanford, CA: Stanford University Press.

Basu, Ellen. 1991. "Profit, Loss, and Fate: The Entrepreneurial Ethic and the Practice of Gambling in an Overseas Chinese Community." *Modern China* 17(2): 227–59.

Basu, Paul. 2007. *Highland Homecomings: Genealogy and Heritage Tourism in the Scottish Diaspora*. London: Routledge.

Belting, Hans. 2011[2001]. *An Anthropology of Images: Picture, Medium, Body*. Princeton, NJ: Princeton University Press.

Biancheng Huashi. 2008. "Jieshou xinjie huozaiqu qingkuang." (Conditions in the Fire Damaged Area Near Xinjie, Jieshou). *Matsu Online*, January 21. www.matsu.idv.tw/topicdetail.php?f=5&t=51121. (Accessed October 3, 2010).

Biehl, Joao, Byron Good, and Arthur Kleinman. 2007 "Introduction: Rethinking Subjectivity." In Joao Biehl, Byron Good, and Arthur Kleinman eds., *Subjectivity: Ethnographic Investigations*. Berkeley: University of California Press, pp. 1–23

Boellstorff, Tom. 2008. *Coming of Age in Second Life: An Anthropologist Explores the Virtually Human*. Princeton, NJ: Princeton University Press.

2012. "Rethinking Digital Anthropology." In Heather Horst and Daniel Miller eds., *Digital Anthropology*. London: Bloomsbury, pp. 39–60

Bosco, Joseph, Lucia Huwy-Min Liu and Matthew West. 2009. "Underground Lotteries in China: The Occult Economy and Capitalist Culture." *Research in Economic Anthropology* 29: 31–62.

Boyer, Dominic and Claudio Lomnitz. 2005. "Intellectuals and Nationalism: Anthropological Engagements." *Annual Review of Anthropology* 34: 105–20.

Cai, Yixuan, Xinhong Li, Defeng Ceng, and Zaixin Tang. 2013. "Guo Taiming chu fazhan boyi: Tamshui she tequ genghao." (Guo Taiming Urges Development of Gambling: Better to Do It in Tamshui). *Liberty Times*, February 19. https://news.ltn.com.tw/news/life/paper/654798. (Accessed February 10, 2014).

Cao, Changbi. 2011. *Fujian changle tantou houfu caozhu caoxing zupu.* (The Geneaology of the Cao Lineage from Caozhu Village, Tantou (Houfu) Town, Changle City, Fujian Province) Self-published.

Cao, Chongwei. 2009a. "Tiaozhan shengmufeng, Li xiaoshi bei Mazu jinshen chufa." (Challenging Mt. Everest: Li Xiaoshi Sets Out Carrying the Statue of Goddess Mazu on His Back). *Matsu Daily,* March 14.

2009b. "Bei Mazu deng shengmufeng, Li xiaoshi zaiyu fanxiang." (Climbing Mt. Everest with the Statue of Goddess Mazu on His Back: Li Xiaoshi Returns with Honor). *Matsu Daily,* June 7.

2012a. "Taiwan Weidner gongsi: 'Yazhou dizhonghai jihua.'" (Taiwan Weidner Co.: "Asian Mediterranean Plan"). *Matsu Daily,* March 2.

2012b. "William Weidner yihui xianshen, shuoming houxu zuowei ji shixian sida chengnuo juexin." (William Weidner Appears at Legislative Meeting to Explain Follow-Up and Reaffirm Commitment to His Four Big Promises). *Matsu Daily,* September 15.

Cao, Eryuan. 1988. "Chaoliu dangbuzhu." (You Can't Stop the Tides). In Jiaguo Liu ed. *Wode jiaxiang shi zhandi: jinma wenti mianmian guan.* (My Hometown is a Military Frontline: A Comprehensive Analysis of the Jinmen-Matsu Question). Taipei: Liu Jiaguo, pp. 160–1

"Cao Qijie yukuai biaoshi, yudai xiaojian hexiao naishi yi da dezheng." (Cao Qijie Is Pleased to Announce that Loans Will Be Reduced or Forgiven in an Act of Benevolent Governance). 1964. *Matsu Daily,* October 29.

Cao, Shunguan. 1978. "Cong Matsu renkou waiqian lun defang jingji fazhan." (Local Economic Development through the Lens of Matsu Emigration). *Matsu Daily,* June 7.

2012. "Matsu boyi gongtou gongtinghui: zhengfang Cao Shunguan." (Public Hearing on Public Investment in Gaming on Matsu: Cao Shunguan Speaks in Favor). July 1. www.youtube.com/watch?v=nIwQSsqPJBg. (Accessed July 17, 2014).

Cao, Yaping. 2017. *Buyu hao ku a! Zhandi zhengwu tizhi xia de Matsu yuye ji yumin jiating chujing.* (Fishing Is Hard! Matsu's Fishing Industry and Fishing Households under the WZA). Master's thesis, Department of Social Development, Shihhsin University.

Cao, Yifeng. 2011. "Luyu de jijie, jiajia huhu douhui kandao." (It's Perch Season —And Everyone Knows It). *Matsu Online,* April 2. http://tw.myblog.yahoo .com/tsaoifeng-blog/article?mid=14569&prev=14575&next=14566. (Accessed May 1, 2011).

Cao, Yuanzhang. 2012. "Naxienian, women yiqi fan junguan." (Back in Those Days, We Resisted Military Control Together). *Matsu Daily,* November 7.

Cappelletto, Francesca. 2005a. "Introduction." In Francesca Cappelletto ed., *Memory and World War II: An Ethnographic Approach.* Cambridge: Cambridge University Press, pp. 1–37.

2005b. "Public Memories and Personal Stories: Recalling the Nazi-fascist Massacres." In Francesca Cappelletto ed., *Memory and World War II: An Ethnographic Approach.* Cambridge: Cambridge University Press, pp. 101–30.

Castells, Mannuel. 1996. *The Rise of Network Society.* Oxford: Blackwell.

Casey, Edward. 1976. *Imagining: A Phenomenological Study*. Bloomington: Indiana University Press.

Castoriadis, Cornelius. 1987. *The Imaginary Institution of Society*. Cambridge, MA: The MIT Press.

Chang, Hsun. 2003. *Wenhua mazu: Taiwan Mazu yanjiu Xinyang lunwenji*. (Constructing Mazu: Selected Paper in Mazu Cult). Taipei: Academia Sinica.

"Chedi genjue dubo xingwei, zhengweihui kai zuotanhui." (Eradicating Gambling: Government Committee Forum Commences). 1965. *Matsu Daily*, August 13.

Chen, Caineng. 2010. "Xiangqin jiayou! 'huan wo zuxian tudi' quanxian lianshu yida 687 ren!" (Keep It Up, Neighbors! 'Return My Ancestral Land' Signed by 687 People Across the County!). *Matsu Online*, October 4. www.matsu .idv.tw/topicdetail.php?f=180&t=83706#411465. (Accessed June 6, 2011).

2011a. "Yikuai bu de Liliang!" (The Power of a Piece of Cloth!). *Matsu Online*, May 16. www.matsu.idv.tw/topicdetail.php?f=180&t=89999#429468. (Accessed August 1, 2011).

2011b. "Boyi zai Matsu, buru Mazu zai Matsu!" (Gaming in Matsu isn't As Good As Mazu in Matsu!). *Matsu Online*, September 29 www.matsu.idv.tw/ topicdetail.php?f=180&t=94497&p=1. (Accessed May 10, 2012).

Chen, Chi-Nan. 1990. "Gongmin guojia de zongjiao xinyang he shehu lunli: cong lusuo de 'sheyuelun' tanqi." (The Religious Beliefs and Social Morals of a Civil Nation: On Rousseau's 'Social Contract'). *Dangdai* 54: 66–83.

1992. *Gongmin guojia yishi yu Taiwan zhengzhifazhan*. (Civil National Consciousness and Taiwan's Political Development). Taipei: Yunchen Publishing.

1996a. "Shequ yingzao yu wenhua jianshe." (Community Building and Culture Cultivation). *Lilun yu zhengce* 10(2): 109–16.

1996b. "Taiwan shehui de fazhan yu zhuanxing: shequzongtiyingzao yu difangshengcheng xuexitizhi de jianli." (The development and transformation of Taiwan society: Community building and the construction of local learning mechanisms). In Guoli lishi bowuguan ed., *Jianguan sishizhounian wenhua yishu xueshuyanjiang lunwenji: Taiwan guangfu hou zhonghuawenhua fazhan zhi huigu yu xingsi* (A retrospective on Chinese cultural development since Taiwan's Recovery: Lectures and dissertations on the 40th anniversary of the National Museum of History), (National Museum of History). Taipei: National Museum of History, pp. 19–48.

"Chen Chi-Nan cuisheng xin wenhua yishu gongtongti" (Chen Chi-nan Triggered the Birth of New Community of Arts and Culture). 2004. October 6. http://210.69.67.46/MOC/Code/NewListContent.aspx?id= d8293db2-9d6b-410c-85d4-5be8be1d80dd#. (Accessed December 18, 2012).

Chen, Chi-Nan and Rui-Hua Chen. 1998. "Taiwan shequ yingzao yundong zhi huigu." (A Retrospective on the Community Development Projects in Taiwan). *Yankao baodao* 41: 21–37.

Chen, Chung-Yu. 2013. *Liangdaoren yanjiu* (The Study of Liangdao man). Nangan: Lianjiang County Government.

Chen, Pengxiong. 2011. "Minhang juzhang Yin Chengpeng: Matsu jichang kuojian queding chao Beigan jichang guihua." (Head of the Civil Aviation Bureau Yin Chengpeng: Plans to Expand Matsu's Airports Focus on Beigan Airport). *Matsu Daily*, July 30.

Chen, Qimin. 2009. "Huangguayu de gushi." (The Story of Yellow Croaker). https://blog.xuite.net/andwer1972/twblog/127811900-%E9%BB%83%E7% 93%9C%E9%AD%9A%E7%9A%84%E6%95%85%E4%BA%8B-%E4% BD%9C%E8%80%85%E9%99%B3%E5%85%B6%E6%95%8F. (Accessed January 11, 2018).

Chen, Tianshun. 2008. "Guanbing yu qiangdao." (Government Troops and Bandits). *Matsu Online*, May 15. www.matsu.idv.tw/topicdetail.php?f=2& t=55386. (Accessed May 10, 2012).

Chen, Yiyu. 1999. "Xilun Matsu liedao zhumin qianqi de jiaoyu gaikuang (shang)." (An Analysis of Education in Early Matsu (Part 1)). *Matsu Daily*, May 3.

Chen, Yunru. 2010. *Liangan junshi duizhi xia Matsu Nangan haifang judian junshi kong jian zhi diaocha yanjiu.* (Study of the Military Affairs in the Coastal Defense Strongholds in Matsu's Nangan during the Hostilities across the Taiwan Strait). Master's thesis, School of Architecture, National Taiwan University of Science and Technology.

Chen, Zhilong. 2013. *Xiajiang taohai: Matsu de chuantong yuye.* (Making a Living at Sea: Matsu's Traditional Fishing Economy). Nangan: Lianjiang County Government.

Cheng, Shiyuan. 2010. *Matsu liedao juluo yu minju bianqian zhi yanjiu.* (A Study of the Villages of the Matsu Archipelago and Changes in Local Architecture). Master's thesis, Department for Architecture and Environmental Design, Shu-Te University.

Chengzhi. 1968. "Matsu yizhou." (A Week in Matsu). *Matsu Daily*, July 1.

Chi, Chang-Hui. 2009. "The Death of a Virgin: The Cult of Wang Yulan and Nationalism on Jinmen, Taiwan." *Anthropological Quarterly* 82(3): 669–90.

2015. "Governance and the Politics of Exchange in Militarized Jinmen, 1949–1992." *Taiwan Renlei Xuekan* 13(2): 1–20.

Chiang, Bo-Wei. 2009. "Zongzu, zongci jianzhu jiqi shehui shenghuo: yi fujian jinmen weili." (Lineages, Temple Construction, and Social Life: Jinmen and Fujian). In Weiwen Lin ed., *Haixia liang'an chuantong wenhua yishu yanjiu* (An Exploration of Traditional Cultures and Arts across the Taiwan Strait). Fuzhou: Haichao sheying yishu, pp. 364–98.

2011. "Hunza de xiandaixing: Jindai Jinmen difang shehui de wenhua xiang-xiang jiqi shijian." (Hybrid Modernity: A Study of Cultural Imagination and Practice of the Overseas Chinese in Modern Kinmen). *Minsu Quyi* 174: 185–257.

Chu, Julie. 2010. *Cosmologies of Credit: Transnational Mobility and the Politics of Destination in China.* Durham, NC: Duke University Press.

Chuang, Ya-Chung. 2005. "Place, Identity, and Social Movement: *Shequ* and Neighbourhood Organizing in Taipei City." *Positions* 13(2): 379–410.

Collinson, Richard. 1846. "Navigation of the Min." *The Chinese Repository* 15(5): 230–2.

Comaroff, Jean and John Comaroff. 1999. "Occult Economies and the Violence of Abstraction: Notes from the South African Postcolony." *American Ethnologist* 26(2): 279–303.
    2000. "Millennial Capitalism: First Thoughts on a Second Coming." *Public Culture* 12(2): 291–343.
    2002 "Alien-Nation: Zombies, Immigrants, and Millennial Capitalism." *The South Atlantic Quarterly* 101(4): 779–805.
Crapanzano, Vincent. 2004. *Imaginative Horizons: Literary-Philosophical Anthropology*. Chicago, IL: Chicago University Press.
CTC. 2011. "Matsu zhengfu jiguan xiaolv zhenshi bang! Zhenzheng bang!" (Matsu Government Efficiency Is Terrific! Really Terrific!). *Matsu Online*, April 27. www.matsu.idv.tw/topicdetail.php?f=2&t=89382. (Accessed June 5, 2011).
Dafang. 1969. "Dendai xiapi wangyan yuchuan." (Eagerly Awaiting the Shrimp). *Matsu Daily*, January 13.
Das, Veena. 2008. "Violence, Gender, and Subjectivity." *Annual Review of Anthropology* 37: 283–99.
Davis, Rede. 2006. "All or Nothing: Video Lottery Terminal Gambling and Economic Restructuring in Rural Newfoundland." *Identities: Global Studies in Culture and Power* 13: 503–31.
Deleuze, Gilles and Felix Guattari. 1987. *A Thousand Plateaus: Capitalism and Schizophrenia*. Minneapolis: University of Minnesota Press.
Dijck, José van. 2007. *Mediated Memories in the Digital Age*. Stanford, CA: Stanford University Press.
Donghai shilu bianzhuan weiyuanhui. 1998. *Donghai budui fendou shilu*. (History of the Efforts of Troops in the East China Sea). Yonghe: The East China Sea Association.
"Dongyin diqu huangyu jijie shiqi sou yuchuan hezuo zuo jiedui qianwang zuoye." (Yellow Croker Season in Dongyin: Seventeen Fishing Boats Combined Forces, Working Together Yesterday). 1976. *Matsu Daily*, April 9.
"Du nai baihuozhiyuan, cong fangweibu fenhui duju shuoqi." (Gambling is the Root of Many Evils: Beginning with the Burning of Gambling Paraphernalia by the Health and Welfare Ministry). 1970. *Matsu Daily*, July 4.
Du Zhen. 1684. *Yuemin xunshi jilue* (A Brief Account of Inspecting Tours of Guangdong and Fujian). *Siku quanshu zhenben*, part 4, vol. 113. Taipei: Shangwu, 1973. Reprint.
"Dujue xiansan duanzheng fengqi, fangqu jiang guanzhi duju, bing yange zhixing jindu." (Putting an End to Laziness and Bringing Back a Proper Atmosphere: Garrisons Will Control Gambling Paraphernalia and Strictly Ban Gambling). 1970. *Matsu Daily*, August 2.
Duara, Prasenjit. 1991. "Knowledge and Power in the Discourse of Modernity: The Campaigns against Popular Religion in Early Twentieth-Century China." *The Journal of Asian Studies* 50(1): 67–83.
Enloe, Cynthia. 2000. *Maneuvers: The International Politics of Militarizing Women's Lives*. Berkeley: University of California Press.
Fang, Wenling. 2012. "Weidner kaifa Taipei bangongshi kaimu, yizhi Macau jingyan dao Matsu." (Weidner Opens New Office in Taipei, Bringing its

Experience in Macau to Matsu). *Xin Media*, December 7. Reprinted on https://n.yam.com/Article/20121207038794. (Accessed November 2, 2017).

Feimaotui. 2012. "Qi nianji Matsu ren de xinsheng." (The Voice of Matsu's Seventh Graders). *Matsu Online*, June 13 www.matsu.idv.tw/topicdetail .php?f=2&t=103007. (Accessed February 7, 2015).

Feng, Quanzhong. 2011. "Zhi Matsu jing tianhougong zeng qianzhuwei daoqian qishi." (A Public Apology to the Former Committee Head of the Mazujing Goddess Mazu Temple). *Matsu Online*, January 12. www.matsu.idv.tw/ topicdetail.php?f=2&t=86577&p=1. (Accessed February 1, 2011).

Festa, Paul. 2007. "Mahjong Agonistics and the Political Public in Taiwan: Fate, Mimesis, and the Martial Imaginary." *Anthropological Quarterly* 80: 93–125.

Foucault, Michel. 1977. *Discipline and Punish: The Birth of the Prison*. New York: Vintage.

1985. *The History of Sexuality*. Vol. II: The Use of Pleasure. New York: Pantheon.

1998. *Ethics: Subjectivity and Truth (Essential Works of Michel Foucault, 1954–1984)*. New York: New Press.

Fujian shengli (Regulations of Fujian province). 1873. *Taiwan wenxian shiliao congkan*. Taipei: Taiwan yinhang, 1964. Reprint.

Fujiansheng lianjiangxianzhi bianzhuan weiyuanhui. 1986. *Fujiansheng lianjiang-xianzhi*. (Fujian's Lianjiang County Records). Nangan: Lianjiang County Government.

Fujian tongzhi (A General Gazetteer of Fujian Province). 1737. *Wenyuan ge siku quanshu*. Beijing: Shangwu, 2006. Reprint.

Fuzhou fuzhi (A General Gazetteer of Fujian Prefecture). 1754. *Zhongguo fangzhi congshu*. Taipei: Chengwen, 1967. Reprint.

Gammeltoft, Tine. 2014. "Toward an Anthropology of the Imaginary: Specters of Disability in Vietnam." *Ethos* 42(2): 153–74.

Gaonkar, Dilip. 2002. "Toward New Imaginaries: An Introduction." *Public Culture* 14(1): 1–19.

"Gaozong chunhuangdi shilu." (Veritable Records of the Gaozong Emperor's Reign). 1985. In *Qing shilu*. Beijing: Zhonghua shuju.

Gates, Hill. 1996. "Owner, Worker, Mother, Wife: Taibei and Chengdu Family Businesswomen." In Elizabeth Perry ed., *Putting Class in Its Place: Worker Identities in East Asia*. Berkeley: Institute of East Asian Studies, pp. 127–65.

1999. *Looking for Chengdu: A Woman's Adventures in China*. Ithaca, NY: Cornell University Press.

Geertz, Clifford. 1973. "Deep Play: Notes on the Balinese Cockfight." In *The Interpretation of Cultures*. New York: Basic Books, pp. 412–53.

1980. *Negara: The Theatre State in Nineteenth-century Bali*. Princeton, NJ: Princeton University Press.

Gell, Alfred. 1998. *Art and Agency*. Oxford: Blackwell.

"Genjue dubo exi, Juecai youxiao cuoshi" (Eradiating the Vice of Gambling, Resolving to Choose Efficacious Measures). 1972. *Matsu Daily*, October 9.

Gongzhongdang Jiaqingchao zouzhe (Secret Palace Memorials of the Jiaqing Period). 1993. Taipei: National Palace Museum.

Goossaert, Vincent and David Palmer. 2011. *The Religious Question in Modern China*. Chicago, IL: Chicago University Press.

Guan, Xiuru. 2008. *Matsu diqu baosong zhidu zhi yanjiu* (A Study of the Guaranteed Admission Program in Matsu). Master's thesis, Graduate School of Education, Ming Chuan University.

Guofangbu shizheng bianyiju. 1996. *Guojun waidao diqu jieyan yu zhandi zhengwu jishi*. (The KMT Imposition of Martial Law on Outer Islands and Records of the WZA). Taipei: Ministry of Defense Department of Compilation and Translation of Historical Documents

Gupta, Akhil and James Ferguson. 1997. "Beyond 'Culture': Space, Idenity, and the Politics of Difference." In Akhil Gupta and James Ferguson eds., *Culture, Power, Place: Explorations in Critical Anthropology*. Durham, NC: Duke University Press, pp. 33–51.

Habermas, Jürgen. 1989[1962]. *The Structural Transformation of the Public Sphere: An Inquiry into a Category of Bourgeois Society*. Cambridge, MA.: MIT Press.

"Haixi: cong di fang zhengce dao guojia juece." (The "Strait Economic Zone": from Local Policy to National Decision). 2009. *Fujian Daily*, June 26.

"Haixi tengfei zheng dangshi." (The Strait Economic Zone is ready to soar). 2009. *Fujian Daily*, June 26.

Hampton, Keith and Barry Wellman. 2003. "Neighboring in Netville: How the Internet Supports Community and Social Capital in a Wired Suburb." *City & Community* 2(4): 277–311.

Harvey, David. 1990. *The Condition of Postmodernity: An Enquiry into the Origins of Cultural Change*. Oxford: Blackwell.

2005. *A Brief History of Neoliberalism*. Oxford: Oxford University Press.

Hatfield, D. J. 2010. *Taiwanese Pilgrimage to China: Ritual, Complicity, Community*. New York: Palgrave Macmillan.

2019. "Remediation and Innovation in Taiwanese Religious Sites: Lukang's Glass Temple." *Asian Ethnology* 78(2): 263–88.

Herzfeld, Michael. 1996. *Cultural Intimacy: Social Poetics in the Nation-State*. London: Routledge.

Holland, Dorothy and Kevin Leander. 2004. "Ethnographic Studies of Positioning and Subjectivity: An Introduction." *Ethos* 32(2): 127–39.

Holober, Frank. 1999. *Raiders of the China Coast: CIA Covert Operations during the Korean War*. Annapolis: Naval Institute Press.

Hong, Jingyun. 2013. "Tebie qihua / zhuanfang Taiwan Weidner zongcai William Weidner." (Special Business Plans: In-Depth Report on Taiwan Weidner United Director William Weidner). *Xin Xinwen*, April 3 https://news.xinmedia.com/news_article.aspx?page=2&newsid=4006&type=3#magText. (Accessed February 17, 2014).

Hongbeiwang. 2012. "Huiying." (Response). *Matsu Online*, June 13 www.matsu.idv.tw/topicdetail.php?f=2&t=103007. (Accessed July 17, 2014).

Hsia, Chu-Joe. 1995. "Quanqiu jingji zhong de Taiwan chengshi yu shehui." (Taiwan Cities and Societies with the Global Economy). *Taiwan shehui yanjiu jikan* 20: 57–102.

1999. "Shimin canyu han difang zizhuxing: Taiwan de shequ yingzao." (Community Development in Taiwan: Citizen Participation and Regional Autonomy). *Chengshi yu sheji xuebao* 9/10: 175–85.

Hsu, Chia-Ming. 1973. "Zhanghua pingyuan fulaoke de diyu zuzhi"(Territorial Organization of Hoklorized Hakka in the Changhua Plain). *Zhongyang yanjiuyuan minzuxue yanjiusuo jikan* 36: 165–90.

Huang, Jinhua. 2005. "Huiying 'Leimengdi: anye sanbuqu'." (Response to 'Leimengdi—Nighttime Trilogy'). *Matus Online*, December 9 www.matsu .idv.tw/topicdetail.php?f=226&t=25434&p=1. (Accessed December 9, 2005).

Huang, Ying-Kuei. 2006a. *"Daolun."* (Introduction). In Ying-Kuei Huang and Wen-Te Chen eds., *21 Shiji de difang shehui: Duozhong difang rentong xia de shequnxing yu shehui xiangxiang* (Local Societies of the 21st Century: Sociality and the Social Imaginary for Multi-local Identities). Taipei: Qunxue, pp. 1–45.

2006b. "Shehui guocheng zhong de zhongxinhua yu bianchuihua." (Centralization and peripheralization in the social process). In Ying-Kuei Huang ed., *Renleixue de shiye* (Visions of Anthropology). Taipei: Qunxue, pp. 127–47.

2006c. "Nongcun shehui de bengjie? Dangdai Taiwan nongcun xinfazhan de qishi." (The Collapse of Agricultural Society? Thoughts of New Agricultural Developments in Modern Taiwan). In Ying-Kui Huang ed., *Renleixue de shiye* (Visions of Anthropology). Taipei: Qunxue, pp. 175–91.

Huang, Zhongzhao, ed. 1485. *Bamin tongzhi* (Gazetteer of the Prefectures of Fujian). *Beijing tushuguan guji zhenben congkan*. Beijing: Shumu wenxian, 1988. Reprint.

"Huigu 101 - Xianzheng guanjianshike xiliebaodao: Matsu xin 'liang' dian! Liangdaoren chutu, gaixie Matsu lishi ye zhenhan taimin kaoguxuejie." (Review 101 - List of Critical Moments for County Government: Matsu's New "Bright" Spot! Liangdao Man Unearthed, Rewrites Matsu History and Shocks Taiwan/Fujian Archeological World). 2012. *Matsu Daily*, December 21.

Ingold, Tim. 2013. "Dreaming of Dragons: on the Imagination of Real Life." *Journal of the Royal Anthropological Institute* 19: 734–54.

"Jiabin huilin." (Honored Guests in Attendance). 1970. *Matsu Daily*, January 24.

"Jinju chahuo dutu, duoda wushiliu ren, qizhong gongwurenyuan liangming." (Police Track Down Gamblers: Up to 56 People, Including Two Government Employees). 1972. *Matsu Daily*, October 7.

Jing, Jun. 1996. *The Temple of Memories: History, Power, and Morality in a Chinese Village*. Stanford, CA: Stanford University Press.

"Junguan hongpishu: Matsu yumin shouce." (Military Control of Red Books: A Manual for Matsu Fishermen). 2002. *Matsu Online*, July 28. http://board.matsu.idv.tw/board_view.php?board=25&pid=5253&link=145 89&start=20. (Accessed July 17, 2012).

Kapferer, Brian, Annelin Eriksen, and Kari Telle. 2009. "Introduction: Religiosities toward a Future—In Pursuit of the New Millennium." *Social Analysis* 53(1): 1–16.

"Keelung-Matsu-Ningde zongjiao jinxiang lishi shouhang." (Keelung-Matsu-Ningde historic pilgrimage). 2008. *Matsu Daily*, July 5.

Kelly, Liz. 2000. "Wars against Women: Sexual Violence, Sexual Politics and the Militarised State." In Susie Jacobs, Ruth Jacobson, and Jennifer Marchbank eds., *States of conflict: Gender, Violence, and Resistance*. London: Zed Books, pp. 45–65.

Kelty, Christopher. 2005. "Geeks, Social Imaginaries, and Recursive Publics." *Cultural Anthropology* 20(2): 185–214.

Kenny, Michael. 1999 "A Place for Memory: The Interface between Individual and Collective History." *Comparative Studies in Society and History* 41(3): 420–37.

Kleinman, Arthur and Erin Fitz-Henry. 2007. "The Experiential Basis of Subjectivity: How Individuals Change in the Context of Societal Transformation." In Joao Biehl, Byron Good, and Arthur Kleinman eds., *Subjectivity: Ethnographic Investigations*. Berkeley: University of California Press, pp. 52–65.

Kwon, Heonik. 2010. "The Ghosts of War and the Ethics of Memory." In Michael Lambek ed., *Ordinary Ethics: Anthropology, Language and Action*. New York: Fordham University Press, pp. 400–15.

Lambek, Michael and Paul Antze. 1996 "Introduction: Forecast Memory." In Paul Antze and Michael Lambek eds., *Tense Past: Cultural Essays in Trauma and Memory*. New York: Routledge, pp. xi–xxxviii.

Latour, Bruno. 1993. *We Have Never Been Modern*. Cambridge, Mass.: Harvard University Press.

2005. *Reassembling the Social: An Introduction to Actor-Network-Theory*. Oxford: Oxford University Press.

Leayang. 2005. "Huiying 'zuihao de shiguang'." (Response to 'The Best of Times'). *Matsu Online*, November 7. www.matsu.idv.tw/print.php?f=226& t=23801&p=1. (Accessed July 17, 2012).

Lee, Anru. 2004. *In the Harmony and Prosperity: Labor and Gender Politics in Taiwan's Economic Restructuring*. Albany: State University of New York.

2015. "Place-making, Mobility, and Identity." In Julie Cidell and David Prytherch eds., *Transport, Mobility, and the Production of Urban Space*. London: Routledge, pp. 153–71.

2017. "Taiwan." In Akihiro Ogawa ed., *Routledge Handbook of Civil Society in Asia*. London: Routledge, pp. 79–94.

Lee, Teng-Hui. 1995. *Jingying da Taiwan* (Managing Taiwan). Taipei: Yuan-Liou.

Leimengdi. 2005. "Yuanfang de tongnian" (A Distant Childhood). *Matsu Online*, October 27. www.matsu.idv.tw/topicdetail.php?f=226&t=23601. (Accessed July 17, 2012).

2006. "Huiying 'Leimengdi: jiyi de weidao'." (Response to 'Leimengdi—The Flavor of Memory'). *Matsu Online*, January 2. www.matsu.idv.tw/topicdetail .php?f=226&t=26261&p=1. (Accessed July 17, 2012).

Li, Lingling. 2012. "Zhiyao boyifa tongguo, Weidner jihua yong 600yi kaifa Matsu." (If Gaming Laws Pass, Weidner Plans to Spend 60 Billion to Develop Matsu). *Now News*, July 9. www.nownews.com/n/2012/07/09/ 143176. (Accessed February 17, 2014).

Li, Shih-Te. 2006. *Zhuixun mingqing shiqi de haishang Matsu*. (Pursuing the Oceanic Matsu in the Ming and Qing periods). Nangan: Lianjiang County Government.

Li, Shiyun (author), as recounted by Suisheng Yang. 2014. *Chulu.* (Way Out). New Taipei City: Ruifeng.

Li, Shiyun, Zhilong Chen, and Xinfu Qiu. 2014. *Liuzhuan shiguang:Matsu koushu lishi.* (The Time of Wandering: An Oral History of Matsu). Nangan: Liangjiang County Government.

Li, Yuanhong. 1998. *Junshihua de kongjian kongzhi: zhandi zhengwu shiqi Matsu diqu zhi gean.* (Militarized Spatial Control: Matsu under the WZA). Master's thesis, Graduate Institute of Architecture and Planning, National University of Taiwan.

Li, Yuefeng. 1965. "Nanwang de juhui: Matsu jixing zhi qi." (An Unforgettable Meeting: Seventh Record of Matsu). *Matsu Daily*, August 3.

Liang, Jiefen and Zhaoxing Lu. 2010. *Zhongguo Macau tequ: bocaiye yu shehui fazhan.* (The Autonomous Region of Macau, China: Gambling and Social Development). Hong Kong: Hong Kong City University.

Liang, Kejia. 1182. *Sanshan zhi.* (Gazetteer of Fuzhou). *Siku quanshu zhenben.* Taipei: Shangwu, 1976. Reprint.

Liangshanding. 2010. "Magang tianhougong weiyuan xuanju shifou he qing, li, fa?" (Were the Mazu Temple Committee Elections in Magang Suitable, Fair, and Legal?). *Matsu Online*, December 14. www.matsu.idv.tw/topicdetail.php?f=2&t=85751. (Accessed February 1, 2011).

Lianjiang xian wenxian weiyuanhui. 1980. *Lianjiang xianzhi.* (Records of Lianjiang County). Nangan: Lianjiang County Government.

"Lianjiang xianzheng huiyi, zuo yuanman jieshu." (Lianjiang District Council Session Comes to Successful End Yesterday). 1959. *Matsu Daily*, February 1.

Liao, Zhi-Long. 2008. *Taoyuan xian bade shi juluo fazhan zhi yanjiu.* (A Study of Settlement Development in Bade City, Taoyuan). Master's thesis, National Hsinchu University of Education.

Lin, Jinguan 2012. "Boyi jiangzhuang Matsu?! Luntanhui fayan yingting, huo baxiang jielun." (Dress Matsu Up with Gaming?! Opinions Are Divided: Eight Arguments). 2012. *Matsu Daily*, April 22.

Lin, Jinyan. 1991. *Matsu liedao zhi.* (The Record of Matsu Archipelago). Banqiao: Lin Jinyan.

2006. *Juguang xiangzhi.* Juguang: Juguang Town Office.

2007. "Matsu haishang wangchao: Ji wei heping jiu guo jun zhang yizhou bu." (Matsu maritime dynasty: an account of Zhang Yizhou's army of the pseudo-Peace National Salvation Army). *Matsu Online*, January 1. www.matsu.idv.tw/topicdetail.php?f=165&t=38657. (Accessed March 20, 2013).

2013a. "Matsu shouzhuang yuye daikuan." (Matsu's First Fishing Industry Loans). *Matsu Online*, April 23. www.matsu.idv.tw/topicdetail.php?f=183&t=112250. (Accessed July 20, 2014).

2013b. "Matsu jiaoyu dianji shilue: minguo 38~45 nian jiaoyu tuohuang qi." (A Brief History of the Foundation of Education in Matsu: The Beginnings of Education, 1948–1955). *Matsu Online*, May 15. www.matsu.idv.tw/topicdetail.php?f=183&t=112897. (Accessed July 20, 2014).

Lin, Li-Ying. 2007. *Taoyuan gongye fazhan yu Taoyuan shehui bianqian: 1966–1996.* (The Industrial Development and the Social Transformation of Taoyuan). Master's thesis, Department of History, National Central University.

Lin, Meirong and Weihua Chen. 2008. "Matsu liedao de fushi limiao yanjiu: cong Magang tianhougong tanqi." (Matsu Temples for Drifting Corpses: Beginning with the Magang Goddess Mazu Temple). *Taiwan renleixue kan* 6 (1): 103–32.

Lin, Shuping. 2013. "xingfu de kuxingseng – Liu Jiaguo." (The Happy Ascetic— Liu Jiaguo). *Matsu Daily*, December 18–19.

Lin, Wei-Ping. 2009. "Bianchui daoyu zai zhongxinhua: Matsu jinxiang de tantao" (Recentralizing the Marginal Islands: Pilgrimage in the Frontline Islands in Taiwan). *Kaogu Renleixue Kan* 71: 71–91.

2009. "Local History through Popular religion: Place, People and Their Narratives." *Asian Anthropology* 8: 1–30.

2013. "Weihe yao jianmiao? cong miaoyu xingjian de wuzhihua guocheng tantao Matsu shequn zaizao" (Why Build a Temple? Materializing New Community Concepts in the Frontline Islands of Taiwan). *Taiwan Shehui Yanjiu Jikan* 92: 1–33.

2014. "Virtual Recentralization: Pilgrimage as Social Imaginary in the Demilitarized Islands between China and Taiwan." *Comparative Studies in Society and History* 56(1): 131–54.

2015. *Materializing Magic Power: Chinese Popular Religion in Villages and Cities.* Cambridge, MA: Harvard University Asia Center.

2016. "Xianshang Matsu: wanglu shequn yu difang xiangxiang." (Internet Matsu: Online Community and the Reimagination of Place). *Kaogu renleixue kan,* 85: 17–50.

2017. "Why Build a Temple? The Materialization of New Community Ideals in the Demilitarized Islands between China and Taiwan." *Material Religion* 13(2): 131–55.

2018. "Mother Ghost Seeks a Human Son-in-Law: Ghost Shrines in Taiwan." *Magic, Ritual, and Witchcraft* 13(2): 190–211.

Lin, Wei-ping and Wang Chun-Hui. 2012. "823 Matsu ren wei tudi shang jietou: wangle yu shehui yundong chutan." (The 823 Matsu Land Protest: An Initial Exploration of the Internet and Social Movements). *Minzuxue Yanjiusuo Ziliao Huibian* 22: 125–57.

Liu, Chun. 1965. "Yulao de chuangju PP sujiaoguan xiapichuang shiyan chenggong." (Successful Experiments in the Fishing Industry Using PP Plastic Piping to Harvest Shrimp). *Matsu Daily,* May 30.

Liu, Hongwen. 2016. *Xiangyin Matsu.* (Voices of Matsu). Nangan: Lianjiang County Government.

2017. *Wo cong haishang lai: Matsu yimin gushice.* (I Come from the Sea: A Collection of Matsu Immigrant Stories). Taoyuan: Taoyuan County Government.

Liu, Jiaguo. 1988. *Wode jiaxiang shi zhandi: jinma wenti mianmian guan.* (My Hometown is a Military Frontline: A Comprehensive Analysis of the Jinmen-Matsu Question). Self-published.

1994. "Tudi de beige: zuchan mei taohui lai, wo si bu mingmu!" (Elegy for the Land: If Our Ancestral Land Isn't Returned, I Can't Die in Peace!). *Matsu*

Report   18.   http://board.matsu.idv.tw/board_view.php?board=25&pid=
4741&link=14581&start=20. (Accessed February 1, 2011).

1996a. "Gucuo ying luori, Niujiao xiang hangdong." (An Ancient Home
Reflects the Setting Sun, Ox Horn Village Faces a Hard Winter). *Matsu
Report* 33, January 10. www.matsu.idv.tw/topicdetail.php?f=176&t=37096.
(Accessed January 2, 2018).

1996b. "Canghai sangtian, menghui sunlong." (The blue sea turned into mul-
berry fields, the memories lingered in Sunlong). *Matsu Report* 36. May 17. www
.matsu.idv.tw/print.php?f=176&t=37908&p=1. (Accessed September 2011).

1996c. "Da haidao cai qian Beigan cangbao chuanqi." (The great pirate
Cai Qian and his legend of treasure hidden in Beigan). *Matsu
Report* 42. December 24. www.matsu.idv.tw/topicdetail.php?f=176&t=
37936. (Accessed September 2011).

2003. "Jiekai dongyin dao limai dawang zhi mi." (Unveil the mystery of
Wheat-Field-Plowing King on the Dongyin Island). *Matsu Report* 42. July
22 http://board.matsu.idv.tw/board_view.php?board=15&pid=9899&link=
9898&start=0. (Accessed September 2011).

2004a. "Haidao wu chuanqi renwu chen zhongping." (The legendary figure of the
pirate house – Chen Zhongping). *Matsu Report* 103. February 23.www.matsu
.idv.tw/topicdetail.php?f=165&t=161788. (Accessed November 25, 2013).

2004b. "Gantang xiaoxiong lin yihe." (The Ringleader in Gantang – Lin Yihe).
Matsu Report 106/7. May 22. http://board.matsu.idv.tw/board_view.php?
board=15&pid=21134&link=0&start=. (Accessed November 25, 2013).

2004c. "Cao Xiaofen, fanxiang wei ziji er huo." (Cao Xiaofen Returns Home
to Live for Herself). *Matsu Online*, November 30. www.matsu.idv.tw/
topicdetail.php?f=165&t=161791. (Accessed November 25, 2013).

2006a. "Huiying 'Leimengdi: baba bujian le'." (Response to 'Leimengdi—Dad
Has Disappeared'). *Matsu Online.* February 6.Awww.matsu.idv.tw/
topicdetail.php?f=226&t=27516&p=1. (Accessed November 25, 2013).

2006b. "Xideng ganyan: wo haiyou yige meng." (An Extinguished Lamp:
I Still Have a Dream). *Matsu Report* 143. March 6. http://board.matsu.idv
.tw/board_view.php?board=25&pid=23270&link=23248&start=0.
(Accessed October 25, 2017).

2015. "Taimazhixing 8 yue 12 ri shouhang zhijin 'guzhang shijian'
dashiji." (Record of Taima Star 'Breakdowns' from August 12 to Today).
Matsu Online. December 20. www.matsu.idv.tw/topicdetail.php?f=176&t=
144746&k=%E8%87%BA%E9%A6%AC%E4%B9%8B%E6%98%9F#892
665. (Accessed October 25, 2017).

Liu, Jiaguo and Xinfu Qiu, eds. 2002. *Dongyin xiangzhi.* Dongyin: Dongyin
Town Office.

Liu, Qiuhua. 2010. "Matsu haiyou jinian keyi deng? Matsu ren ni hai yuanyi zai
deng ma?" (How Long Can Matsu Wait? People of Matsu, Do You Still
Want to Wait?). *Matsu Daily,* July 23.

Liu, Qiuyue. 2010. "Zhengqu santi gaosu xin taimalun: Yang Suisheng baihui
zhongyang." (Fighting for a New Taiwan-Matsu High Speed Trimaran:
Yang Suisheng Pays a Visit to Chinese Leaders). *Matsu Daily,* February 9.

2012. "Yazhou dizhonghai shuominghui – Weidner: Macau neng chenggong,
Matsu gengju dili youshi." (Informational Meeting on Asian Mediterranean—

Weidner: Macau Succeeded, and Matsu's Geography Is Even Better). *Matsu Daily*, April 27.

2013. "DNA jiemi: tuilun 'Liangdao ren' wei nandaoyuzu zuizao zuxian." (DNA Deciphered—Conclusion: Liangdao Man is Earliest Austronesian Ancestor). *Matsu Daily*, July 18.

LOLO. 2011. "Zheyang de rili, ni gan gua ma?" (Would You Dare Hang This Calendar on Your Wall?). *Matsu Online*, January 7. www.matsu.idv.tw/topicdetail.php?f=2&t=86456. (Accessed May 1, 2011).

Long, Nicholas and Henrietta Moore, eds. 2013. *Sociality: New Directions*. New York: Berghahn Books.

Lu, Hsin-Yi. 2002. *Politics of Locality: Making a Nation of Communities in Taiwan*. London: Routledge.

"Lu zhuwei zuotian canguan, zhandi ge junjing jianshe." (Committee Head Lu Tours Military Construction Yesterday). 1971. *Matsu Daily*, September, 17.

Luhrmann, Tanya Marie. 2006. "Subjectivity." *Anthropological Theory* 6(3): 345–61.

Lutz, Catherine. 2001. *Homefront: A Military City and the American Twentieth Century*. Boston: Beacon Press.

2004. "Militarization." In David Nugent and Joan Vincent eds., *A Companion to the Anthropology of Politics*. New York: Blackwell, pp. 318–31.

Macek, Jakub. 2013. "More than a Desire for Text: Online Participation and the Social Curation of Content." *Convergence: The International Journal of Research into New Media Technologies* 19(3): 295–302.

Mahmood, Saba. 2005. *Politics of Piety: The Islamic Revival and the Feminist Subject*. Princeton, NJ: Princeton Univeristy Press.

Maimian Xishi. 2005. "Huiying 'anye sanbuqu'." (Response to 'Nighttime Trilogy'). *Matsu Online*, December 10. www.matsu.idv.tw/topicdetail.php?f=226&t=25434. (Accessed May 5, 2017).

Malaby, Thomas. 2003. *Gambling Life: Dealing in Contingency in a Greek City*. Urbana: University of Illinois Press.

Mao, Yuanyi, ed. 1621. *Wubei zhi* (Treatise on Military Theories, Armament, Training and Logistics). *Xuxiu siku quanshu*. Shanghai: Shanghai guji, 1995. Reprint.

Marcus, George. 1995. "Introduction." In George Marcus ed., *Technoscientific Imaginaries: Conversations, Profiles, and Memoirs*. Chicago: University of Chicago Press, pp. 1–10.

"Mazu jinshen zhihang Taizhong." (The Direct-sailing of Goddess Mazu's Statue to Taichung). 2008. *Matsu Daily*, September 2.

"Matsu minzhong liu cheng er fandui she guanguang duchang." (62% of Matsu Locals Oppose Casino Tourism). 2003. *Matsu Report*, July 30. http://board.matsu.idv.tw/board_view.php?board=25&pid=10337&link=10336&start=0. (Accessed May Feb 22, 2017).

"Matsu xiangqin liangan zhihang minxin suoxiang." (Matsu Residents Hope for Direct-sailing). 2007. *Matsu Daily*, May 19.

"Matsu zhongxue shoujie biyesheng ban, biye kaoshi juxing wanjun." (For the Inaugural Class of Graduates from Matsu Middle Schools, Graduation Exams are Done). 1960. *Matsu Daily*, June 25.

Mazzarella, William. 2004. "Culture, Globalization, Mediation." *Annual Review of Anthropology* 33: 345–67.

McCullough, Colleen. 1977. *The Thorn Birds.* New York: Harper & Row.

Meyer, Birgit. 2015. *Sensational Movies: Video, Vision, and Christianity in Ghana.* Berkeley: University of California Press.

Miklavcic, Alessandra. 2008. "Slogans and Graffiti: Postmemory among Youth in the Italo-Slovenian Borderland." *American Ethnologist* 35(3): 440–53.

Miller, Daniel. 1987. *Material Culture and Mass Consumption.* Oxford: Blackwell.

2005. *Materiality.* Durham, NC: Duke University Press.

Miller, Daniel and Don Slater. 2000. *The Internet: An Ethnographic Approach.* Oxford: Berg.

Miller, Daniel and Heather Horst. 2012. "The Digital and the Human: A Prospectus for Digital Anthropology." In Heather Horst and Daniel Miller eds., *Digital Anthropology.* London: Bloomsbury, pp. 3–38.

"Minzhong tigong junren dubo changsuo, lianxu sanci chahuo mingqi qianchu." (Gambling Sites for Soldiers Supplied by Ordinary Citizens: Discovered Three Times Before Being Removed). 1983. *Matsu Daily,* October 18.

Mitra, Ananda. 1997. "Virtual Commonality: Looking for India on the Internet." In Steven Jones ed., *Virtual Culture: Identity & Communication in Cybersociety.* London: Sage, pp. 55–79.

Miyazaki, Hirokazu. 2004. *The Method of Hope: Anthropology, Philosophy, and Fijian Knowledge.* Stanford, CA: Stanford University Press.

2006. "Economy of Dreams: Hope in Global Capitalism and Its Critiques." *Cultural Anthropology* 21(2): 147–72.

2013. *Arbitraging Japan: Dreams of Capitalism at the End of Finance.* Berkeley: California University Press.

Miyazaki, Hirokazu and Richard Swedberg. 2015. *The Economy of Hope.* Philadelphia: University of Pennsylvania Press.

Mojieke. 2011. "Ceng zouguo de xiaolu: gei jiezhong 75 ji qianhouqi tongxue." (Paths I've Walked: For My Middle School Classmates from Around 1975). *Matsu Online,* February 1. www.matsu.idv.tw/topicdetail.php?f=4&t=86621. (Accessed July 12, 2012).

Moon, Seungsook. 2005. *Militarized Modernity and Gendered Citizenship in South Korea.* Durham, NC: Duke University Press.

Moore, Henrietta. 1994. *A Passion for Difference: Essays in Anthropology and Gender.* Cambridge: Polity Press.

2007. *The Subject of Anthropology: Gender, Symbolism and Psychoanalysis.* Cambridge: Polity.

2011. *Still Life: Hopes, Desires and Satisfactions.* Cambridge: Polity.

Mou, Hongtong 2008. "Taiwan Minsu Jinxiangtuan shouhang Ningde jiang dailai shenme?" (What will the direct-sail pilgrimage of Taiwan bring to Ningde?). www.ningde.gov.cn/jrnd/ndyw/18945.html. (Accessed January 7, 2013).

Mueggler, Erik. 2001. *The Age of Wild Ghost: Memory, Violence, and Place in Southwest China.* Berkeley: University of California Press.

Munn, Nancy. 1986. *The Fame of Gawa: A Symbolic Study of Value Transformation in a Massim Society.* Durham, NC: Duke University Press.

Murray, Dian. 1987. *Pirates of the South China Coast 1790–1810*. Stanford, CA: Stanford University Press.

"Nanbeigan yumin zuori juxing chuhaizuoye bu weigui xuanshi, silingguan qinlin Nangan tianhougong jianshi." (Fishermen in Nangan and Beigan Swore Yesterday to Abide By Rules at Sea, WZA Chair Personally Attended the Oaths at Mazu Temple). 1974. *Matsu Daily*, March 28.

Nedostup, Rebecca. 2009. *Superstitious Regimes: Religion and the Politics of Chinese Modernity*. Cambridge, MA: Harvard University Asian Center.

"Ningde xiying jin liushi nian lai di yisou zhihang de taiwan kelun." (Ningde welcomes the first direct-sailing ferry from Taiwan in nearly sixty years). 2008. http://big5.xinhuanet.com/gate/big5/www.fj.xinhuanet.com/dszx/2008-08/07/content_14060715.htm. July 6. (Accessed January 7, 2013).

Oakes, Tim and Donald Sutton, eds. 2010. *Faith on Display: Religion, Tourism, and the Chinese State*. Lanham: Rowman & Littlefield Publishers.

Ong, Aihwa. 2006. *Neoliberalism as Exception: Mutations in Citizenship and Sovereignty*. Durham, NC: Duke University Press.

Ortner, Sherry. 2005. "Subjectivity and Cultural Critique." *Anthropological Theory* 5(1): 31–52.

Pan, Xintong. 2010. "Taimalun niandu suixiu, Hefulun daipao." (Annual Repairs for the Taiwan-Matsu Ship: Hefu Travels in Its Place). *China Times*. Reprinted on *Yahoo*, https://tw.news.yahoo.com/%E5%8F%B0% E9%A6%AC%E8%BC%AA%E5%B9%B4%E5%BA%A6%E6%AD%B2 %E4%BF%AE-%E5%90%88%E5%AF%8C%E8%BC%AA%E4%BB%A 3%E8%B7%91-20101213-105326-283.html. December 14. (Accessed March 12, 2019).

2012. "Yifengxin rang defang yulun fanpan: 13 sui nvsheng fandu ganyan, dadong Matsu ren." (One Letter Turns Public Opinion: Thoughts of 13- Year-Old Girl on Gambling Touches Matsu Public). *China Times*, June 24 Reprinted on *Yahoo*, https://tw.news.yahoo.com/%E5%B0%81% E4%BF%A1%E8%AE%93%E5%9C%B0%E6%96%B9%E8%BC%BF% E8%AB%96%E7%BF%BB%E7%9B%A413%E6%AD%B2%E5%A5% B3%E7%94%9F%E5%8F%8D%E8%B3%AD%E6%84%9F%E8%A8% 80-%E6%89%93%E5%8B%95%E9%A6%AC%E7%A5%96%E4%BA% BA-213000814.html. (Accessed March 12, 2019).

Papataxiarchis, Evthymios. 1999. "A Contest with Money: Gambling and the Politics of Disinterested Sociality in Aegean Greece." In Sophie Day, Evthymios Papataxiarchis, and Michael Stewart eds., *Lilies of the Field: Marginal People Who Live for the Moment*. Boulder: Westview Press, pp. 158–75.

Peacock, James and Dorothy Holland. 1993. "The Narrated Self: Life Stories in Process." *Ethos* 21(4): 367–83.

Peng, Ying. 2011. "Liang'an zhihang hou, Ningbo yinlai 450 ren zuidaguimo Taiwan tuan." (With Direct Flights across the Strait, Ningbo Welcomes 450 People in Huge Taiwanese Tour Group). *Xiandai Jinbao*, July 9.

Peter, John. 1997. "Seeing Bifocally: Media, Place, Culture." In Akhil Gupta and James Ferguson eds., *Culture, Power, Place: Explorations in Critical Anthropology*. Durham: Duke University Press, pp. 75–92.

pinkheart. 2012. "Matsu de qingnian, zhan chulai zhichi 7/7 gong tou!" (Calling Young Matsu Residents to Support the 7/7 Referendum!). *Matsu Online,* June 12. www.matsu.idv.tw/topicdetail.php?f=2&t=102939&fb_comment_ id=10151040244155815_25077375. (Accessed February 22, 2017).

Postill, John. 2011. *Localizing the Internet: An Anthropological Account.* New York: Berghahn Books.

Qihaogou. 2010. "Huiying 'Leimengdi: caimin liang fengdeng'." (Response to 'Leimengdi—Colorful Storm Lantern). *Matsu Online,* February 18. www.matsu.idv.tw/topicdetail.php?f=226&t=75766&p=1. (Accessed May 10, 2012).

Qing shilu, Gaozong chunhuangdi shilu. (Veritable records of successive reigns of the Qing dynasty, the Qianlong reign). Beijing: Zhonghua shuju, 1986–7.

Qiu, Xinfu and Guangyi He. 2014. "Renmin Zhi" (Peopole). In Jiaguo Liu et al. eds., *Lianjiang xianzhi* (Lianjiang Gazetteer) vol. 5. Nangan: Lianjiang County Governemnt, pp. 6–151.

Rapport, Nigel. 2015. "'Imagination is the Barest Reality': On the Universal Human Imagining of the World." In Mark Harris and Nigel Rapport eds., *Reflections on Imagination: Human Capacity and Ethnographic Method.* Surrey: Ashgate, pp. 3–22.

Reed, John William and John William King. 1867. *The China Sea Directory.* London: Hydrographic office, Admiralty.

Rigger, Shelley. 1999. *Politics in Taiwan: Voting for Democracy.* London: Routledge.

Robbins, Joel. 2010. "On Imagination and Creation: An Afterword." *Anthropological Forum* 20(3): 305–13.

Rollason, Will. 2014. "Pacific Futures, Methodological Challenges." In Will Rollason ed., *Pacific Futures: Projects, Politics and Interests.* New York: Berghahn, pp. 1–27.

Ruiyun. 2011. "Wode fuqin cao dianzhang." (My Father Cao Dianzhang) *Matsu Online,* March 19. www.matsu.idv.tw/print.php?f=165&t=88211&p=1. (Accessed May 1, 2013).

Sanford, Victoria, Katerina Stefatos, and Cecilia Salvi, eds. 2016. *Gender Violence in Peace and War: States of Complicity.* New Brunswick, NJ: Rutgers University Press.

Sangren, Steven. 1987. *History and Magical Power in a Chinese Community.* Stanford, CA: Stanford University Press.

  2000. *Chinese Sociologics: An Anthropological Account of the Role of Alienation in Social Reproduction.* London: Athlone.

  2013. "The Chinese Family as Instituted Fantasy: or Rescuing Kinship Imaginaries from the 'Symbolic'." *Journal of the Royal Anthropological Institute* 19: 279–99.

Scott, James. 1985. *Weapons of the Weak.* New Haven, CT: Yale University Press.

See, Chinben. 1973. "Jisiquan yu shehui zuzhi: zhanghua pingyuan juluo fazhan moshi de tantao." (Religious Sphere and Social Organization: an Exploratory Model of the Settlement of Changhua Plain). *Zhongyang yan- jiuyuan minzuxue yanjiusuo jikan* 36: 191–206.

Shenhua. 2010. "Weishenme miaoyu chengle xuanju gongju." (Why Does the Temple Become the Tool of Election). *Matsu Online,* June 8. www

.matsu.idv.tw/topicdetail.php?f=2&t=79847&k=%A4%FB%Aep%B9%D2 #399943. (Accessed August 20, 2012).

Shixisheng. 2007. "Niufengjing jianmiao quan jilu~G." (The Complete Record of the Construction of Niufengjing Temple~G). *Matsu Online*, March 18. www.matsu.idv.tw/topicdetail.php?f=4&t=41297&k=#220398. (Accessed April 13, 2012).

Shiyuan. 2011. "Taidian fuzeren de chengnuo zai nali?" (What Happened to Taiwan Power Company's Promises to Take Responsibility?). *Matsu Online*, April 19. www.matsu.idv.tw/topicdetail.php?f=2&t=89113. (Accessed May 1, 2011).

"Silingguan deyi shenzhong, bo shimidai yu yumin." (The WZA Chair Shows His Virtue, Allocates Loans of Rice to Fishermen). 1966. *Matsu Daily*, January 18.

"Silingguan guanxin minmo, hezhun dai mi yu yumin." (The WZA Chair Shows His Concern for the People, Approves Loans of Rice for Fishermen). 1967. *Matsu Daily*, November 18.

Simon, Scott. 2004. *Sweet and Sour: Life-worlds of Taipei Women Entrepreneurs*. Lanham: Rowman & Littlefield Publishers, INC.

Sneath, David, Martin Holbraad and Morten Pedersen. 2009. "Technologies of the Imagination: An Introduction." *Ethnos* 74(1): 5–30.

Song, Jiansheng. 2013. "Canyu Feiguo xin duchang touzi 10%, Weidner touzi Matsu zhi qian dongfeng." (After Investing 10% in Philippines' New Casino, Weidner's Investment in Matsu Lacks One Crucial Thing). *Matsu Daily*, March 17. www.matsu-news.gov.tw/2010web/news_detail_101.php?CMD= open&UID=151315. (Accessed July 2014).

Steinmüller, Hans. 2011. "The Moving Boundaries of Social Heat: Gambling in Rural China." *Journal of the Royal Anthropological Institute* 17(2): 263–80.

Stewart, Pamela J. and Andrew Strathern. 2009. "Growth of the Mazu Complex in Cross-Straits Contexts (Taiwan and Fujian Province, China)." *Journal of Ritual Studies* 23(1): 67–72.

Stolow, Jeremy. 2005. "Religion and /as Media." *Theory, Culture & Society* 22(4): 119–45.

Strauss, Claudia. 2006. "The Imaginary." *Anthropological Theory* 6(3): 322–44.

Sun, Jianzheng. 1966. "Xiapi shengchan zai jinluomigu zhong." (Shrimp Production under an Intense Publicity). *Matsu Daily*, October 17.

Szonyi, Michael. 1997. "The Illusion of Standardizing the Gods: The Cult of the Five Emperors in Late Imperial China." *The Journal of Asian Studies* 56(1): 113–35.

2008. *Cold War Island: Quemoy on the Frontline*. Cambridge: Cambridge University Press.

Tai'an huilu xinji. Taiwan wenxian congkan. Taipei: Taiwan yinhang, 1964. Reprint.

"Tan lühua Matzu." (The Forestation of Matsu). 1962. *Matsu Daily*, March 12.

Taylor, Charles. 2004. *Modern Social Imaginaries*. Durham, NC: Duke University Press.

"Tianhougong zuori luocheng, zhihuiguan qinlin jiancai." (Goddess Mazu Temple Completed Yesterday—Commanding Officer Joins Ribbon Cutting). 1964. *Matsu Daily*, May 5.

Tilley, Charles. 2006. "Objectification." In Charles Tilley et al. ed. *Handbook of Material Culture*. Oxford: Sage, pp. 60–73.

Timing. 2011. "'Qingding shiliu, Matsu haozan,' wuyu chuangguan yue chengnian." ("Loving 16, Mazu is Great," a Coming-of-Age Activity). *Matsu Online*, September 15. www.matsu.idv.tw/topicdetail.php?f=4&t=93989& k=%A4%FB%AEp%B9%D2#438113. (Accessed April 13, 2012).

Tsao, Yi-Hsun and Wei-Ping Lin. 2013. "Matsu juguang huahajie: bianjing daoyu ruhe tansuo weilai." (Matsu's Juguang Clam Festival: How a Frontier Archipelago Explores Its Future). *Minzuxue Yanjiusuo Ziliao Huibian* 23: 179–206.

Tsing, Anna Lowenhaupt. 2005. *Friction: An Ethnography of Global Connection*. Princeton, NJ: Princeton University Press.

2015. *The Mushroom at the End of the World: On the Possibility of Life in Capitalist Ruins*. Princeton, NJ: Princeton University Press.

Turkle, Sherry. 1997 [1995]. *Life on the Screen: Identity in the Age of the Internet*. New York: Touchstone.

Turner, Victor. 1967. "Betwixt and Between: The Liminal Period in Rites de Passage." In *The Forest of Symbols: Aspects of Ndembu Ritual*. Ithaca, NY: Cornell University Press, pp. 93–111.

1968. *The Ritual Process: Structure and Anti-Structure*. Chicago, IL: Aldine Publishing Company.

Turner, Victor and Edith Turner. 1978. *Image and Pilgrimage in Christian Culture: Anthropological Perspectives*. New York: Columbia University Press.

Vice Admin. 2010. "Huiying 'Leimengdi: caimin liang fengdeng'." (Response to 'Leimengdi—Colorful Storm Lantern'). *Matsu Online*, February 4. www.matsu .idv.tw/topicdetail.php?f=226&t=75766&p=1. (Accessed February 17, 2015).

Wang, Changming. 2011a. "Jinnian 8 yue 23 ri zoushang Taiwan jietou, zhengqu zao gai huangei Matsu renmin yingyou de quanyi." (Marching on August 23 in Taiwan, Fighting for the Rights Every Matsu Citizen Has Long Deserved). *Matsu Online*, April 22. www.matsu.idv.tw/topicdetail.php?f= 181&t=89253. (Accessed June 6, 2011).

2011b. "823 kaidagelan dadao youxing jingzuo kouhao, qing dajia yiqi lai tigong." (Everyone Should Suggest Slogans for the 823 March and Sit-in on Ketagalan Boulevard). *Matsu Online*, May 17. www.matsu.idv.tw/topicdetail .php?f=2&t=90033&k=%A4g%A6a#429485. (Accessed May 26, 2011).

Wang, Huadi. 2000. *Matsu diqu miaoyu diaocha yu yanjiu* (The Investigation and Research on Matsu Temples). Nangan: Lianjiang xian shehui jiaoyu guan.

2009. "'Leimengdi' de zhandi tongnian, yeshi women de tongnian." ('Leimengdi's Childhood under Military Rule' Is Also Our Childhood). *Matsu Online*, July 3. www.matsu.idv.tw/topicdetail.php?f=4&t=68733. (Accessed February. 1, 2011).

Wang, Huadi, Jianhua Wang, and Guangyi He. 2016. *Matsu wenhua shidian* (Encyclopedia of Matsu Culture). Nangan: Lianjiang County Government.

Wang, Jianhua. 2010a. "Yikuai xiao shuichi, wuxian shengmingli!" (One Little Pond, Infinite Vitality!). *Matsu Online*, May 12. www.matsu.idv.tw/ topicdetail.php?f=172&t=78957. (Accessed May 12, 2010).

2010b. "Rang haizi xue zhe zuo gengduo: Kaifu ha." (Let Our Young Students
  Do More: Saltwater Clams). *Matsu Online*, June 30. http://tw.myblog.yahoo
  .com/arthur-88001/article?mid=2539&prev=2738&l=f&fid=10. (Accessed
  February 1, 2011).
2011. "Cuoguo zhe jitian, jiuyao deng mingnian!" (Miss These Few Days, and
  You'll Have to Wait Until Next Year!). *Matsu Online*, March 18. http://tw
  .myblog.yahoo.com/arthur-88001/article?mid=5263&next=5251&l=f&fid=
  10. (Accessed May 1, 2011).
Wang, Jinli. 2000. "Matsu de yuye." (The Matsu Fishing Industry). In Jinbao
  Qiu ed., *Diyijie Matsu liedao fazhanshi guoji xueshu yantaohui lunwenji* (The
  First International Symposium on the History of the Matsu Islands'
  Development). Nangan: Lianjiang County Government, pp. 164–86.
Wang, Xuanqing. 2017. "Taimalun waihai shiqu dongle, junren, taidian yuan-
  gong huojiu." (Taiwan-Matsu Ship Loses Power, Military and Taiwan
  Power Company Workers Come to the Rescue). *Liberty Times*, April 29.
  https://news.ltn.com.tw/news/society/breakingnews/2051335. (Accessed
  June 25, 2018).
Wang, Zhihong. 2006. "Yi / zhi renting yu kongjian zhengzhi: Taoyuan huochez-
  han zhoubian xiaofei zuyi dijing yanjiu." (Moving/Settling and Political
  Space: A Study of Consumption and Ethnicity Around the Taoyuan
  Railroad Station). *Taiwan shehui yanjiu jikan* 61: 149–205.
Watson, James. 1975. *Emigration and the Chinese Lineage*. Berkeley: University of
  California Press.
"Weihu shumiao chengzhang, xianfu mingling chu yang." (To Protect the
  Growth of Saplings, the County Government Orders the Elimination of
  Sheep). 1961. *Matsu Daily*, March 24.
Weidner, William. 2013. *Matsu ye wei mian.* (Sleepless in Matsu). Taipei: Shiying.
Weiss, Brad. 2009. *Street Dreams & Hip Hop Barbershops: Global Fantasy in Urban
  Tanzania.* Bloomington: Indiana University Press.
Weller, Robert. 1999. *Alternate Civilities: Democracy and Culture in China and
  Taiwan.* Boulder, CO: Westview Press.
2000. "Living at the Edge: Religion, Capitalism, and the End of the Nation-
  State in Taiwan." *Popular Culture* 12(2): 477–98.
2019. "Goddess Unbound: Chinese Popular Religion and the Varieties of
  Boundary." *The Journal of Religion* 99(1): 18–36.
White, Geoffrey. 2000. "Emotional Remembering: The Pragmatics of National
  Memory." *Ethos* 27(4): 505–29.
2001. "Histories and Subjectivities." *Ethos* 28(4): 493–510.
2004 "National Subjects: September 11 and Pearl Harbor." *American
  Ethnologist* 31(3): 293–310.
Wilkinson, Endymion. 2013. *Chinese History: A New Manual.* Cambridge, MA:
  Harvard University Asia Center.
Winter, Jay and Emmanuel Sivan, eds. 1999. *War and Remembrance in the
  Twentieth Century.* Cambridge: Cambridge University Press.
"Wu Jinzan fang nan Beigan." (Wu Jinzan Visits Nangan and Beigan). 1978.
  Matsu Daily, January 8.

Wu, Mei-Yun, ed. 1995. *Changzhu Taiwan.* (Taiwan for the Long Term). Taipei: Hansheng.

Wu, Shizi. 2006. "Jiejue tudi wenti zhizai zhuzhengzhe de shifou 'yongxin'." (Resolving Land Issues Relies on Whether Leaders 'Really Care'). *Matsu Online,* March 3. www.matsu.idv.tw/topicdetail.php?f=170&t=28369#141400. (Accessed June 12, 2011).

Xia, Shuhua. 2005a. "Yue quan shi." (Total Lunar Eclipse). *Matsu Online,* September 14. www.matsu.idv.tw/topicdetail.php?f=226&t=21926. (Accessed July 17, 2012).

2005b. "Huiying 'yiwang zai qiaozicun de shiguang.'" (Response to 'Forgetting My Time in Qiaozi Village). *Matsu Online,* October 13. www .matsu.idv.tw/topicdetail.php?f=226&t=21931. (Accessed July 17, 2012).

2005c. "Wode wudi xiaojingang." (My Invincible Little Warrior). *Matsu Online,* October 16. www.matsu.idv.tw/topicdetail.php?f=226&t=23143&p=1. (Accessed July 17, 2012).

2005d. "Yuanfang de tongnian." (Distant Childhood Years). *Matsu Online,* October 27. www.matsu.idv.tw/topicdetail.php?f=226&t=23601. (Accessed July 17, 2012).

2005e. "33 sui mama de dishini leyuan." (A 33-Year-Old Mother's Disney Land). *Matsu Online,* November 19. www.matsu.idv.tw/topicdetail.php?f=226&t=24488. (Accessed July 17, 2012).

2006a. "Zhongnian jiaolu." (Middle Age Anxieties). *Matsu Online,* February 9. www.matsu.idv.tw/print.php?f=226&t=27668&p=1. (Accessed July 17, 2012).

2006b. "Manhuo." (The Slow Life). *Matsu Online,* March 6. www.matsu.idv .tw/topicdetail.php?f=226&t=28446&p=1. (Accessed July 17, 2012).

2008. "Huiying 'Leimengdi: haisha de jiyi'." (Response to 'Leimengdi—Oceanside Memories'). *Matsu Online,* June 15. www.matsu.idv.tw/topicdetail.php?f=226&t=56874&p=1. (Accessed July 17, 2012).

Xia, Shuhua and Chen Tianshun. 2009. *Leimengdi de Zhandi Tongnian.* Taipei: Eryu Wenhua.

"Xiapi jue cai zixing yunxiao, bing jiang chengli yunxiao hezuoshe." (Shrimp Harvesters Ship Their Own Goods. Will Establish a Shipping Cooperative). 1974. *Matsu Daily,* June 30.

Xie, Dan. 2014. "Matsu xianzhang: he fuzhoushi yiqi xun 'haisi' zhilu zouxiang shijie." (Matsu County Comissioner: Let's Head Down the 'Maritime Silk Road' Together with Fuzhou). *FZnews,* May 19. http://news.fznews.com.cn/xhsjzkfz/2014-5-19/201451950Nb0P5iXX162731.shtml. (Accessed June 15, 2016).

Xie, Zhaohua. 2016. *Daoju.* (Island Life). Taipei: Lianhe Literature.

Xiong, Shoupai. 2012. "Matsu Liangdao chutu 7,900 nianqian wanzheng renguhai." (Complete 7,900-Year-Old Skeleton Unearthed on Liangdao, Matsu). *Matsu Online,* April 2. www.matsu.idv.tw/print.php?f=4&t=100574&p=1. (Accessed June 15, 2016).

Xu, Yuhu. 1962. "Zheng he xia xiyang hanghaitu kao." (A study on the nautical charts for the Great Voyages of Zheng He). *Dalu zazhi* 25(12): 14–18.

Yan, Zheng. 1977. "Jinnian huangyu yiding henduo, pangda chuandui kaiwang Dongyin." (A Great Year for Yellow Croaker: Huge Fleet of Boats Heads to Dongyin). *Matsu Daily*, April 12.
  1979. "Duju yipi zuo fenhui, zhongwang neng shaodiao waifeng, chajin suijiu qijin wei genjue, genben banfa yinggai fangzhi duju jinkou." (A Cache of Gambling Paraphernalia Destroyed Yesterday: The People Confident the Unhealthy Habit Can Be Suppressed Despite Its Persistence Today, Basic Method Should Be to Control Import of Gambling Paraphernalia). *Matsu Daily*, April 19.
Yang, Bingxun. 2014. "Jingji caishuizhi." (The Economy). In Jiaguo Liu, Shide Li, and Jinyan Lin eds., *Lianjiang xianzhi*, (Lianjiang County Records), vol. 6, Nangan: Lianjiang County Government.
Yang, Ching Kun. 1961. *Religion in Chinese Society: A Study of Contemporary Social Functions of Religion and Some of Their Historical Factors*. Berkeley: University of California Press.
Yang, Hong-Ren. 2007. *Shequ ruhe dongqilai? Heizhenzhu zhi xiang de paixi, zaidi shifu yu shequ zongti yingzao*. (Making Community Work: A Case Study of Linbien). Taipei: Zuoan.
Yang, Mayfair. 2004. "Goddess across the Taiwan Strait: Matrifocal Ritual Space, Nation-State, and Satellite Television Footprints." *Public Culture* 16 (2): 209–38.
  2008. "Introduction." In Mayfair Yang ed., *Chinese Religiosities: Afflictions of Modernity and State Formation*. Berkeley: University of California Press, pp. 1–40.
Yang, Suisheng. 2007. "Niufengjing miao guanli weiyuanhui qishi." (The Notice of the Niufengjing Temple Committee). *Matsu Online*, January 25. www .matsu.idv.tw/topicdetail.php?f=4&t=39501&k=#207510. (Accessed April 13, 2012).
  2008. "Miandui boyi de jiudaode yu xinsiwei." (Old Morals and New Ideas in the Face of Gaming). *Matsu Online*, August 20. www.matsu.idv.tw/ topicdetail.php?f=174&t=59252. (Accessed February 10, 2014).
  2009. "Shiren hua boyi." (A Poet Talks Gaming). *Matsu Online*, July 5. www .matsu.idv.tw/topicdetail.php?f=174&t=68780. (Accessed February 10, 2014).
  2010. "Qidai zongtong shuo yes." (Hoping for the President's Yes). *Matsu Daily*, June 9. www.matsu-news.gov.tw/2010web/news_detail_101.php? CMD=open&UID=113027. (Accessed February 10, 2014).
Yang, Yaxin. 2014. "Dili zhi." (Geograhy). In Jiaguo Liu et al. eds., *Lianjiang xianzhi*, (Lianjiang Gazetteer), vol 2. Nangan: Lianjiang County Governement. pp. 36–202.
Yang, Zhuohan. 2013. "Yao zhuan shijie qian, duchang shezai Matsu bi Tamshui hao." (Make Money from the Rest of the World: Better to Build Casinos in Matsu than in Tamshui). *Business Today* 847, March 14. www.businesstoday .com.tw/article-content-80392-93782-%E8%A6%81%E8%B3%BA%E4% B8%96%E7%95%8C%E9%8C%A2%20%E8%B3%AD%E5%A0%B4

E8%A8%AD%E5%9C%A8%E9%A6%AC%E7%A5%96%E6%AF%94%
E6%B7%A1%E6%B0%B4%E5%A5%BD. (Accessed February 10, 2014).
"Yong santi kuailun du Matsu yige jihui." (Bet on Matsu with Trimarans). 2010.
   Matsu Daily, May 21.
Yu, Hao. 2007. "Matsu hangxian wuyuefen quxiao 135 banci, Uni Air youku
   nanyan." (Uni Air Has Difficulty Explaining Cancellation of 135 Matsu
   Flights in May), *Epoch Times*, June 3. www.epochtimes.com/b5/7/6/3/
   n1731933.htm. (Accessed February 10, 2014).
Yu, Yonghe. 1697. *Bihai jiyou*. (Records of Travels on a Small Sea). *Taiwan
   wenxian congkan*. Taipei: Taiwan yinhang, 1959. Reprint.
Yuan, Binghua. 2009. "Huiying '2009/7/5 Beigan: Xia Shuhua, Leimengdi de
   zhandi tongnian xinshu fabiaohui'." (Response to '2009/7/5 Beigan—Xia
   Shuhua, Leimengdi's Childhood Under Military Rule: Book Release
   Event'). *Matsu Online*, July 4. https://www.matsu.idv.tw/topicdetail.php?f=
   4&t=68733. (Accessed July 17, 2012).
"Yuminzheng yaopai wenda." (Questions and Answers Regarding Licenses and
   Permits for Fishermen). 1961. *Matsu Daily*, June 9.
"Yuye fuzeren zuo jihui, Zhang mishuzhang qinlin zhuchi, shangtao yuju caigou
   wuqi bujiu banfa." (Heads of the Fishing Industry Met Yesterday with
   Secretary-General Zhang Chairing the Discussion of Corrective Measures
   for the Late Arrival of Purchased Fishing Equipment). 1965. *Matsu Daily*,
   May 21.
"Yuye xietiaohui zuo yuanze jueding, caigou yuju yanwu shijian, yuandong
   gongsi peichang shunshi, jiangyi wuxi daikuan fangshi zuowei buchang."
   (The Fisheries Council Resolves that Losses Due to Delays in the Purchase
   of Fishing Supplies Will Be Indemnified by the Far East Corporation,
   Interest-free Loans Will Be Given in Compensation). 1965. *Matsu Daily*,
   April 14.
Zeng, Linguan. 2010. "Zeng Linguan ci Matsu jing tianhougong xinren weiyuan,
   jian huiying gejie zhiyi yu zhijiao." (Ceng Linguan's Statement on the Newly
   Appointed Committee Members of the Mazujing Goddess Mazu Temple,
   and a Response to Numerous Questions and Comments). *Matsu Online*,
   December 16. www.matsu.idv.tw/topicdetail.php?f=2&t=85802. (Accessed
   February 1, 2011).
Zhai, Benrui. 2000. "Xuni shequ de shehuixue jichu: xuni shijie dui xianshi
   shenghuo de shentou" (Sociological Foundations of Virtual Communities:
   Infiltrations of the Virtual World into Real Life). In *Jiaoyu yu shehui: yingjie
   zixun shidai de jiaoyu shehuixue fanxing*. Taipei: Yangzhi Wenhua,
   pp. 223–43.
Zhang, Chi. 1984. "Zhang yizhou hengxing minhai shimo." (The whole story of
   Zhang Yizhou's dominating the sea of Min). *Xian you wenshi ziliao* 2:
   89–117.
Zhang, Longguang. 2012. "Wo ben jiang xin xiang mingyue, naihe mingyue zhao
   gouqu. Siqian: huishou Matsu de guoqu. Xianghou: zhanwang Matsu de
   weilai." (Thinking of the Moon and How It Shines in Ditches—First
   Thinking of Returning to Matsu's Past, Then Looking Toward Matsu's
   Future). *Matsu Daily*, April 25.

Zhang, Peifen. 2012. "Matsu hangban quxiaolyu, jin 2 cheng." (Nearly 20% of All Matsu Flights Cancelled). *China Times.* https://tw.news.yahoo.com/%E9%A6%AC%E7%A5%96%E8%88%AA%E7%8F%AD%E5%8F%96%E6%B6%88%E7%8E%87-%E8%BF%912%E6%88%90-213000369.html. July 10. (Accessed February 10, 2014).

Zhang, Pingguan, ed. 2001. *Lianjiang xianzhi.* Beijing shi: Fanzhi chuban she.

"Zhengweihui chongshen qianling, yanjin jungongjiao dubo." (Committee Reiterates Previous Order Prohibiting Soldiers and Teachers from Gambling). 1982. *Matsu Daily,* January 20.

Zheng, Zhiren. 2003. *Matsu minju: Lianjiangxian xiangtu jianzhu yanjiu baogao.* (Matsu-style Houses: A Study of the Architecture of Lianjiang County Villages). Nangan: Lianjiang County Government.

"Zhihuiguan guanhuai yumin, jiang juban yuye daikuan, dai yu benqu ge pinku yumin." (Demonstrating Concern for Fishermen, the Commander Will Offer Fishing Industry Loans to Needy Fishermen across the Area). 1962. *Matsu Daily,* August 15.

"(Zhihuiguan) jian zhuwei guanhuai pinku yumin, zhishi chunjie qian daikuan." (The (Commander and) WZA Chair Shows His Concern for Impoverished Fishermen, Indicating Loans Will Be Made Before the Spring Festival). 1964. *Matsu Daily,* February 3.

Zhongge. 2010. "Magang tianhougong xuanju zhuduo yiwen?" (Question Surrounding the Mazu Temple Elections in Magang?). *Matsu Online,* December 12. www.matsu.idv.tw/topicdetail.php?f=2&t=85701. (Accessed May 1, 2011).

Zhongguo keji daxue. 2007. *96 niandu lianjiangxian wenhua jingguan pucha jihua.* (The 96th Annual Survey of the Cultural Landscape of Lianjiang County). Unpublished report.

Zhonghe Afang. 2008. "Huiying 'Kuaixun: shanlong xinjie yu jinwan fasheng dahuo, huoshi lishi 3 xiaoshi cai shou kongzhi'." (Response to 'News Flash: Huge Fire Tonight on Xinjie in Shanlong, Raged for Three Hours). *Matsu Online,* January 20. www.matsu.idv.tw/topicdetail.php?f=1&t=51090. (Accessed March 10, 2010).

Index

For EU product safety concerns, contact us at Calle de José Abascal, 56–1°,
28003 Madrid, Spain or eugpsr@cambridge.org.

www.ingramcontent.com/pod-product-compliance
Ingram Content Group UK Ltd.
Pitfield, Milton Keynes, MK11 3LW, UK
UKHW020309140625
459647UK00015B/1809